Managing People in Charities

Managing People in Charities

SECOND EDITION

John Burnell

Published by ICSA Publishing Ltd
16 Park Crescent
London W1B 4AH

© John Burnell 1997, 2001

First published 1997
Second edition 2001

All rights reserved. No part of this publication may be reproduced, stored in a retrieval system, or transmitted, in any form, or by any means, electronic, mechanical, photocopying, recording or otherwise, without prior permission, in writing, from the publisher.

Designed and Typeset in Swift and Bell Gothic by
Paul Barrett Book Production, Cambridge

Printed and bound in Great Britain by
TJ International Ltd., Padstow, Cornwall

British Library Cataloguing in Publication Data

A catalogue record for this book is available from the British Library

ISBN 1 86072 125 7 2nd edition
(ISBN 1 86072 029 3 1st edition)

Contents

Preface vii
Acknowledgements ix
Foreword x

Chapter 1 The uniqueness of the voluntary sector and the challenge for the people who work in it 1

Introduction 1
The role of the charity sector 1
A growing sector 2
A unique and diverse sector 3
A changing personnel profile 6
In summary ... 8

Chapter 2 Managing staff – the responsibilities of trustees and chief executives 10

Introduction 10
Legal constraints and obligations 11
Conflicts of interest 12
Delegation: getting the mix right 14
In summary ... 24

Chapter 3 Managing staff – the legal framework 25

Introduction 25
Employment law sources 25
The contract 26
Statute law 28
European legislation 28
Employment Tribunals 35
A word or two about case law 36
In summary... 36

Chapter 4 Managing staff – rules, procedures and best practice in times of change 37

Introduction 37
What is best practice? 38
Pointers to determining good practice: how do we get there? 42
Why do we need rules? 43

Disciplinary procedures 47
Incapability 54
Grievances 57
In summary ... 62

Chapter 5 Communication and staff involvement 64

Introduction 64
A framework to believe in 64
Equal opportunities employment 66
All that, and openness too 68
Communication, consultation and negotiation 70
To recognise or not to recognise ... 71
... Management is still responsible 74
Coping with industrial disputes 75
Do trustees have a role? 78
In summary ... 80

Chapter 6 Staff conditions – what you have to do 81

Introduction 81
A raft of rights 81
Statement of particulars 84
Making payments 96
In summary ... 97

Chapter 7 Staff conditions – what you may want to do 98

Introduction 98
Towards good practice 98
Developing a salary policy 99
Rewarding performance 104
Job evaluation 107
Salary levels and reviews 111
... But there's more to life than money 114
And that's not all ... 122
Giving staff the choice 122
In summary ... 124

Chapter 8 Effective recruitment 126

Introduction 126
Why make such an effort? 127

Job analysis 127
Finding the candidates 134
Consultancy or do-it-yourself? 134
Why advertise? 138
The detailed planning 140
Where have we got to so far? 147
In summary ... 147

Chapter 9 Selecting fairly and efficiently 148

Introduction 148
So what's wrong with interviewing? 149
But doesn't that mean a great deal more effort? 151
The recruitment assessment centre 152
What techniques are available? 152
So how do you make up your mind? 166
The great equal opportunities in recruitment debate 170
In summary ... 172

Chapter 10 Developing staff – motivation and training 174

Introduction 174
Theories of motivation 174
Motivational management 176
Some key issues for charities 177
Equal opportunities, motivation and development 180
Investing in your staff 182
Why train at all? 183
A SWOT analysis approach 186
A training policy 187
Training needs identification 193
Training techniques 198
Measuring training effectiveness 204
In summary ... 206

Chapter 11 Developing staff – supervision, appraisal and personal development 207

Introduction 207
Staff development in context 207
The need to be involved 208
Target-setting and performance evaluation 210
All you need is love? 212
It's not just when things go wrong ... 215
Formal appraisal 219
Linking performance to pay and benefits 224
In summary ... 227

Chapter 12 Taking the tough decisions 228

Introduction 228
We don't all see things the same way 228
Reasonableness 229
Grasping the nettle 230
A procedure a day keeps your troubles away? 231
Redundancy 233
Outplacement and career management 236
Responding to complaints – Employment Tribunals and sacking fairly 240
Responding to and dealing with industrial action 244
Going for win-win 247
In summary ... 248

Chapter 13 Managing volunteers 250

Introduction 250
Who are these volunteers? 250
Let's get organised 252
Designing the jobs 253
Recruitment and selection of volunteers 256
Induction and training 263
Supervision and evaluation 265
Retaining volunteers 266
De-selecting volunteers 267
The legal position of volunteers 269
Some other issues 270
Some final remarks 272
In summary ... 272

Chapter 14 Developing a personnel strategy 273

Introduction 273
Matching a personnel strategy to your organisational needs 274
The changing nature of work 275
Delivering a personnel service 282
Personnel consultants 283
In summary ... 284

Directory 285

Further reading 285
Useful addresses 286
Networks and trustees 291

Epilogue 291

Preface

When my book first came out four years ago, I was worried that it would not really be possible to offer anything meaningful on addressing personnel issues in the voluntary sector in such a slim volume. After all, you only have to visit the library at the Chartered Institute of Personnel and Development to realise the depth and breadth of thinking and advice that is available.

Events proved me wrong. Many colleagues in the voluntary sector have been very flattering about what I wrote, telling me that it was just what they needed – something not too heavy, but a basic guide to an area where they knew they had to get it right but were often afraid to ask. Building on that basic guidance, they have gone from strength to strength in the management of their charities, and if I have been a small catalyst in that process, then it has all been worthwhile.

The new edition retains the basic aims of the original book: to provide a guide to personnel management for non-personnel managers or specialists, which also takes into account the added complexities faced by voluntary sector managers.

Of course, the voluntary sector, even more than anywhere else, cannot afford to stand still. In the past four years, we have seen the election of a Labour government that seems far more committed to employee rights and a more co-operative approach to work. Trades unions have moved towards a partnering model of industrial relations and, true to form, employment law, now even more heavily influenced by Europe, the Social Chapter and significant equalities legislation, gets ever more complicated. We have also been faced with a world of work that, compared with even ten years ago, is changing out of all recognition.

I have sought to reflect these developments in the second edition. The revised chapter on employment law has been pared down to the essentials as an introduction to more detailed coverage featured elsewhere in the book. I have also given some thought to the new challenges that will face charity managers as they come to terms with work practices that are still rapidly evolving, and so have included references to the increasing use of information technology, remote working and flexible careers, matters about which we would not even have dreamt a generation ago. New, too, is extended coverage of managing volunteers, with a chapter dedicated to the issues involved. Finally, in response to requests from several quarters, I have offered new case studies and other models – I hope they are thought provoking.

The book is in a revised format, but its core message remains the same – that managing people in charities is an enormous challenge, but one which, if you get it right, can offer enormous satisfaction. I wish the reader well in rising to that challenge.

John Burnell, FCIPD

Acknowledgements

It is always difficult to provide a list of acknowledgements for a book like this. Much of what I have written comes from my own experience and knowledge in the personnel profession and from observing the work of countless voluntary sector managers and volunteers, and I doubt whether I could pinpoint now where most of what is contained in the book has come from.

However, I am particularly grateful to the following: my solicitor colleague, John Esplen of Barnes and Partners, and barrister Simon Perhar for their rigorous assistance in revising the chapter on employment law, Terry Rollinson, of the Youth Hostels Association (England and Wales) for contributing the new chapter on managing volunteers, and the senior psychologists at Saville and Holdsworth Ltd for their assistance in preparing the case study on selection techniques and for their comments on the recruitment and selection chapters.

I would also like to thank my wife, Jan, whose work as a charity chief executive has shown me time and again that compassion, professional care standards and high quality management can be combined in equal measure, and to make specific mention of Tessa Baring, whose powerful, thought-provoking talk, given as the 1996 Arnold Goodman Lecture, was extremely influential on my thinking.

John Burnell
February 2001

Foreword

One of the things they forget to tell you when you become a chief executive in a charity is that you're going to have to deal with all those tricky personnel questions that previously you could rely on your personnel department to provide answers to.

You may be an expert in the provision of advice services; you may well have done a course in charity finance management; you'll certainly have experience in campaigning and public relations. But dealing with the complexities of staff motivation, contracts of employment, training programmes, disciplinary procedures, salary setting and all the rest of it? You'll be lucky if you spent a couple of hours in the dim and distant past on your course to be a general manager, and anyway, the world has become a lot more complex since then.

It's little wonder, then, that with the best will in the world, smaller charities with few specialist management resources can sometimes make serious mistakes in dealing with their staff – mistakes that can cost thousands of pounds and which have been known in some cases to bankrupt them.

Fortunately, at last there is somewhere to turn. With this book, now published in its second edition in an even more accessible form, John Burnell has met a gaping need, and has done so with the sensitivity that can only come from long association with the voluntary sector. For every manager in every charity who has any responsibility for staff, this book is an invaluable tool in helping you through the minefield – and, just as importantly, helping you to avoid the minefield in the first place. Most significantly, far from being frightened by what lay ahead, once I had the book to hand, I knew I now had the confidence to tackle those little and not so little problems that, like others, I had been tempted to put off for far too long.

I am therefore delighted to have been invited to write the foreword to this second edition, and I recommend it highly to my management colleagues at every level throughout the voluntary sector.

Eric Appleby
Director, Alcohol Concern
Chair, Association of Chief Executives of Voluntary Organisations

The uniqueness of the voluntary sector and the challenge for the people who work in it

CHAPTER 1

INTRODUCTION

There are many different types of organisation that are neither private sector, profit-making concerns nor part of the statutory or quasi-statutory public sector. It is in a sense far easier to define the voluntary sector by what it is not than by what it is; but that is a rather negative way of starting what I hope will be a positive book. So let's accept that this book is about managing people in any organisation that is either a registered charity, a friendly society or other recognised independent organisation such as a housing association or private school; that has objectives other than profit making; and that has a mixture of voluntary workers and paid employees. The real point is that people who work in the voluntary sector know it, and therefore have the attitudes and expectations that this brings – if you think that this book applies to you, then the odds are that you are right. This chapter sets the context for what follows by outlining the key dynamics of the sector and the unique challenges facing the people who work in it.

The role of the charity sector

The charity sector has always been a vital component of British society, and it is rapidly also becoming a vital component of the British economy. Its traditional role has been to provide a wide range of services to those in need, either because the state did not do so itself or because people with specialist skills and understanding, coming together in a voluntary capacity, could do so better. More recently, the sector has moved from providing largesse to the deserving (and sometimes also to the rest) towards campaigning for social change to remove the causes of the issues it has always needed to face, drawing together the common threads of provision into an educational process both for the people who benefit from its activities and for society as a whole that supports them. And it provides a third role – a focus for people who want to do their bit both to help others and to change society, but who feel that traditional political activity is inadequate for the purpose or inappropriate for them. (Interestingly, by my definition political parties are themselves part of the sector!) Perhaps the most important thing that the sector is, or should be, doing is drawing together this myriad of energy, experience and understanding to build links between people, organisations and widely differing parts of society, both to lobby effectively for resources and to maintain pressure on our leaders to build social cohesiveness. This is preferable to allowing the continuing drift towards the divisiveness and fragmentation we have witnessed during the last twenty years at least, as the rich get richer and the poor poorer, and compartmentalisation and the cash nexus mean that government is run like business, but with diminishing social objectives or welfare considerations. If that sounds like a political agenda, then so be it. But it is not a party political one. All mainstream strands of political opinion are moving towards the disengagement of the state, and the debate is over the pace and extent, not the principle.

A growing sector

The sector is huge, and is growing by the day. Every week at least 100 new charities are registered, and even allowing for closures, the sector is growing by 4,000 organisations a year. Estimates of its revenue income suggest figures ranging between £12 and £20 billion each year amongst the 180,000 charities on the Charity Commissioners' books. But whilst it is huge, truly a third sector, it is also enormously skewed, which makes it very difficult for any one person or any single organisation to be able to claim with great confidence that they can speak for it. Its very nature and diversity make that hard enough anyway; the geographical and interest spread don't help, and the best that organisations such as the Charities Aid Foundation and the National Council for Voluntary Organisations can do is to seek to set the standard and use their membership bases of approaching 1,000 charities as a platform from which to launch ever-more intense efforts at being representative.

The diversification and skewedness of the sector are pointers to best practice management within it. For the vast majority of charities, organising volunteers and representing their views is the only thing they do. Of the 180,000, only 30,000 have any staff at all, and most have just one worker, very often part-time. Only 6,000 charities (three per cent) have five or more staff, but there are altogether 425,000 staff employed in the sector – more than in agriculture, fisheries and the armed forces. And there are well over 100 charities with more than 1,000 staff – big employers by anyone's standards, sometimes larger than the local authorities with which they have a range of service delivery contracts. With size of the workforce comes, increasingly, an awareness of the nature of employment and the rights of employees: one union alone – MSF (the Manufacturing, Science and Finance Union) – now claims over 20,000 members in the sector; others have a similar level of involvement.

The diversity of employment is mirrored in the financial statistics. The huge majority (over ninety per cent) has less than £10,000 income a year. At the other end of the spectrum, only 2,000 earn more than £1 million, and a minuscule 700 get more than £10 million. Not surprisingly, there is a close correlation between income and staff size, although some of the biggest charities still rely on volunteers for most of their work. Perhaps the most significant figure of all is that the top two per cent of charities own eight-seven per cent of the sector's assets.

What this tells us is that whilst there may be a few charities out there vying with ICI in the size stakes, with complex managerial infrastructures and support systems, including expert personnel departments, the large majority are neither cash-rich enough nor sufficiently developed to be able to afford the comfort of in-house personnel advice. Typically, small charities (those with fewer than five staff) and even medium-sized ones (anything up to fifty or sixty employees) struggle to get their personnel practices right in an increasingly complex employment world, but usually without professional help. If this book offers them and their fellow workers in the very small organisations at least some glimpses into how they can go about their role as employers with the same degree of professionalism that they already demonstrate in setting service delivery standards, then it has made a useful contribution to the work of the voluntary sector. If it can also help those larger charities that already have policies in place to review their practices, then so much the better.

A unique and diverse sector

As I shall be stressing throughout this book, managing people in the voluntary sector is a particularly complex yet enormously rewarding challenge. That is because, unlike other sectors of the economy, the charity manager has to deal with at least two additional factors: the involvement of volunteers with their interaction with paid staff, and the altruism of those paid staff, whose dedication to the cause is often tested by their status as relatively poorly paid employees. I shall come back to these themes throughout the book, and at this point will do no more than set the scene, describing the typical management arrangements any charity trustee, director or other executive is likely to confront, all within the overall context of 'It's more than a job – it's a commitment, and a lot more besides.'

Within the sector there is an intricate web of management relationships that is not reflected to anything like the same degree elsewhere. There is a parallel with local government, in that trustees have their counterpart in councillors – but councillors are publicly elected for a fixed term, whereas trustees at best are selected from amongst a narrower constituency – in effect often appointed and re-appointed by their peers – and have a chain of accountability that is rarely transparent. These are the aspects that have generated most concern by politicians and service users alike against some parts of the sector, particularly in recent years against housing associations and other successor social housing providers. In general, however, the concerns are rather less vociferously expressed by volunteers and supporters, which does lead to consideration of the question: whom is the charity for? Obviously, the biggest stakeholders have to be the service users but, particularly in campaigning charities, there is a healthy tension between their competing demands and those of the members and staff. It is not for this book to provide answers to this issue, but rather to point it out as part of the context in which voluntary sector personnel management needs to be set.

Then there are all the different styles of organisation that are both possible and observable throughout the sector – a rich tapestry of management structures that reflects the very diverse nature of how charities go about their business. Some charities remain comfortable with an autocratic, top-down approach: they may be small bodies with a few founder members with a mission still at the helm, or large bureaucracies with a powerful senior management team that has to pay only token regard to its trustee board. They can and do succeed by the depth of their commitment, their enthusiasm which generates almost unquestioning loyalty, or through a tough managerial regime, which will not allow the charity to be diverted from its service delivery objectives.

At the other end of the organisational political spectrum, there are many charities operating virtually as collectives, all the members having an equal say and progress being achieved through consensus. Such organisations tend to be rather small, since the more members there are, generally the less the chance of agreement, and they tend to be volunteer-dominated. They often experience quite painful conflicts when paid staff are taken on who begin to see themselves either as the same as the trustees – which they cannot be – or as second-class citizens – which, however much the voluntary members might try to avoid or deny it, they often become. In between, there is every possible combination of staff, volunteer and trustee relationship.

This diversity is much wider than in the rest of the economy, which is one of the reasons why a prescriptive personnel textbook is inappropriate (the other is that there is a natural resistance, which I fully endorse, amongst voluntary sector managers and staff to being told how to do their business better!). The voluntary sector differs, at least in employment terms, from the rest of the economy in other ways.

Staff in the voluntary sector are paid less than their counterparts in corporate organisations, for example in 1999 chief executives and other directors were paid about fifteen per cent below the market rate. The same is also true of most other positions – only the lowest graded posts earn above their comparators, surely an example of charity beginning at home. Underpaid the staff may be, but all the survey data indicate that nearly all staff get a great deal more job satisfaction than their private and even public sector counterparts. It all adds up to a considerable motivational challenge.

The sector has a much better track record in other areas than the rest of the economy. Of the more than 600 members of the voluntary sector chief executives' professional association, no less than 40 per cent are women, and rather more than a handful come from minority ethnic communities. The sector also has several leading executives with significant disabilities. Compare that with elsewhere: amongst local government chief executives, only about 5 per cent are women, and fewer are black or disabled. The situation is far worse in the private sector. These statistics show how, and perhaps why, the sector is rather different – they also demonstrate that equal opportunity is a factor to be reckoned with at all times and at all levels.

But are voluntary sector staff all that different? Do they differ from their colleagues elsewhere – that is, is a special type of person attracted to working in the sector? Or is it the nature of the sector that produces rather different types of people working in it? Where do they come from?

One answer is that all (well, nearly all) have personal experience of the kind of issues being addressed and a keen sense of commitment, very often a burning passion to right an injustice, to improve society or simply to make a real difference to someone's life. Typically, a volunteer has all those attributes, attitudes that go well beyond the Victorian patronising approach to the 'deserving poor'. Very often, that commitment translates into professionalism as small charities grow and need to take on paid staff. Probably the biggest bridge that anyone in the voluntary sector has to cross is becoming an employee when previously they had been a volunteer, Of course there are similarities, but there is also a world of a difference, and it is a great tribute to the strength of the sector that so many make the crossing successfully.

A changing personnel profile

Whilst that process to a great extent accounts for the development of small charities, when founders become employees and administrative staff are taken on to support them, the pattern is rather different, and getting more so in larger organisations. The bigger charities generally operate open recruitment processes, do it very effectively and spread their nets wide in an attempt to catch the best quality staff that their meagre remuneration and bountiful satisfaction packages can offer. With an increasing emphasis on the need for professional management and high-quality technical skills, particularly at the top, it is hardly surprising that more and more posts are being filled by people from outside the sector. Chief executives are the most likely to be recruited from beyond the rarefied atmosphere of the charity world – one study suggested up to forty-five per cent over a five-year period. Other managers, especially finance and computer specialists, are also likely to be recruited from outside.

But that still leaves a great number of people appointed from within the sector. Typically, a shortlist for a chief executive position will have a panel of candidates that includes a couple of current or former heads of smaller charities, deputies in larger ones, a redundant captain of industry and someone who has taken early retirement and thinks that running a charity is a good way of winding down towards the twilight years (they are soon disabused of that notion). Posts at lower levels tend to be dominated far more by charity workers on the move, developing careers in a sector to which they have made a comprehensive commitment. Recruitment at the bottom of the ladder is a mixture of starry-eyed idealists and people who see it as just another job. The former soon get the shine knocked off them, whilst the latter, if they stay, rapidly take on the ideals and ideology of the sector.

And there is a great deal of that for them to share. There has always been the opportunity to demonstrate missionary zeal and, in some areas, in support of some causes, zeal is still a vital component. Without it, campaigning charities can easily lose a sense of direction, their sharp edge, the difference that makes government ministers listen to them, local councillors respect them, the people who share their ideals continue to support them with money and effort through thick and thin. The issue for the voluntary sector manager is always to channel enthusiasm in ways that are cost effective, without dampening the spirits.

The politics of the voluntary sector are, however, about much more than zealous enthusiasm, however important that may be. They need to be about presentation too, about not only being professional, but about being *seen* to be professional. Charity managers are learning a whole new range of skills as they come to terms with the need to compete and get their case over for a bigger slice of what may be a diminishing cake – whether it is to win a community care competitive tender bid, a lottery handout or a change in legislation.

With that agenda, most charities cannot keep out of the political arena and remain effective. Of course, some of them will always be comfortable relying on rich benefactors and providing the same services to the same clientele. If they can survive like that, then that's fine as far as it goes. What their chances are, only time can tell; but within the broader voluntary sector, a failure to recognise what the movement is about, to accept that they are part of a wider campaign for social improvement and not just social stability, is likely to lead to a degree of isolation.

For the sector cannot fail to ignore the political realities of the day and keep hold of its greatest strength – an acute awareness of injustice and a desire to do something about it. The simple fact is, there is increasing poverty in Britain and increasing inequality in a society that is fragmenting; and these are areas where the charity world has a key role to play. Just one set of government statistics which highlights all this: since 1979, the poorest twenty per cent of our society have seen no real increase in their standard of living, and the bottom 10 per cent are actually worse off. Charity managers can wring their hands, and charity staff and volunteers can want to change this, but it's no use unless they all develop to bridge the gap between, on the one hand, the narrow, bottom-line business view of knowing the cost of everything and the value of nothing; and on the other, the equally myopic state welfarists who know the value of everything and the cost of nothing. The challenge for charity personnel management is to equip the sector's staff with the skills to provide sensitive, caring services efficiently, to make sure that the rest of society wants to do the same, and to put pressure on our leaders to ensure that we do.

For if that change is not achieved, all that the voluntary sector will ever be able to achieve is a holding back of the floodgates, a series of fingers in the dike or a continuing papering over of the cracks. We will still be faced with the attitudes of the Hooray Henries passing an alcoholic collapsed in the street, telling each other that some people will do anything to jump the queue in the local hospital. However much looking after that drunk may give the people of the sector a sense of importance, it can never offer the same kind of job satisfaction gained by knowing that you have made a significant and long-term difference and that, rather than curbing the excesses of society, you have helped society come to terms with them and reduce them, as well as helping those selfsame Hooray Henries to understand their responsibilities. That is the challenge for staff and their managers – a challenge that can only be met if those staff have a quality of personnel management that supports them in the task.

I hope this book will help you to realise that managing your staff effectively, making the best of personnel skills in the voluntary sector, will be a key part of your plan to secure your own organisation's strategic objectives and, with it, to make a real difference to society as a whole. I do not offer any (or at least not many) prescriptive proposals, since that is for you to decide. After all, it is *your* charity. It is how it can be made to work better that you have to determine, and only *you* will know what will and what won't work. But I hope that I will at least be able to give you a taster of what best employment practice can be about, and offer some of the techniques to implement it. If that has started you thinking, if it helps you to identify the issues and further work you need to do, and the help that you may need to do it, then the book has served its purpose, and you will be joining the growing band of competent people managers in the voluntary sector who have recognised that to give the best to one group of people – their clients – they need to get the best from another group – their employees.

In summary ...

- The charity sector has developed from the voluntary provision of services by those who can afford them to those whom they think need them. It is now part of a wider, vibrant society that provides complementary and alternative services to the state, and offers an outlet for those concerned to see social change.
- It is now truly a third sector, with an annual turnover of up to £20 billion and more than 400,000 employees.
- There is a vast range of different management structures, sizes and approaches to service delivery which is not even approached by the public or commercial sectors.
- Staff in the sector are generally paid significantly less than their counterparts elsewhere, but employment patterns show a rather more progressive approach, with women in particular well represented at all levels.
- Staff, both paid and volunteer, offer a commitment to their employing organisation and a personal professionalism that is not matched elsewhere in the economy, and their charities are becoming increasingly professionally organised.

- Charities are both responding effectively to the major political issues of the day such as poverty, and increasingly leading on setting that agenda, through greater political awareness and more effective presentation.
- Effective management of a charity's staff is, in the end, the only way of ensuring that the sector remains able to play these key roles.

CHAPTER 2

Managing staff – the responsibilities of trustees and chief executives

INTRODUCTION

Charity trustees sometimes like to think of themselves as company directors. Whilst there may be some parallels – they have overall responsibility for direction, they employ staff, they have legal obligations – there are also enormous differences, and not just in terms of statutory requirements. Even with all the talk nowadays about the socially aware profit-making organisation, ultimately the directors of private companies have an underlying commitment to maximising income for their owners, whether these are shareholders or partners.

That is the crucial difference between private companies and charities. Most charities exist to provide services, rather to make money, (although by making money they may help towards that end). Many charities seek to apply sound business and management principles – but in order to maximise their effectiveness and impact, not their income. And whilst the private sector company may adopt a personnel strategy of best salaries and conditions to get the best staff to secure those marginal improvements that lead to greater profit, charities sometimes get confused between ends and means, and lose sight of their objectives. Any board of trustees that decides it will be generous to its staff just because the organisation is a charity, without considering how this will affect the quality of their services, runs the risk of being in breach of their charitable objectives.

So, the message is clear. Just as in the private sector, staff in charities are not employed for the sake of employing them, but for a greater purpose. But whereas in the private sector you can probably justify any policy as long as it seems to be contributing to the organisation's survival, as a trustee of a charity you will be under much greater scrutiny. After all, people didn't put money into your collecting tins to pay your staff fat salaries; they thought it was all going to the children/animals/poor. So any and every personnel policy in the voluntary sector has to be aimed at securing maximum staff performance for minimum use of charitable funds. It's a very fine tightrope, which apparently stretches into infinity. This chapter looks at the role trustees play in directing and managing personnel policy and management, and how they can work alongside the organisation's chief executive to the benefit of both staff and clients alike.

Legal constraints and obligations

It has always been the case that charity trustees have been supposed to spend the money they raise on the purposes for which the charity was established (or in accordance with any revised objectives the trustees have persuaded the Charity Commissioners to allow them to adopt). This has, in many cases, been done by using some of the money to employ staff to carry out the work the volunteers might not be available or able to do, or by purchasing services (such as those of personnel consultants!) that cannot otherwise be provided. As long as the money kept rolling in and the services rolling out, it was largely left to the trustees to get the balance between services and salaries right.

In theory, that was tightened up by the 1992 Charities Act. There is now a much greater obligation on trustees to ensure that charitable funds are used for the purposes for which they are intended, and the Charity Commission now has a clearer policing role to make sure this happens. This is meant to happen in two ways. First, there is a clearly spelt-out fiduciary duty on all trustees to ensure that funds are spent effectively in accordance with the charity's objectives. Secondly, all money received as charitable donations (and, by implication, from public funds) must be spent on charitable activities. So not only must trustees be good managers, they must also be absolutely clear that the expenditure they incur is fully in accordance with the charity's objectives. The size of salaries and the benefits enjoyed by staff have to be justified and proportional to the needs of the charity employing them. And as for trustees benefiting, if you were thinking of offering free chauffeur services or subsidised dinners at gala performances for the chair's relatives, forget it – unless, of course, you're not using charitable funds to pay for them!

In practice, of course, the Charity Commission cannot possibly hope to scrutinise the activities of 180,000 charities, and it has to rely to a great extent on self-policing. But if there is a hint of impropriety, it is likely to take a long, hard look at what's been going on. Although its powers are limited it can, ultimately, remove trustees, and of course the damage to a charity's credibility and fundraising capacity from such public scrutiny is likely to be severe. It is still early days, but the signs are that, as trustees slowly (sometimes very slowly) get to hear about the more rigorous obligations imposed on them by the Act, they are becoming more prudent in the disbursement of funds.

In the same way that the 1992 Act put charity financial management in a tighter statutory framework, there is also legislation on the statute book covering the activities of registered housing associations, which to all intents and purposes can be considered as charities and certainly have many of the characteristics of other organisations in the voluntary sector – despite the best efforts of some housing association chief executives to turn them into private housing companies! The 1985 Housing Act, in particular, places onerous responsibilities and constraints on associations and how they can spend 'their' money.

What does all this mean for charity personnel management? It certainly suggests that a more considered and structured approach is necessary to the employment of staff and the service conditions they enjoy. The 1985 Housing Act actually states, in Section 15, that trustees will be personally liable for any payments to or on behalf of staff that are not specifically provided for under their contracts of employment. Whilst housing associations can go cap in hand to the Housing Corporation to secure approval for a non-contractual payment, it is a long process with no guarantee of success. It has meant that employment contracts, and all the various elements of service conditions that are implied in those contracts, have been far more carefully written in recent years, creating a mini-industry and boom in the numbers of personnel staff in that part of the sector.

It is not quite as tight as that for the rest of the voluntary sector, but the principle remains the same: the best way of ensuring that you are spending money on staff wisely is to make all payments in accordance with contractual rights and obligations; and the best way of ensuring that those contracts make sense is to have a clear personnel strategy and set of personnel policies. This book aims to help you get to that position.

Conflicts of interest

Before we launch into the world of employing and managing staff, there is one area where trustees have faced problems in the past, and on which it may be helpful to offer some guidance. This is when, to all intents and purposes, they employ themselves or derive some benefit from someone else's employment. Just consider some of the following examples:

- A paid chief executive who attends and votes at the trustee board.

- A trustee who fundraises for the charity on a commission basis.
- A trustee who at a meeting of the board appoints her partner to undertake consultancy work for the charity.
- A trustee who marries the charity's director of finance.
- A trustee who is a builder and charges for work done for the charity.

These are all areas that can cause major concerns in the charity, housing association and public sectors.

In general, the law says that you cannot simultaneously be a trustee and a paid employee of the same organisation (although there are some exceptions related to umbrella organisations and trading subsidiaries). One definition of a trustee is someone who has voting rights at a meeting of trustees – so our chief executive must make up her mind: either she gets paid or she votes; she can't do both.

The law also makes it clear that trustees cannot personally benefit from their charitable activities (apart, of course, from the satisfaction of doing good works). A trustee taking a cut from fundraising activities would therefore be acting illegally, although he could legitimately recover out-of-pocket expenses – nobody expects you to be worse off from charitable work.

If you know that someone close to you may benefit from a decision you take as a trustee, then you should take no part in any decision-making process related to that person. Your partner may well be the best consultant available in their field, but it must be for others to determine that, not you – everyone expects you to tell them that anyway, and they must be free to make up their own minds. In those circumstances, the prudent thing to do is to withdraw until the decision is made, and if they conclude that your partner is the best thing since sliced bread, after the decision has been made, as far as practicable, never get involved in parts of the charity's work affected by his activity. Similarly, if a trustee establishes a relationship with a member of staff, or their partner seeks employment with the charity, that trustee should avoid involvement in their partner's areas of responsibility – and should be absent when the recruitment decision is made.

These conflicts of interest are far more difficult to avoid in small charities, where the organisation's work is harder to compartmentalise. Although there are no hard and fast rules, I really would urge trustees and staff alike to consider very carefully if they can ever genuinely avoid any suggestion of conflicts of interest in such situations. If they can't, then my advice is simple – one of you has to resign. It's tough, but in the end it's in the best interests of the charity – and that's what we're all here for.

Finally, awarding contracts to yourself, however good a builder, lawyer, accountant, or whatever you are, always looks suspect, even if you have not taken part in the decision-making. The 1992 Act makes it quite clear – you should always seek to avoid such appointments; indeed, it is only ever permissible if you have such a specialist skill that the charity is unlikely to be able to find it elsewhere, but is still desperate to have it. It is difficult to envisage many circumstances where trustees are likely to have such rare skills that are in such high demand.

The basic point in all this is simple: charity trustees and their staff – particularly their senior staff – are under an absolute moral (and to some extent legal) obligation to act with total probity in all of their actions, particularly when what they are doing affects, directly or indirectly, the use of charitable funds. It is fine to act properly, but you need to go further and be seen very publicly to be acting properly. So if there could ever be the slightest suspicion, however ill-founded, that as a trustee or senior employee you are acting out of motives that are anything other than altruistic or professional – DON'T. Declare an interest and withdraw, then others will defend you against those baseless allegations. Stay, and they may cease to be baseless.

Delegation: getting the mix right

Except in the smallest of charities, people tend to specialise in different areas, whether it is fundraising, delivering services, keeping in touch with members and supporters or providing support to everyone else. All these activities are equally important (yes, even personnel management!), because they all rely on each other to make the charity work efficiently. In that respect, charities are little different from other organisations. But where the differences do arise is in the distinction between the roles of the professional staff and the trustees – one that to a very large extent mirrors the delineation of roles in local authorities between councillors and chief officers. In local government, of course, much of this is enshrined in law, notably in the 1989 Local Government and Housing Act. Apart from the obvious issues of conflict of interest, discussed above, in the voluntary sector it is left largely to good sense. Sometimes this seems to be rather conspicuous by its absence – trustees often struggle to delegate effectively.

There are many models of charity management practice around, some drawn from the business sector, others from theories of public accountability developed for pluralist democracies. Yet others, it would appear, have been developed from first principles specifically with the voluntary sector in mind. What most of them have in common is an attempt to distinguish between governance and management.

Broadly, governance is about determining the overall policy direction of a charity, and taking such steps as are necessary to ensure that the appropriate resources are available to allow it to be carried out. Management is about implementing those major policy decisions. It's not that straightforward of course; someone has to advise the policy-makers and help them develop new ideas, and the trustees need to be able to measure the effectiveness of management. But generally, I find the distinction between governance and management a useful one, which at the very least offers a benchmark against which charities can measure their operational structures and effectiveness.

The key to effective operation, I would suggest, is effective and appropriate delegation. The more complex the organisation, the more you need to delegate, since not only can one person not possibly hope to make all the decisions, but even just by trying to do so, inefficiencies quickly creep in and people who have the ability to deliver soon become frustrated and demotivated. Delegation will mean different things to different people, and there is a whole debate to be had (not in this book) about delegation or devolution, empowerment or decentralisation. Every charity will need to determine what style and model is appropriate for its trustees, its finances, its staff and, by far the most important, its beneficiaries. I would simply argue that, as a general rule, the greater the delegation of authority (with whatever safeguards the trustees feel they must retain), the better the chance of a highly motivated workforce, fast and effective decision-making and quality control of service delivery.

Understandably, it is often difficult for trustees to let go and delegate to paid staff anything other than routine administrative tasks. This is particularly the case in voluntary sector bodies which are, primarily, member organisations, the prime purpose of which is to service the needs of members, and which usually operate through a democratic structure. Members who are recipients of the services, who then become trustees ultimately responsible for the provision of those same services, will, in my experience, want to maintain an interest in the detail, confusing their role as consumers with that of providers. The problem is that such organisations also tend to employ professionals to run them (sometimes from amongst the ranks of the membership, often originally because of their commitment to the cause, but usually people who very quickly take on the qualities of managers), and there can be a considerable degree of conflict between the paid staff and the volunteers. The former can become resentful about what they see as interference in the day-to-day running of the organisation whilst the volunteers resent the fact that people are being paid for what they used to do – or think they could do – for nothing.

> **CASE STUDY 2.1** The manipulating manager
>
> A member organisation had ten branches, each sending one representative to a management committee, which also had external organisations represented. From this a trustee board was appointed, comprising four plus the chief executive, who was both paid and a full trustee. There were thirty staff in the head office and a similar number scattered around the country.
>
> There was a great deal of organisational politics, with major conflicts between the committee and the board, and between the chief executive and the staff. The chief executive had been in post for twelve years but, by all reports from funders and key senior staff, was only effective when he had good second-tier support. He had been recently bereaved and had inherited a large personal fortune, but had not retired. Rather, he had decided to work casual hours but still on a salaried basis until he decided what his future would be. The operations director, one of four second-tier posts, was appointed by the trustees to act up in the chief executive's stead while he contemplated his career, although at first he had wanted all four to share the role. Although at least one of the others would have liked to do the job, they were united in the view that there needed to be just one person, and eventually the operations director was appointed – but on the basis that the arrangement would be reviewed monthly. She was expected to keep doing her other job, was given only a partial acting-up allowance and did not have access to the chief executive's PA for support.
>
> In the meantime, the chief executive continued as a trustee, and in that guise continued to come into the office unannounced and sporadically. There, he still sought to influence what was going on, retained some duties and openly criticised the operation director's actions.
>
> The trustees were, with just one exception, all placemen of the old chief executive, and the operations director believed that he had had a close personal relationship with at least one of them. As a body, the trustees were either uncritical or cowering of the

A similar problem arises when an organisation experiences 'Founder Member Syndrome'. We all admire the single-handed efforts of individuals who have been fired by compassion, injustice or a disaster to 'do something about it'. Their enthusiasm knows no bounds, they operate like human dynamos and, in next to no time, vast sums are raised, the world's conscience is pricked and people start to benefit. Whether they are from amongst the great and the good, or a bloke from the pub down the road, they rightly receive the thanks of a grateful community.

But then time passes, the nature of the challenge changes and either the task is completed and the organisation is wound up or, far more likely, the organisation seeks new goals and settles down on the road to maturity. The founder's vision is still there, but now new ways of doing things and skills that go beyond that vision and enthusiasm are needed. Staff are appointed, job

chief executive, whose management style was authoritarian. Before the acting-up arrangement started, there was a great deal of staff discontent and high turnover – both matters improved under the operations director's more inclusive style, despite the difficulties placed in her way.

A bombshell was dropped without warning after one of the chief executive's sporadic visits – the board decided to terminate the acting-up arrangement, return the operations director to her substantive duties and let the chief executive co-ordinate the work in his guise as a trustee, now unsalaried. All four senior managers objected, but to no avail. They spoke privately to the Charity Commission, who were so appalled that they started along the road of withdrawing charitable status, so seriously did they take the breaches of good practice and the inability and unwillingness of the trustees to address them.

Not surprisingly, the operations director came very quickly to feel that her position was impossible, and concluded that the reversion had arisen because the chief executive did not like the thought of her being so successful. She concentrated her efforts on improving her CV. She had never been allowed to feel at the helm, her hands were tied, it was debilitating and demoralising for her and now for the rest of the staff team. But she was still, amazingly, totally committed to the aims of the organisation, for whom she would wish to continue as a volunteer after she had left.

Such tales are not uncommon in the voluntary sector, and many readers will doubtless acknowledge that this is by no means one of the most extreme examples around. It touches upon some key points, which are easy to understand but difficult to correct:

- Ensure a clear division between trustee and management roles.
- Keep on the right side of charity law.
- Ensure that when you delegate, it stays that way.
- Separate personality issues from the needs of the organisation.

descriptions are written, new developments are proposed. But the founder still wants to be in there – 'It's my idea, my baby, I should say what it does'. Babies grow up and become independent. So do charities.

Both these scenarios describe a similar problem – a need but an inability to let go. Unless beneficiary members and founders are prepared to delegate, however, they run a grave risk of stifling the very organisation they have nurtured. There is no simple or single solution to this issue, which is only too prevalent in the British voluntary sector, with its heavy emphasis on self-help and philanthropy, and each organisation needs to work through the problem in its own way. But unless it does so, there will almost inevitably be internal tensions so great that they will lead to schisms and trustee board *coups d'état* – which rarely, if ever, are to the benefit of service users.

> **CASE STUDY 2.2** Trustees as managers
>
> Some twenty years ago, a group of twenty parents, all of whom had children with a particularly disfiguring but not life-threatening condition, got together because they were upset about the social attitudes towards their children and the low priority the medical profession gave to treating and ameliorating the condition. They formed a charity to educate the public towards greater tolerance and understanding and to campaign to increase resources being directed towards the condition. For some years they remained a small, tight knit group, but gradually their numbers grew, they started to get some doctors interested, and then got a great boost in publicity when a media star had a child with similar symptoms. All of a sudden, the money started rolling in, and they took on an administrator to support their work.
>
> As time went by, doctors and representatives of pharmaceutical and cosmetic companies offered to join, the whole campaign took off, and there were frequent demands for media appearances and involvement with other organisations. The charity broadened its activities from being merely a self-help group to offering counselling and support to a large number of parents and to children with the condition, some of whom were now adults and keen to get involved. The founders, most of whom were still trustees, were unable to meet all the media and professional demands themselves, were not trained therapists, and gradually found that the administrator was taking on these roles herself and supervising other volunteers who were offering their services. As more money came in, these roles were increasingly provided by paid staff, all appointed by the trustees. However, the trustees still sought to maintain direct and detailed involvement in the work of the charity through the day to day management of the administrator.
>
> She felt that the job had grown beyond what she had wanted, and so moved on to a senior office manager post in another charity. The trustees decided to recruit a replacement, but were not sure how to go about it. One of their number volunteered, but he was not a popular choice, so they decided to advertise and let him take his chance. He applied (but did not resign as a trustee) and two other external candidates, both experienced charity managers, were available for consideration.
>
> The best candidate by far was offered the job, but she accepted only on condition that her post was recognised as a chief executive, not an administrator; that the trustee board considered its own structure to take account of perspectives other than those of service users; and that there was a clear understanding of the distinction

Fortunately, not all problems between trustees and the staff they employ are this extreme: the key is to recognise boundaries, to agree a protocol on appropriate relationships, and to relate to each other as fellow professionals, particularly when dealing with senior managers in sensitive positions. Quite how far delegation should go, that is, where the boundary between governance and management should be drawn, is for each organisation to determine, taking into account its history, the

between governance and management roles. Keen to appoint her and worried about filling the post, the trustees agreed, but there was little enthusiasm for the changes and the trustee who had been unsuccessful in his application remained on the board.

Eighteen months into her appointment, not much had changed. Individual trustees, and the board collectively, still wanted to know everything that was happening on a day to day basis; they had failed to recruit any new members, but still made all appointments of both staff and volunteers; and the chief executive had to refer all decisions on expenditure above £100 to the treasurer. The unsuccessful trustee applicant was particularly critical of the chief executive's public (and very effective) appearances, promoting the charity and generally seeking to take a lead in its development. When he discovered that she had authorised a staff member to attend as a last minute delegate to a conference, at the much discounted fee of £275, he insisted that the board take disciplinary action for not referring the matter to them.

The chief executive resigned rather than go through that humiliation, complained to an Employment Tribunal of constructive unfair dismissal, won a high profile case with a substantial reward, and several major funders, alarmed at the situation, pulled the rug out from the organisation. It could no longer afford to employ the therapists and other staff, made them redundant, and within six months had collapsed. Everyone had made some pretty fundamental mistakes:

- The original trustees had failed to recognise that the nature of the organisation had changed and that they needed to apply a much lighter touch – they did not secure for themselves adequate training in their governance role.

- The major funders applied insufficient scrutiny until it was too late.

- The new chief executive was too bombastic in making her initial demands and then failing to follow through on securing the necessary changes – a more subtle approach would probably have got better results.

- The unsuccessful trustee candidate should not have been allowed to continue in a position of pernicious influence.

- Both the trustees and the chief executive should have maintained a much more open dialogue and should not have allowed their differences to get to the point of a humiliating Employment Tribunal case.

nature of the services it provides and of the people who receive them, its size and resources, the spread of its operations, and so on. From a personnel perspective, I would argue that staff will be best motivated if they are given a clear sense of direction and then given free rein to get on with it. (The whole issue of motivation is discussed in more detail in chapter 7.) But I also recognise – and the case study above demonstrates – that there are factors other than staff in the equation; indeed, in the voluntary sector, it can be argued that whilst staff are its most valuable asset, they should come a long way behind service users, donors and perhaps even trustees when meeting individuals' needs. Having made that clear – after all, staff, personnel and personnel management are but tools in the only purpose of any charity, to be charitable – I shall return again and again to the main theme of this book, namely that a well-managed workforce is the best asset a charity can possibly have, and that this book seeks to help you secure just that.

> **CASE STUDY 2.3** Delegation: A study of how not to do it
>
> An old-established family business recognised the need for a fundraising operation to support a network of service providers in a field that did not readily secure public acceptability and which was a low priority for statutory funding. It therefore established a trust whose work would be to provide infrastructure support while the local service providers raised money for their own efforts. It was therefore necessary to proceed sensitively but effectively, supporting local organisations whilst at the same time raising the general profile of the cause.
>
> For the first few years, the business partners and some of their retired former employees worked voluntarily, with some young (poorly) paid enthusiasts, but the time came when they felt, because of their advancing years, that they needed someone professional at the helm. They therefore appointed a chief executive.
>
> Unfortunately, whilst she brought with her many good ideas and an excellent track record for effective fundraising, she had the reputation of acting as a loose canon (or, as she put it, taking the initiative). The trustees therefore told her that she must refer everything to them and appointed one of their number to work full-time, on a voluntary basis, to be a point of reference for her, as they put it (or keep a close eye on her, as they privately reassured themselves). At the same time the founder, still acting as chair, insisted on continuing in his previous role, not only as a figurehead for fundraising but also dealing with a great deal of the detailed work of the trust as an unpaid volunteer.
>
> The chief executive kept trying out ideas, most of which were successful. But she was always acutely aware of the presence of the supervisory trustee, to whom she was meant to refer everything for decision, including matters of staff management (another thing she was rather good at). The trustees had been used to instructing the junior staff direct, and it was therefore rather difficult for her to manage with any authority.
>
> The time came when the trust needed to move forward or degenerate; other organisations were springing up with more modern ideas, and the local network of service providers was becoming unclear about the trust's role. So the chief executive started to explore new options for fundraising and operations. In accordance with what had been her unspoken but successful practice up to then, she did not tell the supervisory trustee everything from day one, but rather decided to go to him only when ideas had been firmed up. Unfortunately, some of them went wrong,

Whichever way you go, it is critical to ensure that everyone understands that there is a distinction between governance and management, that who is responsible for what is clearly communicated, and that, as far as is humanly possible, people stick to their side of the line. It is equally important that everyone recognises the distinction is not always clear-cut and that no one can foresee every issue that is likely to come up – sometimes delegation decisions have to be made on the spur of the moment. There

including when the chief executive was off sick, and the trustees found out about these exploratory initiatives from outsiders. They then questioned the staff closely, only to learn that the chief executive had taken the staff into her confidence, but had not yet shared her thinking with the trustees.

Thinking that they had been deceived, the trustees started looking back over the chief executive's previous five years of service, only to discover that whilst there had been a series of successes, there were also some projects that had not been pursued or shared with them, and that in some cases there had been a risk of losses to the charity. They did however acknowledge that, on balance, the chief executive had been remarkably successful in developing the charity – it was just that this was not necessarily in the direction they would have liked. She had been too enthusiastic, too pro-active; they felt she had taken their charity away from them.

They therefore concluded that the chief executive had to go, because she had deceived them. She felt equally strongly that they had hampered her in the execution of her duties. The court case continues.

There are many lessons to be drawn from this sad case, and there are many charities in a not dissimilar position to this one. Some of the key points are:

- If you are going to appoint someone to run an organisation, let them run it, particularly when giving them the responsibility for managing staff.
- If you have doubts about whether someone is right for the job, either don't appoint them or accept the consequences of their being different from what you had planned – a compromise to keep them to your agenda is unlikely to be successful.
- Make sure that you are absolutely clear about the limits of authority on all sides, and support people in keeping to them.
- See new ideas as an opportunity, not a threat.
- Learn to distinguish between key policy matters and operational issues, however complex the latter may be.
- Recognise that the world is constantly changing, and respect the advice of professional managers on how most effectively to respond to change.
- Accept that, even as a founder trustee, there will come a time when you have to let go, and that you must delegate to an appropriate level if you are not going to tread on toes – let trustees set the policy and leave the managers to carry it out.

are particular issues for trustees in smaller charities where there remains a need for rather more volunteer involvement in direct management, simply because there's nobody else to share the load with the chief executive. But if you accept the premise that you should go for the maximum of delegation commensurate with the nature and needs of your charity – and if you don't, perhaps you had better stop reading this book now – how do you achieve that happy state of affairs? Again, there is no simple answer, but I offer below a few pointers for you to take up. Very often, charities achieve a satisfactory outcome from going through the process of addressing these issues, without even realising that they have been considering them. On other occasions, they recognise the need for some form of support to facilitate the process. Those that do neither of these things tend to run into trouble, and sooner rather than later.

Checklist 2.1 Issues to consider in securing effective delegation

- ☑ Do you have a clear delineation as to who does what – between managers and staff, between trustees and the chief executive?
- ☑ Are levels of authority – financial, disciplinary, publicity, etc. – clearly spelt out between trustees and staff, and what fall-back arrangements exist?
- ☑ How do trustees review the performance of the organisation and its staff?
- ☑ Do the trustees have a code of conduct and a description of their own duties, and do they stick to them?
- ☑ In a geographically dispersed organisation, have you maximised opportunities for local decision-making, and/or have you put in place an effective internal communications system?
- ☑ Are staff and trustees encouraged to pass ideas and information openly, up, down and sideways through the organisation?
- ☑ Does your organisation encourage innovation at all levels, and in particular how do trustees consider new ideas and policy proposals?
- ☑ Is appraisal a positive, enabling and target-setting process encouraging good performance, or one that staff approach in fear of their jobs if they put a foot wrong?
- ☑ Are your procedures, rules, standards and guidelines intended to be very prescriptive, or are staff encouraged to learn by their mistakes?

Irrespective of your answers to this perhaps challenging list of questions, there remains one area where trustees cannot get away from their direct responsibilities as employers, and that is in respect of the chief executive herself. Even if you have delegated absolutely everything to her, you still, as a trustee, must have in place a framework for her own employment – because, despite this frequently being forgotten by all and sundry, chief executives are employees too, with employment rights and a perfectly reasonable expectation to decent treatment by trustees.

Although this book has been written primarily for employed managers in charities, there is of course no reason why trustees should not consider the issues I cover and then apply them in the most appropriate way to their relationship with the chief executive. That is an approach that has worked successfully when recruitment, review or even discipline of the chief executive has been on the agenda. However, while in a managerial context most issues are dealt with on a one-to-one basis by a small management team dealing with collective processes, there can be a danger of the whole trustee board becoming involved in personnel management problems when it comes to dealing with their one key employee, and that can be cumbersome and often intimidating for the chief executive.

I would suggest that a preferable approach would be for the chair of the board (or, in particular circumstances, another designated trustee) to be the line manager of the chief executive, and for a small body of trustees to deal with all general aspects of her employment, rather along the lines of the Cadbury principles of transparent supervisory arrangements and independent advice on remuneration matters. In that way, there is a day-to-day reference point and framework that should ensure a smooth flow of communication and overall control, as well as a body charged for considering more complex issues, one that can take expert advice as appropriate.

In order for trustees to be confident that they have got the employment of their chief executive right, I offer the following checklist – each of the areas covered is discussed in terms that relate to the whole staff team elsewhere in this book.

Checklist 2.2 Employing your chief executive

- ☑ When recruiting your chief executive, are you clear about what you want, where you will go to find it and how you are going to conduct an open, fair and effective selection process?

- ☑ Do you know how much the job is worth, where you can get advice on appropriate salary levels and how you can operate an independent remuneration review process?

- ☑ Are you clear that, although the chief executive can be seen as 'just another employee', the relationship with trustees is usually subtly different, so that more sensitive arrangements need to apply?

- ☑ How is the work of the chief executive evaluated? Is she subject to an appraisal process like other staff and how is this managed?
- ☑ Who amongst the trustees deals with problems of underperformance and indiscipline, and are there mechanisms for a review of any decisions made?
- ☑ As well as accepting the public acclaim for your charity's successes and praising the staff for achieving them, do you remember that, very often, without the chief executive none of it would have happened?

Once you have given thought to these issues, either in a structured way through a process of internal audit and analysis, or more casually as they occur to you, then you are well on the way to securing a maximum of delegation and delineation that is suitable to your charity. And once you have done that, you will be in a position to be much clearer about the kind of personnel policies and procedures that will suit your organisation. That is the subject of the rest of this book.

In summary ...

All staffing policies in the voluntary sector need to be justified in terms of service delivery outcomes, and there is a general presumption that trustees should not authorise any more expenditure than they have to – although where that level is to be found is a matter for fine judgement in each organisation.

- Charity law expects that trustees will not benefit, directly or indirectly, from their positions. The exceptions to this are so limited that they can in general be ignored.
- Unless every effort is made to avoid conflicts of interest and to allay any suspicion, however ill-founded, trustees and charity managers are likely to run into difficulties.
- Charities should seek to distinguish between governance and management, ensuring that they maximise delegation of decision-making to the lowest possible and appropriate level. In particular, trustees should try to avoid taking detailed operational decisions, and managers should provide a framework in which trustees are enabled to make effective policy decisions.
- Recognise that managing the chief executive needs a similar but distinct approach, with special responsibilities for the trustees to carry out.
- Both trustees and managers need to recognise that they have complementary roles, and need to work together to enable them to come to terms with these roles, thereby maximising their contributions and the charity's effectiveness.

Managing staff – the legal framework

CHAPTER 3

INTRODUCTION

All organisations that employ staff must be aware of the increasing importance of employment law and how it applies to them. It is therefore essential for any personnel book to include a chapter that highlights employers' legal obligations towards staff. This chapter aims to make you aware of the complexities of employment law and provide you with basic information.

It is important that any personnel or charity manager who has the task of employing staff makes sure that there is a clear system in place that considers these principles. The Arbitration, Conciliation and Advisory Service (ACAS) will give guidance on most employment procedures, which should be available for all employees to see. Further useful information regarding the basics can be obtained in literature supplied by the Employment Tribunal (see the Directory).

Employment law is complex, too complicated to address in any detail in one chapter. However, it is important that you read this chapter carefully, as it will start to make you think the correct way when considering employment issues.

The chapter starts by describing the contract of employment and goes on to outline the most significant pieces of employment legislation. If you want to look at the law in greater depth I recommend you consult an employment law textbook or seek qualified legal advice.

Employment law sources

The law relating to employment comes from three primary sources:

- Contract law – the laws of contract and tort (wrongdoing).
- Statute, i.e. Acts of Parliament.

- European legislation and judgements of the European Courts of Justice.

The contract

The contract of employment is the starting point of the relationship between employer and employee. It can be written or oral or a mixture, but in the interests of clarity and to avoid disputes it is advisable for the contract to be in writing. Where there is a dispute over whether a contract exists, the courts will apply a multiple test, considering all the surrounding features before they classify a relationship as one of employment rather than that of self employment, independent contractor or agent. They will consider features such as payment of wages, national insurance, income tax, holiday pay and power to suspend and dismiss. No single factor is conclusive and all the relevant circumstances surrounding the employment relationship must be considered.

Once it is established that a contract of employment exists, the next stage is to consider the terms of the agreement.

The terms of the contract

Every contract of employment consists of a number of terms – 'express', 'implied' and statutory. The parties are free to agree any terms.

- *Express terms* – those that have been agreed between the parties and are included in the contract.
- *Implied terms* – based on the presumed intention of the parties, but not included in the contract.
- *Statutory terms* – implied by statute, such as equal pay for equal work for men and women. An employer will often extend and improve upon the minimum statutory rights.

In a dispute over implied terms the Employment Tribunal will decide the nature of the term after hearing evidence from both parties. The courts will consider all the facts and circumstances before implying a term into the contract and will only do so if it is absolutely necessary, or if it is clear that the employer and employee would have agreed to the term had it been discussed.

If an employer (or employee) tries to terminate a contract of employment before the end of a fixed-term contract or without giving the requisite notice period, this will lead to the possibility of an action being brought for wrongful dismissal.

Written statement of the terms of contract

After agreeing the contractual terms anyone employed for more than one month has the right to receive a written statement of the most important terms of the contract of employment – the statement of particulars – within two months of starting work. It must include:

- The names of employer and employee.
- The date when the employment began.
- Job title or a brief description of the work for which the employee is employed.
- The scale or rate of remuneration.
- Whether remuneration is to be paid weekly, monthly or at some other interval.
- Normal hours of work.
- The place of work or, where the employee is required or permitted to work at various places, an indication of that fact and the address of the employer.

There is a range of other information that must also be given to employees within the same timescale, including details of sickness procedures, pension provision, the length of a fixed-term contract and notice periods. Although this doesn't have to be provided at the same time as the above particulars it would be good practice to include all terms of employment within one document.

Any changes in the terms of employment must be notified by the employer, in writing, within one month of the change.

The requirement for such a statement was introduced by the Employment Rights Act 1996. The status of such a statement is to encourage the development of clear terms. It is intended to be a full reflection of the contract but is not the contract itself. This is a further example of the growing importance of having clear terms and procedures available to the employee.

When drafting the statement it is prudent to build some flexibility into the terms. For further information about the statement of particulars see chapter 6.

The duty of care

Once the contract is identified as a contract of employment the courts attach certain duties to the parties (i.e. the employer and employee):

- The employer has a duty to act reasonably and with care, for example, to provide a safe working environment (whether under health and safety or common law), to keep to his side of the bargain by paying in accordance with the contract and to treat the employee with respect.

- The employee has a duty to obey the employer's reasonable instructions and not wilfully to damage the employer's interest.

This duty of care is at the basis of all contracts, but is particularly important in employment matters, where we are talking about people's livelihoods, their future, the business of the employer and (particularly in the voluntary sector) a group of clients or customers who rely upon the employment relationship working properly for them to benefit.

Liability

The responsibility for all actions of any charity or, for that matter, any organisation, rests firmly with the employer as a corporate entity. Exactly what is meant by a 'corporate entity' will vary depending on the administrative arrangements in place in each organisation, but in the voluntary sector trustees are normally ultimately liable for their employees' actions.

Trustees may choose to delegate responsibility for most staffing matters to a chief executive or other senior manager and indeed, as argued in chapter 2, such delegation if properly managed, may well be the way to get the most out of staff. But the cost of any actions, right or wrong, still usually falls to the organisation and not to the individuals who have carried out those actions.

Disciplinary procedures

Once a person is employed it is important that all the charity's rules and procedures are made clear. The ACAS Code of Practice on Discipline and Grievance Procedures stresses the importance of having a fair disciplinary procedure and that all staff are made aware of it (and this is a legal obligation if you have twenty or more employees). ACAS also publishes the handbook, 'Discipline at Work'. The Employment Appeal Tribunal has stressed the importance of having regard of the ACAS Code. Disciplinary procedures are covered in further detail in chapter 4.

Statute law

The main statutory provisions will be mentioned very briefly here – some are expanded in other chapters.

European legislation

It is not possible to consider the main statutory provisions without also considering European legislation.

European Union (EU) law plays a vital role. There are two main sources: Treaty Provisions and Directives. Provisions of EU Treaties give clear, precise and unconditional rights to individuals, which can be directly enforced in English courts. For example, Article 119 of the Treaty of Rome provides for each member state to maintain the application of the principle that men and women should receive equal pay for equal work. A Directive is secondary EU legislation. It is not directly applicable as it must be implemented by national legislation. However, employees can seek to enforce rights conferred by EU Directives that have not been properly implemented by asking the UK courts to interpret UK legislation in the light of the EU Directive. Public sector employees can sometimes also seek direct enforcement of Directives against the State.

EU law will therefore often be, and sometimes *must* be, incorporated within national legislation.

The following are the main statutory provisions.

Equal pay

- The Equal Pay Act 1970 establishes, where necessary, equal terms and conditions of employment.
- The principle of equal pay was subsequently extended by an EU Directive: work of *equal value* (not necessarily the same work) must be remunerated at the same rate, although when deciding whether it has been, the courts are entitled to take into account the overall benefits package, not just the basic salary rate.
- The equal pay principles apply to non-wage conditions as well as to pay packets so that, for example, variations in working hours between men and women (with a very few exceptions that are now being phased out) are also illegal. How salaries are determined is also a key factor; if your salary bands disproportionately favour one sex amongst your workforce (e.g. residential care workers – usually women – are paid consistently less than accountants – usually men), then you should have a job evaluation scheme (see chapter 7) that can justify the differences by comprehensive factor analysis that genuinely reflects organisational culture and values.

Health and safety

- The Health and Safety at Work Act 1974 established joint employer and employee responsibility for safe working, and imposed a general duty of care on everyone towards each other and towards anyone who may be affected by their actions.
- Ultimate responsibility for employee safety lies with senior management and cannot be delegated. All organisations with

five or more employees are required to prepare and revise as appropriate a written statement of general policy. It may be necessary in larger organisations, indeed desirable, to ensure that many people are responsible for safety management, but they must be fully trained and safety conscious if they are to carry out their duties effectively.

- The 1974 Act provides the basis for, and operates through, a range of subsequent codes, EU Directives and consolidating legislation controlling workplace environment, including:
  - *Control of Substances Hazardous to Health Regulations 1999* (COSHH) – covers substances from Tippex to copier toner, from petrol to paint: if it can be swallowed, breathed, absorbed through the skin or otherwise consumed, then you have to take care. Unless you have a full inventory identifying risks, ensuring there are precautions for safe handling, deployment and storage, and proposing a safer alternative whenever possible, you're not allowed to use the substance. And your initial risk assessment needs to be updated every time you introduce a new substance into the workplace.
  - *Electrical Appliance Inspection Regulations* (EIR) – anything that gets plugged into a power supply needs to be regularly tested by a qualified electrician and must be earthed and only used in accordance with manufacturers' instructions.
  - *Health and Safety (Display Screen Equipment) Regulations 1992* – these flow from an attempt to standardise operations as a result of a 1993 EU Directive. They set down operating standards for the hardware (light levels, radiation emissions, etc.), and offer strict guidelines for location, view and working angles, posture, and so on, as well as working practices such as breaks, length of work time and the obligation on the employer to provide free eyesight tests for 'frequent and habitual' users of VDUs – and to pay for special glasses if they are subsequently needed.
  - *The Manual Handling Operations Regulations 1992* – cover the safe handling of heavy materials – how to lift, stack and load, and so on. Any employer who doesn't ensure that staff know what they are doing is liable to damages if staff get hurt.

Working hours

The Working Time Regulations 1998 cover issues such as the maximum weekly working time (generally forty-eight hours in a seven day period) and entitlement to paid annual leave (see chapter 6).

Anti-discrimination legislation

All employees – regardless of length of service – have a right in law not to be unfairly discriminated against. The three Acts that cover this area are the Sex Discrimination Act 1975 (SDA) (subsequently amended by Sex Discrimination Act 1986), the Race Relations Act 1976 (RRA) and the Disability Discrimination Act 1995 (DDA). These Acts have been supplemented by various secondary legislation including the Sex Discrimination (Gender Reassignment) Regulations 1999.

The SDA and RRA cover:

- *Direct discrimination* – where someone is treated less favourably than others in comparable circumstances because of their sex, race or marital status, for example refusing to appoint a woman to a post because it is 'a man's job'.
- *Indirect discrimination* – imposing a condition or a circumstance that cannot be justified and which puts a racial group, one sex or married people at a disadvantage, for example where there is a proportion of minority ethnic workers who meet the criteria to achieve promotion, but never have the opportunity to apply.
- *Victimisation* – treating someone less favourably because that person has brought, or intends to bring, proceedings or give evidence or information or make allegations in connection with the SDA or RRA.

The DDA covers the same areas of discrimination as the SDA and RRA, but currently only applies to organisations employing fifteen or more staff.

It is therefore important that every selection criterion, every procedure and every action taken by an employer, is carefully scrutinised. It is a clear multi-stage process:

- Does this action have the effect of making some people less able to comply than others? If not, fine, but if yes ...
- Can it really be justified? If yes, it is legitimate, but over time it may no longer be so – you need to review it, and think of other ways of acting.
- If it cannot be justified, you are guilty of indirect discrimination – change your practices now before it is too late.

Unfair dismissal

The Employment Rights Act 1996 ss 94-107 states that all employees have a right not to be unfairly dismissed – i.e. when the employer terminates the contract of employment unilaterally, in circumstances which the employee feels to be unfair. Unless the employment had come to its end anyway as a fixed-term contract, there was a redundancy situation or a significant breach of contract, any such termination is potentially unfair.

Any employee who has been in post for at least one year can complain to the Employment Tribunal if they feel they have been unfairly dismissed. It is then it is up to the employer to show that the reason for the dismissal was fair. This could be for the following reasons:

- *Employee inability* – the employee couldn't do the job.
- *Long term sickness* – an employee who is absent from work for a long period because of sickness or ill-health is entitled to sympathetic consideration by the employer, but only within a reasonable limit.
- *Employee misconduct* – the employee's actions had been such that, over time they had accumulated to the point where they were intolerable, for example continuing absenteeism or lateness, or they amounted to gross misconduct – for example, major theft from the employer. In either case it is essential that the employer followed the correct procedure and dealt with the matter in accordance with the guidance given in ACAS' Code of Practice for disciplinary procedures (see chapter 4).
- *Some other substantial reason* – very difficult to prove and should be entered into very carefully after taking advice.

Not only must the reason for dismissal be shown to be fair, so also must the way it was carried out. However badly an employee has behaved, there is no excuse for the employer to behave equally badly in dismissing them. Proper consideration needs to be given to the case, and the employee's story considered, if a dismissal process is going to gain credibility. This highlights the need for a good and fair disciplinary procedure to be in place.

An employee who is dismissed, either with or without notice, or by the expiry of a fixed-term contract, is entitled to receive a written statement of the reasons for dismissal within 14 days of a request.

Constructive dismissal

This is where the employee terminates the contract, with or without notice, because of the employer's conduct. To be able to claim constructive dismissal the employee must make it clear that she is treating the contract as having been repudiated by the employer.

Compensation

Unfair dismissal awards are composed of two payments: an automatic basic award calculated on the employee's length of service and age (as of February 2001 a maximum of £7,200) and a compensatory award – what the Employment Tribunal considers just and equitable, up to a maximum of £57,000.

Staff transfers

Far reaching rules for the protection of employees' rights on the transfer of a trade or business are contained in the Transfer of Undertakings (Protection of Employment) Regulations 1981 (TUPE) and Collective Redundancies and Transfer of Undertakings (Protection of Employment) (Amendment) Regulations 1995–1999. It is a difficult area of law, with a complex and continuing argument over exactly what constitutes transfer and I recommend you get specialist advice if you are going to provide a service that was previously provided by someone else. If you are covered by the above Regulations the following will apply:

- Staff transferring are entitled to bring with them the service conditions they enjoyed immediately before transfer, including salaries and other benefits, non-wage conditions and procedures (pensions are the only exception). They are also treated as if they have continuous service with you from when they started with the previous employer, so may well have employment protection rights. The law's basic position is that their access to these conditions and rights will continue for as long as they would have done with their previous employer.
- You also inherit any obligations of the previous employer, such as redundancy costs if you need to slim down the workforce once it has transferred; however, selection for redundancy simply on the grounds of having been transferred is likely to be considered unfair.
- You may finish up with two sets of employment conditions – yours and the previous employer's. There is therefore a key industrial relations issue of whether you wish to integrate, and if so, how you intend to achieve this. Staff transferring can be bought out, but they do not have to agree, and you could well finish up with a partially integrated workforce. A great deal of effort may need to be spent dealing with very few employees.
- If the group transferring does not impact on the rest of your operations, some of the problems of integration may be avoided. However, one of the reasons that you were awarded the contract may be that you appeared more efficient than an in-house proposal. So you are now stuck with staff on service conditions that do not enable you to operate in the way you had anticipated. It is at this point that the protection that employees and their unions imagined they had been offered by TUPE starts to break down.

- If you need to change the contracts of employment of transferring staff, you can do so if you give them due notice under those contracts of your proposed changes. If they accept the changes, so much the better. But if they resist, your only option is to dismiss them and then offer re-engagement under new contracts on your terms. Whether you can successfully defend the subsequent unfair dismissal claims will largely depend on how sensitively you have handled the process, and whether you can demonstrate that the changes were genuinely forced on you out of economic necessity. If you find yourself in a situation involving this area then seek professional advice immediately.

Unions

The main Act governing trades unions and trade disputes is the Trade Union and Labour Relations (Consolidation) Act 1992, as amended by the Trade Union Reform and Employment Rights Act 1993. Union membership is covered in chapter 5.

Employment Rights Act 1996

This is a major piece of employment legislation that was mentioned earlier in the context of unfair dismissal. This Act also covers a number of other areas, including maternity and redundancy rights.

Maternity

A pregnant employee has a number of specific rights, in particular the right to maternity leave and the right not to be dismissed for any reason connected with the pregnancy or maternity leave. The precise rights will depend on various factors such as length of service and salary level prior to going on leave. The whole area of maternity rights is very complex for all employers. In addition to statute there are also contract and European law considerations. Increasingly there are also issues such as paternity rights to consider. Some further information is included in chapter 6, but if in any doubt you should take specialist advice.

Redundancy

There will be times when, due to changes in the location or nature of the employer's work, a legitimate reduction in staffing levels needs to be made. It is important that an employer adopts the correct procedures when faced with a situation that may lead to redundancies. An employer cannot make staff 'redundant' and get away with such action unless the relevant criteria for a true redundancy situation are met. Specialist advice should be taken.

An eligible employee dismissed by reason of redundancy will be entitled to a statutory redundancy payment from his employer. Redundancy is covered further in chapter 12.

Employment Relations Act 1999

This Act has made changes to trade union law and has simplified provisions relating to maternity pay and time off work for domestic emergencies, to care for dependants and parental leave. The Act also introduced the right for an employee to be accompanied in grievance or disciplinary proceedings.

Human Rights Act 1998

This came into force in October 2000. The Act provides that any new legislation must be compatible with European law. It applies to the actions of public bodies and those bodies carrying out public functions – which could include charities if they carry out functions on behalf of public bodies. At the time of writing the impact of the Act was unclear but it is important that you are aware of it and the impact it may have on your organisation's policies, practices and procedures.

National Minimum Wage Act 1998

This created the Low Pay Commission and entitles employees to be remunerated at a rate which is not less than the minimum wage. The Commission sets the level.

Employment Tribunals

An Employment Tribunal (previously an Industrial Tribunal) is concerned with two main issues: liability and remedies. If successful on the former, the Tribunal will look at what remedies are available to the ex-employee – re-instatement (old job back), re-engagement (different job with the same employer, or a successor or associated employer), financial compensation or a combination.

The rules under which Tribunals operate are complex. It is not practicable to describe them here, but it is worth being aware that one of the key points is that, within reason, Tribunals can vary their own rules if it makes industrial good sense to do so, or if the interests of natural justice so demand. Tribunal decisions are persuasive but not binding on other Tribunals. Judgements of the Employment Appeal Tribunal (EAT) and of higher courts are binding. Cases will go to the EAT if there is a point of law to be determined – either because the Tribunal has misapplied the law as it currently stands, or its procedures were perverse or unjust.

Employment Tribunals are covered in more detail in chapter 12.

A word or two about case law

Lawyers often quote cases, usually those that have been to the Employment Appeal Tribunal or to a higher court. These give guidance on how common law, statutory provisions and European law should be interpreted. The cases will often be about different interpretations at different times on what is considered reasonable.

In summary ...

I hope that you will see this chapter as a concise introduction to the complex world of employment law and that it has started you thinking about the employment practices that are adopted by your organisation. The chapter provides a framework to make you aware that the rules of law must be considered very seriously and that they are neglected at your peril.

Some areas are covered in more detail in other chapters. If you are in any doubt about any aspect of employment law it is essential to take specialist advice.

Managing staff – rules, procedures and best practice in times of change

CHAPTER 4

INTRODUCTION

There is always a danger, when considering such issues, to wander into the realms of philosophy, an area where many personnel managers would feel distinctly uncomfortable. I shall try to avoid that fate here; but in the voluntary sector in particular, where style and culture are important – indeed essential – parts of what you are doing, it is impractical to try to separate out completely the pragmatism of the 'how to secure the best results from our people' from the 'why are we here and how can we be sure that the way we do it fits in with our quality standards?' debate.

The private sector is just beginning to discover ethical management. The voluntary sector has been practising it for years – although not consistently. Some of the worst employers in the sector, certainly in terms of how they treat their employees and the conditions they grant, are trades unions and campaigning bodies seeking to enhance workers' rights. And they, of course, are always faced with the classic voluntary sector dilemma – how can they maximise the quality and quantity of the outputs to their beneficiaries, whilst at the same time offering conditions that are advantageous to their staff? The short answer is, of course, that they can't. Like everyone else, charity managers have to strike compromises. How they do this, without surrendering their principles and keeping to best practice, is the essence of the first part of this chapter. It also outlines the necessary procedures for handling disciplinary and grievance procedures.

What is best practice?

It is not my intention to offer prescriptive models for best practice; every charity will need to consider its own position. But there are methodologies available, and there are, I believe, some underlying principles that most voluntary sector managers would recognise, principles that can perhaps be described as the keys to best practice in voluntary sector employment. I would argue that the most successful charities will have secured their success if they have approached the management of their staff, and particularly developmental issues, having taken account of the following aspects:

- *A willing adherence to the current state of the law, both of cases that establish current application, and of the statutory requirements that underpin them.* There is always a game to be played in trying to get round the law, but in general to play it gives employers a bad name. It is a bit like the distinction between tax evasion and tax avoidance – the former is illegal, the latter clever, but both are undesirable. I do not even comment on those employers who deliberately flout the law – they deserve everything they get. But there are also those organisations that are willing to exploit the grey areas, to push the boundaries out in their favour and against the interests of their employees. They may gain short-term advantage, but employees' memories are long, and when legislation does change, there will always be people around who find that revenge is sweet.
- *A willingness to embrace optional elements of legal matters.* For example, on the one hand, employment codes, and on the other, extending contractual rights to employees who aren't statutorily entitled to them. Employers declaring that they are prepared to treat all their staff equally will usually find that in terms of increased employee commitment and effort this far outweighs the marginal cost of the benefits themselves. Now that the Social Chapter has been adopted in Britain, the same is already beginning to happen, with many of our more enlightened employers are following their European counterparts and acceding to their employees' requests for consistency of treatment.
- *Efforts to encourage employee involvement.* European employment practice places considerable emphasis on a commitment to staff involvement, consultation, empowerment and development. The British situation is rather different, with an adversarial political and legal system spilling over into our industrial relations. The more enlightened private sector organisations, particularly in the commercial sector, are already well down the road of employee involvement, and

their profit margins are generally reaping dividends. So also can a lesson be learnt by Britain's charity sector. Involve the staff in planning their working lives, identifying organisational objectives and determining new areas to operate, and you will have a good chance of securing greater commitment and efficiency. Ignore them or tell them who's boss, and you could find yourself with a disgruntled workforce – or no workforce at all. But do be sure that you distinguish between employee involvement and consultation on the one hand, and what can amount to employee veto and control on the other. Unless you take an extreme left-wing perspective, the latter is probably inappropriate for the voluntary sector, which, above all others, needs to put first and foremost the needs of its end users.

- *Staff should be remunerated appropriately and fairly.* The voluntary sector has, with virtually no exceptions, never been a good payer. Data from the Charity Appointments/Reward salary survey have shown that charity managers earn fifteen per cent less than their commercial counterparts, and that pattern is repeated throughout the sector. Only the most junior staff seem to do a little better than in the general world of work. This pattern clearly reflects a concern to ensure that charitable donations are targeted at end-users, coupled with the social conscience about its own low-paid staff for which the sector is renowned. But the historic situation does not offer a justification for unnecessarily low wage levels and unnecessarily onerous employment conditions, and many managers in the sector will argue, as they do over any tendency towards a lack of staff involvement, that they are, in the longer term, counterproductive.

- *Employment practices should be underpinned by a genuine acceptance of effective equal opportunities practice.* The final element in voluntary sector best practice is one which is increasingly shared with the public sector, but only slowly with the rest of the world of work. This does not mean the knee-jerk mechanistic processes of the 1980s, but rather a clear understanding of how disadvantage arises in society, together with a commitment to remove blockages and to provide sensitive services through high-quality staff to a disadvantaged client group. After all, charities are all about addressing disadvantage, particularly in dealing with concerns over poverty, health and education. By their very existence, they are seeking to deliver greater equality of opportunity to the groups they seek to assist. It makes absolute sense that they are positively self-critical in equal opportunities terms on how they go about it.

So, to sum up, best practice in the voluntary sector is based on four pillars:

- Willing acceptance of the current state of the law.
- Embracing optional good employment practices.
- Avoiding exploitation.
- Commitment to equal opportunities.

Putting these together as an underpinning set of values will enable charity employers to develop their staff resources in the best way available to the charities and to the staff themselves. Applying them in practical terms to your own situation should enable you to move towards working models of best practice.

Employment practice can perhaps be best described by:

- What you *must* do – the legal requirements on both employers and employees.
- What you *could* do – taking things as far as is appropriate for your organisation.

MODEL 4.1 Contents of a staff handbook for a small charity

Note: You may not wish to have policies and procedures to cover all the following issues, but it should serve as a tool for you to decide what you wish to include, and what to leave out.

Section 1: The overarching framework

- The role and use of the staff handbook
- *The Charity's* overarching personnel policies:
  - principal objectives
  - guidelines for operation and good practice

Section 2: Staff management

- Management and staff responsibilities:
  - management style
  - expectations of staff
  - standards of work
  - staff dress code
  - confidentiality policy
- External relationships:
  - the role of *The Charity*
  - dealing with the public and service users
- Equal opportunities in employment
- Health and safety policy and management
- Risk assessment, safety inspections and good practice:
  - operational guidelines
  - checklists
- Smoking and alcohol policy
- Code of conduct and disciplinary rules
- Disciplinary procedure
- Capability procedure
- Grievance procedure
- Dealing with harassment at work

Section 3: Staff development

- Recruitment procedure:
  - policy and administrative arrangements
  - model job description
  - model person specification
- Training and staff development policy
- Training objectives and priorities
- Staff supervision and appraisal:
  - regular management arrangements
  - appraisal procedure
  - standard appraisal documentation

Section 4: Staff conditions

- Employee consultation and representation:

MANAGING STAFF – RULES, PROCEDURES AND BEST PRACTICE

What you must do has already been set out in chapter 3 and will be looked at again in chapter 6. Extending this into practice and procedures is further discussed in chapter 7, and I also offer some advice below on why you need rules and how they should be implemented. Put together, they will give any charity manager a comprehensive framework for best employment practice that suits both her organisation and its staff. That framework can and should contain what you must do, what you think it is right that you should do, and a way of ensuring that everyone knows about both. The classic way forward on that is to prepare and publish a staff handbook that draws all the threads together. Set out below is a possible table of contents for a handbook, that you can modify to suit your own operational needs; many of the items suggested are discussed in further detail throughout this book.

- individual rights
- union recognition
- trade union procedural agreement

■ Standard statement of particulars of terms and conditions of employment

■ Salary review policy:
- salary scales
- annual review and incremental progress
- job evaluation

■ Hours and annual leave:
- flexitime scheme
- time off in lieu
- annual entitlements

■ Sick leave and pay:
- absence and sick pay entitlements
- reporting procedure
- review arrangements

■ Special leave:
- maternity leave
- partner/parental leave
- adoption leave
- carer's leave
- time off for public duties
- unpaid leave
- sabbaticals
- study leave

■ Employee expenses and transport:
- petty cash
- entitlements
- car allowances
- cycle allowance
- other transport arrangements

■ Notice, pensions and retirement:
- periods of notice
- normal retirement arrangements
- access to and details of pension scheme(s)

■ Redundancy:
- policy
- redundancy agreement

You may also want to publish the following, although not as part of a staff handbook, but instead making reference in the handbook to their importance and location:

■ Office administrative procedures

■ Financial regulations

■ Job description bank

■ Person specification bank

Pointers to determining good practice: how do we get there?

Managing the process

Every employer will need to determine individually to what extent employment practices should go beyond the legal minimum, in order to be satisfied that good practice criteria have been met. Every charity is different, and so no two charities are likely to agree completely on their service conditions and practices. Throughout the rest of this book, therefore, I offer pointers to good practice in specific areas and checklists on what to consider when determining employment arrangements – it is then up to you to apply them to suit your own circumstances.

One key to effective personnel management is to adopt a strategic approach, and ensure that, as far as the law allows (and best practice too if, as is usually the case, that is your choice), every element of the employer-employee relationship fits within the strategy. This is easier to do if you're starting from scratch, or if you are in the commercial sector, where profit maximisation objectives are clear, and everything that you do is subsumed by and targeted on that goal. And it is fairly straightforward in the public sector, with its (relatively) ready acceptance of bureaucratic processes, sometimes apparently almost for their own sake.

But in the voluntary sector, probably more than anywhere else, the more general experience is that a strategic approach to production or service delivery, including the management of staff to achieve charitable objectives, was not determined from the outset. Rather, a few like-minded people got together to tackle a social problem, then they took on an administrator to support their own voluntary efforts. The administrator generated more income and the charity grew, so she took on an assistant, and only then did the volunteers start thinking about their role as an employer. By that time, in many cases, it was too late, and they were already faced with their first Employment Tribunal case. A case of 'If I were you, I wouldn't start from here in the first place!'.

Nevertheless, a strategic approach will pay dividends in the end, even if that sounds like the wisdom of hindsight. It will enable you to consolidate and manage if you've been going for some time, or think more clearly if you are just setting out – or, in common with the rest of the sector, you are having, however reluctantly, to face up to the enormous changes that the pincer movements of more regulatory legislation and a more demanding public and group of service users have imposed on the sector. You may therefore consider it worthwhile to develop an overall personnel policy strategy document, and incorporate all rights, obligations and procedures into a comprehensive staff handbook. Such a handbook is no substitute for good management, but it can serve as an invaluable tool and support for it. Then, even the most anarchic of situations can, with the right determination, be managed successfully.

Why do we need rules?

Personnel isn't completely – or even mainly – about rules. It is far more about motivation, development and reward. These key topics are discussed in later chapters. But since all voluntary sector organisations are communities of some kind, and since all communities continue to exist, ultimately, through the consent of those who comprise them, clearly some rules are necessary to cement together that consent, and to deal with situations when breaches of those rules occur. So the rest of this chapter addresses the thorny questions of disciplinary rules and procedures to cope when people break them – disciplinary procedures when employees deliberately do what they shouldn't, capability processes when they are unable to do what they should, and grievance arrangements for when the organisation itself gets it wrong. And when you've got to the end of this chapter, you can pass on to the more positive parts of this book, in the hope that the only problems you'll ever have to address will be those of success and how to be even more successful. You'll be lucky! It might be worth your while noting this page number, just in case you have to come back to it at any time.

There are many issues that any organisation has to consider, but they can be broken down very simply into three stages: determining what the rules are; making sure that everyone knows about them; and what you do when they are broken. Grievance procedures are a variation on the last of these stages, and capability is a different approach, often with the same outcome.

Every organisation is slightly different, and so the rules will inevitably vary to reflect the nature of the operations. The larger the organisation, the more likely is it that the 'rule book' will be complex. The smaller it is, the greater chance of informality being acceptable and workable. And you can try to operate different sets of rules for different parts of the charity, or for different types of employees – but beware, Employment Tribunals tend to look at large charities as one employer, not a series of small ones (even when you have a federated structure). So unless you can demonstrate an overwhelming need for different rules and different emphasis in different places, they may consider your actions to be unfair if you treat indiscipline amongst one group of workers in a more severe way than in the case of others. And if one group is predominantly female or black, then not only will you have unfair dismissal claims lodged against you, you run the risk of discrimination allegations even if nobody gets sacked!

This all points to the need for good communication of, and justification for the employer's requirements. That can best be done within the context of a disciplinary policy that sets out why the charity has the rules it does, and sets out those rules clearly. In formulating such a policy, I suggest that you take the following points into account:

Checklist 4.1 Formulating a disciplinary policy

- ☑ Have you sought the staff's views on what rules are appropriate? Very often they have just as keen a sense of right and wrong as their managers, perhaps even more so. It's always worth seeking agreement on the rule book, and getting a joint commitment to its validity and enforcement. But remember that a rule book is not a description of how to do (or not to do) a job, it should be a positive underpinning guide on how to offer your best efforts. Make it the former, and the charity soon loses control of its operations and anarchy reigns.

- ☑ Are there generally understood rules and standards that operate in charities like yours (such as a code of professional conduct for certain staff, like the Chartered Institute of Personnel and Development's or that operated by the Bar Council?) If so, they can be useful benchmarks, and staff will have great difficulty in resisting them, since they will already have signed up to the code to maintain their membership of the professional institute. If you have made it a requirement of the job that they qualify for such membership, the obligation on the employee is plain.

- ☑ Because the charity is ultimately responsible for its actions and those of its staff, it has to be the charity corporately that sets the rules, preferably after full consultation. And so it must also be able to make changes in those rules when it appears prudent to do so. Thus you need to consider a mechanism whereby such changes are made and promulgated, and whereby the rules form part of staff's contracts of employment. Otherwise, there will be arguments about whether they apply to individual employees in individual circumstances.

- ☑ Much industrial relations practice is sound common sense. It is obvious, and should perhaps go without saying, that you shouldn't steal from your employer. The twin duties of care and fidelity discussed in chapter 3 underpin this. But sometimes it's worth stating the obvious all the same, if only for the sake of completeness, or to head off barrack room lawyers. Unfortunately, completeness is

MANAGING STAFF – RULES, PROCEDURES AND BEST PRACTICE

never fully possible – there will always be some employee somewhere who commits an offence that nobody had anticipated. That's why it is important in any set of rules to include a disclaimer clause, to cover the unexpected. How you then respond is subject to the tests of reasonableness, and Employment Tribunals will judge accordingly. They will also judge how you respond even with offences clearly set out in the rules since, as I have explained before, the test of reasonableness is not just the response to the accusation of misconduct, but how you conduct that response.

- ☑ Does your organisation clearly understand the meaning of gross misconduct? In law, it is when an employee has done something so bad that by so doing, they have rendered their contract of employment null and void, there and then. They probably aren't entitled to consideration under the full disciplinary process, including accumulating warnings and so on, because you can't afford to keep them on, but rather they will be summarily dismissed. Whilst even in these cases they need to be handled sensitively (and how you do that is discussed below), it is worth setting out in your disciplinary policy that you do draw the distinction between gross and other types of misconduct, and that you will respond accordingly. Your own charity's definition of gross misconduct could therefore feature in your rules policy, as a precursor to the rules themselves. If you set out the kind of actions that could lead to summary dismissal and those lesser concerns that are unlikely to do so, everyone knows where they are. And it is always worth putting in the caveat that in some circumstances, lesser offences may amount to gross misconduct, and vice versa.

- ☑ As for the rules themselves, the emphasis will vary between voluntary sector organisations, reflecting their cultural norms. Violence and theft are likely to feature high in most lists, but confidentiality may be more important in some than in others, and for certain organisations, creativity may be the price worth paying for disobedience. Offences against equal opportunity policies are more important for some charities than for others, and breaches of health and safety arrangements will play a more prominent role in higher risk organisations.

- ☑ Many breaches of rules tend to be petty and a nuisance, but little more. These do, however, need to be dealt with before they get worse and again, an indication of what is, and what is not, acceptable, is very useful. Thus a list of potential offences falling short of gross misconduct serves to set standards, and how breaches are dealt with will then vary depending on the charity's view of how the early stages of its disciplinary procedure should operate.

- ☑ One particularly tricky area is criminal convictions or allegations not connected with work. Motoring offences normally should not worry you (unless the employee is paid to drive for your charity), but what about theft or fraud if they are employed as an accountant? And how would your donors feel if you were a child care charity and you discovered you were employing a paedophile, even if he didn't have unsupervised access to children? Again, there is no simple rule: you do need to work out what behaviour, in work and out, is acceptable to you, and then make it clear to your staff. And you also need to act promptly when allegations are made. Whether you do so before or after a conviction is a sensitive area, and there is a great deal of case law beyond the scope of this book. But it is worth remembering that if you have genuine reason to believe that a criminal offence has been committed, you may have a fair defence if you take action now, even if there is a subsequent finding of innocence. There are many cases to prove this, and again it all turns on reasonableness, but each case does need to be considered on its

---

MODEL 4.2 Code of conduct and disciplinary rules

1. *The Charity* shares with its staff a commitment to upholding the highest standards of professional conduct.

2. To this end, its professional staff will abide by the various codes of conduct of the *ABC Institute*, and all staff will accept the disciplines required for the effective management of the organisation and the most effective delivery of services to clients.

3. All paid staff and volunteers are expected to apply themselves diligently to their responsibilities, and to take every reasonable step to ensure that they are capable of carrying out these responsibilities in the manner prescribed by *The Charity*.

4. All employees will at all times observe *The Charity's* policies and procedures as agreed and developed by the trustee board, will abide by the terms and conditions in their contracts of employment, and will follow such disciplinary rules as may be adopted from time to time.

5. To this end, *The Charity* has adopted the following disciplinary rules. It is stressed that this list is not exhaustive, but indicative of what may constitute misconduct. Other issues may arise which may also be subject to the disciplinary process; areas indicated as potentially gross misconduct may on occasion be treated as a lesser offence, and vice versa.

6. Gross misconduct is defined as an action so serious that *The Charity* would be justified in dismissing a member of staff on the first offence without notice, behaviour that makes further trust between *The Charity* and the employee impossible and thus destroys the contract of employment. Other misconduct is indiscipline that falls short of this definition.

7. Examples of potential gross misconduct are:
   - Theft or unauthorised possession of, or wilful damage to, *The Charity's*, another employee's or a client's property, including fraud, deceit or dishonesty.
   - Continued refusal to carry out reasonable management instructions.

MANAGING STAFF – RULES, PROCEDURES AND BEST PRACTICE

merits, and you are well advised to seek support from lawyers or personnel specialists if you are faced with such a problem.

You will need to work out your own rules to suit your own organisation and its staff. You may choose to do it alone, in consultation with your staff, or with the help of outside advice. I can offer little more than a model code of conduct and set of rules, which, if nothing else, should serve as a prompt for your further consideration.

Disciplinary procedures

So you've decided what your rules are. You've communicated your decisions to your staff and you've told them about all the

- Extreme rudeness or abuse towards managers, colleagues, clients or members of the public.
- Unbecoming conduct at work which would threaten workplace relationships, including:
  - fighting or assault in or connected to the workplace
  - being under the influence of alcohol or unprescribed drugs
  - endangering the health or safety of others
  - indecent behaviour or sexual misconduct
  - harassment or direct discrimination on the grounds of race, gender, religion, sexuality, disability, marital status or age.
- Criminal convictions where the credibility of *The Charity* is threatened by its connection with the convicted employee.
- Significant and unauthorised breach of confidentiality.

8   Examples of other types of potential misconduct are:
- Poor timekeeping, absenteeism or failure to work to a pattern acceptable to *The Charity*.
- Failure to follow *The Charity's* policies and procedures, where not covered under the gross misconduct rules.
- Deliberately working below an acceptable standard.
- Abuse of the sick pay, annual or special leave arrangements.
- Failure to carry out reasonable instructions.
- Disruption of the work of colleagues.
- Damage to property arising from negligence.
- Milder examples of offences listed under the gross misconduct rules.

9   It is not necessarily possible to determine whether an offence should be classified as gross or other misconduct without investigation. The severity of the misconduct, if proven, is a finding of the disciplinary process, not in itself an accusation. *The Charity* has therefore adopted its own disciplinary procedure to provide a framework for investigation and decision.

changes you've made in the light of experience. Still someone is foolish enough to do something wrong. How do you handle the situation? You need a disciplinary procedure.

Each charity will have separate arrangements, depending on considerations such as size, how far authority is delegated to managers, the degree of involvement of trustees, whether unions are recognised, the extent of formality or informality of management style, and so on. But these are all matters of emphasis. For a disciplinary process to be defensible as fair, if you've used it to sack someone and find yourself at an Employment Tribunal as a result (and remember, the process as well as the reason for dismissal must be fair), it should normally have taken account of the following key aspects:

Checklist 4.2 Testing your disciplinary policy

☑ Does it ensure that complaints against the employee are fully set out, and does it have provision for allegations to be fully investigated before formal accusations are made? Unless the employee knows what she is being accused of, and has adequate time to prepare her defence, no process is likely to be seen as fair.

☑ Are you abiding by the legal requirement for the employee to be properly represented (by a colleague or union official, for example) at every formal stage of the process? Some employers fight shy of allowing representation by lawyers – normally a reasonable reaction, because an internal proceeding is not a court of law, and industrial common sense is what should govern it, not fine points of law. But if an outside lawyer is brought in, it is worth reminding them that they are there to operate within the procedures and rules as a representative, not as a solicitor.

☑ Does the employee have adequate opportunity for putting her side of the story and cross-examining the evidence, and those putting it, against her? If not, any decision on that evidence is likely to be seen as biased.

☑ As far as practicable, is the person making the accusation different from the person who makes the decision on the evidence? In smaller organisations, it may be difficult to avoid one person playing both roles of prosecuting counsel and judge (and even taking initial managerial decisions such as whether to suspend the employee pending investigations), but in such circumstances, all the other safeguards described here must come into play if you are not to be accused of running a kangaroo court.

☑ Is care taken to ensure that, if proven, the punishment fits the crime, and that there is a chance for all extenuating circumstances to be taken into account?

☑ Do you have provision for an independent appeal against any finding of misconduct, conducted by someone not involved in the original consideration of the case?

If you are able to respond positively to all items in this checklist, you are well on the way to having an effective and fair disciplinary procedure. But even if you cannot – and the only real excuse is the size of your organisation – then provided that you have made every effort to act reasonably, you are unlikely to fall foul of the law. Remember that the golden rule is reasonableness in all circumstances, taking into account the employer's size and resources available.

Because of the issue of size, two rather different models for a disciplinary procedure are offered below. The first gives a framework for small organisations, typically with a flat management structure and maybe no more than a dozen staff. In such situations, it is unlikely that different people will be able to play the roles of manager deciding to suspend, of investigating the complaint, presenting the accusations, listening to and deciding on the evidence, and providing expert advice. For the small charity – and depending on your definition, this covers perhaps 95 per cent of all organisations in the sector – the manager/chief executive/ director is likely to have to suspend, investigate and then listen to the arguments. In these circumstances, she will have to be very careful to be objective and, if you do nothing else, you must have provision for a separate appeals process to test that objectivity.

In larger organisations, it is possible, indeed desirable, to separate these various roles, and Employment Tribunals would be very critical if you did not do so. But however you do it, it is important to maintain managerial control of the process. It is generally unwise to place any part of the decision-making process outside your charity, since that way, you will have to live with the consequences of someone else's decisions, someone who may not be accountable to your charity, its trustees or its clients. Of course, this is very different from bringing in an outside party, such as ACAS, to help resolve a dispute arising from disciplinary action having been taken: this is an industrial relations matter (which can often benefit from outside intervention) following on from a decision that has, quite properly, been taken by management.

So base your procedures, however loosely, on one of the models set out on the following pages, depending on your organisation's size.

MODEL 4.3 Disciplinary procedure – small charities

1. *The Small Charity* recognises that in an organisation of its size, informal resolution of concerns about an employee's behaviour is usually the best way of maintaining effective working relationships. It is therefore incumbent upon the chief executive, who has full responsibility for all disciplinary issues, to seek to resolve matters of minor misconduct quickly and without recourse to this procedure.

2. However, it is also recognised that more serious incidents of indiscipline, or the repetition of minor incidents, may need to be dealt with under this formal procedure. Such matters are likely to be of the kind indicated in the code of conduct and disciplinary rules.

3. If, in the chief executive's opinion, there has been a breach of good discipline serious enough to warrant formal action, then the employee shall be so advised in writing, setting out the grounds of concern, and indicating how the chief executive intends to proceed to investigate the allegation. In the event of most disciplinary complaints short of gross misconduct, the chief executive shall conduct the disciplinary hearing; for issues of alleged gross misconduct, or where accumulated misconduct could result in an employee's dismissal with notice, the chief executive will investigate the complaint and present findings to the staffing sub-committee of the trustee board.

4. At least three working days prior to any formal disciplinary hearing, the full details of the complaint against the employee and of any evidence or witnesses that will be brought to substantiate the complaint should be provided in writing to the employee and (if appropriate) the employee's representative, who may be a work colleague or a trade union official. The employee should provide in writing at least 24 hours before the hearing details of any witnesses and evidence to be called to refute the allegations.

5. At the hearing, the complaint and evidence to support it will be presented first, the chief executive explaining her/his concerns, setting out the details, and presenting such evidence and witnesses as may be appropriate to substantiate the allegations. The defence to the allegations will then be offered in the same way by the employee or her/his representative. Both sides may cross-examine evidence and witnesses. A decision on the substance of the complaint will then be made, sitting alone, by either the chief executive or the staffing sub-committee as appropriate, who may seek such advice in reaching their conclusions as may be necessary, which may include inviting advisers to attend as observers during the disciplinary hearing itself. The decision will be made on the balance of probability.

6. The decision will then be communicated to the employee. If the case has been found not proven, the matter will end there, and all reference to it will be expunged from *The Small Charity's* records. If the case has been found proven, the employee will be invited to make a statement in mitigation. A final decision will then be made on the outcome of the disciplinary process, which may take one of the following forms:

- **First written warning** – when the offence is a first and relatively minor one.
- **Further written warning** – where there has been a continuation of misconduct.
- **Final written warning** – where, if the employee offends again, dismissal is likely to be the result.
- **Dismissal with notice** – where the employee has consistently failed to remedy misconduct.
- **Summary dismissal** – where the employee has been found guilty of gross misconduct, and there are no substantial mitigating factors.

7 Although it is intended that, in general, this process is cumulative, in cases of early instances of serious misconduct short of gross misconduct, a finding more severe than a first or subsequent written warning may be considered appropriate.

8 Warnings will normally stay on an employee's record as follows:
- **First written warning** – one year from the date of issue.
- **Further written warning** – two years from the date of issue.
- **Final written warning** – indefinitely.

The duration of these warnings may in exceptional circumstances be varied by the staffing sub-committee.

9 An employee may appeal against the outcome of a disciplinary hearing on the grounds either of its findings or the severity of the action. An appeal against a decision by the chief executive will be heard by the staffing sub-committee; an appeal against a decision of that body by the full trustee board, excluding members of the staffing sub-committee. The same procedure will generally apply as at the original hearing, save that only evidence and findings in dispute will be considered, and that the person who chaired the original disciplinary hearing shall present the findings, calling other managers as witnesses as appropriate. The appeal body may substitute any alternative outcome, or uphold the original decision.

10 In cases of alleged gross misconduct, it will be the norm to suspend the employee on full pay pending the outcome of the process. Suspended employees may have access to *The Small Charity's* premises, records, staff and clients only by prior arrangement with the chief executive, and only to prepare a defence.

11 All employees have the right to be represented by a full-time trade union official, but not by any other person outside *The Small Charity*, at all formal stages of the disciplinary process, although during the earlier investigatory stage, the chief executive has the right to discuss matters alone with them. Employees and their representatives have the right to a reasonable amount of time off with pay to prepare and present the defence to the allegations.

12 In the event of disciplinary action against the chief executive, the procedure set out above will apply, save that the matter will be investigated and the hearing conducted or presented by the chair of the trustee board.

MODEL 4.4 Disciplinary procedure – large charities

1. *The Large Charity* recognises that informal resolution of concerns about an employee's behaviour is usually the best way of maintaining effective working relationships. It is therefore incumbent upon all managers who have delegated responsibility for disciplinary issues to seek to resolve matters of minor misconduct quickly and without recourse to this procedure.

2. However, it is also recognised that more serious incidents of indiscipline, or the repetition of minor incidents, may need to be dealt with under this formal procedure. Such matters are likely to be of the kind indicated in the code of conduct and disciplinary rules.

3. If, in the opinion of a line manager (which shall be taken to mean any employee who has formal responsibility for the direction of the work of other staff of *The Large Charity*), there has been a breach of good discipline serious enough to warrant formal action, then the line manager shall so advise the employee in writing, setting out the grounds of concern, and indicating how the line manager intends to proceed to investigate the allegation.

4. In the event of most disciplinary complaints short of gross misconduct, the manager or the line manager shall conduct the disciplinary hearing; for issues of alleged gross misconduct, or where accumulated misconduct could result in an employee's dismissal with notice, the line manager's manager will investigate the complaint and present findings to the divisional head, with the line manager attending as a witness as appropriate. In the case of a complaint against a divisional head, the case will be investigated by the chief executive, and the disciplinary hearing conducted by the chair of the personnel committee of *The Large Charity*. Where there is a case against the chief executive, it will be investigated by a member of the personnel committee, and the hearing conducted by the other members of the committee.

5. At least five working days prior to any formal disciplinary hearing, the full details of the complaint against the employee and of any evidence or witnesses that will be brought to substantiate the complaint should be provided in writing to the employee and (if appropriate) the employee's representative, who may be a work colleague or a trade union official. The employee should provide in writing at least three working days before the hearing details of any witnesses and evidence to be called to refute the allegations.

6. The disciplinary hearing will be chaired independently by the manager or director appointed to conduct it; she or he will normally be accompanied by an adviser from the personnel department and any other technical advisers as may be appropriate, and arrangements will be made for full notes to be taken. The advisers and notetaker will not normally participate in the hearing, except to seek or offer clarification of points arising from it.

7. The complaint, and evidence to support it, will be presented first, the presenting manager explaining her/his concerns, setting out the details and

presenting such evidence and witnesses as may be appropriate to substantiate the allegations. The defence to the allegations will then be offered in the same way by the employee or her/his representative. Both sides may cross-examine evidence and witnesses. Both complainant manager and defendant employee will then withdraw, and a decision on the substance of the complaint will be made by the manager appointed to conduct the hearing or by the personnel committee or one of its members as appropriate, who may seek such advice in reaching their conclusions as may be necessary. If necessary, both sides may be called back to seek clarification of an issue. The decision will be made on the balance of probability.

8 The decision will then be communicated to the employee. If possible, it should be given orally immediately on the conclusion of the hearing, and confirmed in writing; but in any event, it should be put in writing, setting out full reasons for the decision, within three working days of the decision being made. If the case has been found not proven, the matter will end there, and all reference to it will be expunged from *The Large Charity's* records. If the case has been found proven, the employee will be invited to make a statement in mitigation. A final decision will then be made on the outcome of the disciplinary process, which may take one of the following forms:
- **First written warning** – when the offence is a first and relatively minor one.
- **Further written warning** – where there has been a continuation of misconduct.
- **Final written warning** – where if the employee offends again, dismissal is likely to be the result.
- **Dismissal with notice** – where the employee has consistently failed to remedy misconduct.
- **Summary dismissal** – where the employee has been found guilty of gross misconduct, and there are no substantial mitigating factors.

9 Although it is intended that, in general, this process is cumulative, in cases of early instances of serious misconduct short of gross misconduct, a finding more severe than a first or subsequent written warning may be considered appropriate.

10 Warnings will normally stay on an employee's record as follows:
- **First written warning** – one year from the date of issue.
- **Further written warning** – two years from the date of issue.
- **Final written warning** – indefinitely.

The duration of these warnings may, in exceptional circumstances, be varied by the personnel committee or, in the case of a warning issued by the committee or one of its members, by the chair of the trustee board.

11 An employee may appeal against the outcome of a disciplinary hearing on the grounds either of its findings or the severity of the disciplinary action. An appeal against a decision by a manager will be heard by that manager's own manager (or, in the case of a decision by the chief

MODEL 4.4 Disciplinary procedure – large charities [continued]

executive, by the chair of the personnel committee); an appeal against a decision of the chair of the personnel committee by the full committee, excluding the chair, and against a decision of that body by the full trustee board, excluding members of the personnel committee. The same procedure will generally apply as at the original hearing, save that only evidence and findings in dispute will be considered, and that the person who chaired the original disciplinary hearing shall present the findings, calling other managers as witnesses as appropriate. The appeal body may substitute any alternative outcome, or uphold the original decision.

12 In cases of alleged gross misconduct, it will be the norm to suspend the employee on full pay pending the outcome of the process. Suspended employees may have access to *The Large Charity's* premises, records, staff and clients only by prior arrangement with the chief executive (or, in the case of disciplinary action against the chief executive, with the chair of the personnel committee), and only to prepare a defence.

13 All employees have the right to be represented by a full-time trade union official, but not by any other person outside *The Large Charity*, at all formal stages of the disciplinary process, although during the earlier investigatory stage, the investigating manager has the right to discuss matters alone with them. Employees and their representatives have the right to a reasonable amount of time off with pay to prepare and present the defence to the allegations.

Incapability

It's usually pretty clear when an employee has done something wrong. It's also usually pretty clear when they are in breach of the rules, either overtly or through their general behaviour, and you can deal with that through the disciplinary process. In essence, what you are doing is responding to deliberate or wilful misconduct. But there are also occasions when an employee is not doing what they should be doing, not because they have chosen to rebel, but because they don't have the ability to get it right. The effect of their underperformance may be the same, but if it's not their fault, is it really fair that they should be subjected to the disciplinary process? Most enlightened employers in the voluntary sector would accept that it is not, but many struggle with the problem of how to cope, since their charity is still suffering, and they have an overriding responsibility towards their trustees and their clients to provide the best possible services – and you can't do that with underachieving staff.

Hence in recent years, and encouraged by ACAS through its model disciplinary procedures and codes of conduct, there has been a trend amongst the more enlightened employers to operate separate procedures in cases of underachievement that are not the result of deliberate misconduct, which have come to be known as 'incapability procedures'.

The reasons for employee underperformance are varied, but in nearly every case, are not the fault of the employee, as the following list will demonstrate:

- The original selection process was flawed, and a candidate was appointed who was not up to the job. You can hardly blame them for applying, but you can legitimately criticise the selection process for failing to pick up their inadequacies. Hence the emphasis in the following two chapters on spending the necessary effort on getting recruitment right.
- The world of work has changed, requirements on employees have changed as their jobs become more complex, technical or physically demanding, and they just can't keep up the pace. In effect, their old job has changed and they aren't capable of changing sufficiently themselves. The job is redundant and they can't be either retrained or slotted into another position that matches their abilities.
- Illness – or even just advancing years – means that they can't fulfil the job specification. In most cases, you can hardly blame them for getting ill (there is perhaps a debate to be had about 'self-inflicted' illnesses arising from alcohol or drug misuse, or from debilitating accidents arising from recreational injuries), but you are still faced with the problem of an employee who is either not at work at all, or is only partly there, on either a long-term or permanent basis.
- An employee becomes disqualified from undertaking certain duties or from working at all, either because the law changes or is invoked (for example, a work permit for an overseas worker is withdrawn), or because they are debarred from an activity (most typically, they lose their driving licence). Whilst as an employer, you have to accept the consequences of statute-based changes, which will override your contractual obligations, there is always a question in cases such as the drunken driver as to whether you can find them alternative employment, or alternative ways of doing their old job. Incapability procedures are a useful mechanism to test this out.

Sickness absence

Dealing with sickness absence is particularly tricky without an incapability procedure, and Employment Tribunals are loathe to support employers who have sacked staff simply because they have been absent. You need to treat such cases sensitively, but you do need to deal with them. Here are a few pointers to ensuring that you stand a good chance of treating your staff fairly:

- Look at sickness patterns (e.g. is the employee always ill on Mondays?) to see whether there is genuine illness or unauthorised absenteeism masquerading as sick leave – and if the latter, deal with it through the disciplinary process.
- Consider whether the absence patterns throw up an underlying cause (e.g. women off sick at the same time each month perhaps being caused by menstrual problems) and then, in confidence and sensitively, seek to address that cause.
- Set standards for the level of absence that you can reasonably expect from any employee. We're all ill sometimes, but if the levels get excessive, you have a responsibility to try to curb the problem. Smaller charities are likely to be more seriously affected than bigger ones from an individual's poor sick record, so tighter targets may be reasonable there, but each organisation will want to set its own norms. By way of a guide, the average number of sick days taken throughout the economy is about seven per employee per annum, and that includes people off for months after a heart attack. So five occasional days might be considered a reasonable threshold for action.
- Taking action early, by drawing your concerns to the attention of the employee, very often generates an improvement or produces an explanation. So talk to your employees every time they come back from sick leave, consider asking them to produce a self-certificate for every absence, even a doctor's statement (you'll probably have to reimburse them for the cost of this), and in nine cases out of ten, the absence levels will drop.
- There will always be genuine cases of illness. Unless you're in a medical charity, you are unlikely to have the expertise to examine your staff to identify them. So you need independent medical advice – not the view of the employee's GP, whose job is to look after the interests of their patient, not of the employer. Your medical adviser needs to tell you whether the employee has a real problem, and if so, how it can be resolved (and if not, you need to act firmly); and to offer you a prognosis, particularly if employees are likely to be away sick for a long time.
- In most cases, if an employee has acquired rights to a certain amount of sickness absence, you should avoid considering terminating their contracts until that entitlement is exhausted. But it is usually the case, provided the contract is written properly, that entitlement to sick pay only follows an agreement to take sick leave, it does not offer an absolute right to be absent. So in the case of really key workers, you may well feel the need to act earlier, however reluctant you may be, simply because of

the effect the continuing absence is having on your charity's work. Generally, the smaller the charity and the more senior the employer, the more likely are your actions to be considered reasonable in these circumstances.

If you take all these factors into account, you are unlikely to encounter too many difficulties when dealing with sickness cases through your (in)capability procedure. A model procedure for smaller charities is set out below, and a flowchart indicating the various decisions you will need to take at each stage of handling sickness absence follows it. The capability procedure, based on the disciplinary procedure, seeks to take the sting out of that procedure whilst still leaving the employer in control. In the same way as the model disciplinary procedure for larger charities extended the procedures included in the less formal version, so you may also consider modifying this incapability process if you are a manager of a voluntary sector body with more than, say, twenty staff, and with several layers of management.

Many charities find it helpful to set out for their managers step-by-step guides on how to deal with particular issues. It is not practicable to provide a wide range of such guides in a book like this, nor would it be particularly desirable, since what was proposed could well be considered as too prescriptive and not sufficiently sensitive to an individual organisation's culture or needs. However, simply by going through the process of drawing up a guide, perhaps in the form of a flowchart, you will be able to identify key decision-making points and rights and obligations of both employer and employee. An example of this is the outline sickness procedure handling flowchart set out on the following page.

Grievances

It is not just employees who get things wrong. In the headstrong atmosphere of the voluntary sector, where managers and trustees often get swept up in the enthusiasm of delivering services to the very people the charity is all about, there is a tendency to forget that it is often only through the staff that success can be achieved. People's toes get trodden on and, like any other employee, if charity workers feel aggrieved, they will want to vent their concerns and frustrations. It would be very foolish to seek to prevent them from doing so.

An effective grievance procedure is a safety-valve. It allows staff who feel they have been wronged to have their concerns addressed seriously. Whatever the final outcome of the process, it should, if properly managed, offer them some degree of satisfaction that they have been listened to.

How a grievance procedure works is to some extent self-evident, and you should need to do little more than go through

FIGURE 4.1 Handling sickness flowchart

It should be noted that this model does not necessarily cover every stage of the procedure, and should be considerably adapted to suit local circumstances.

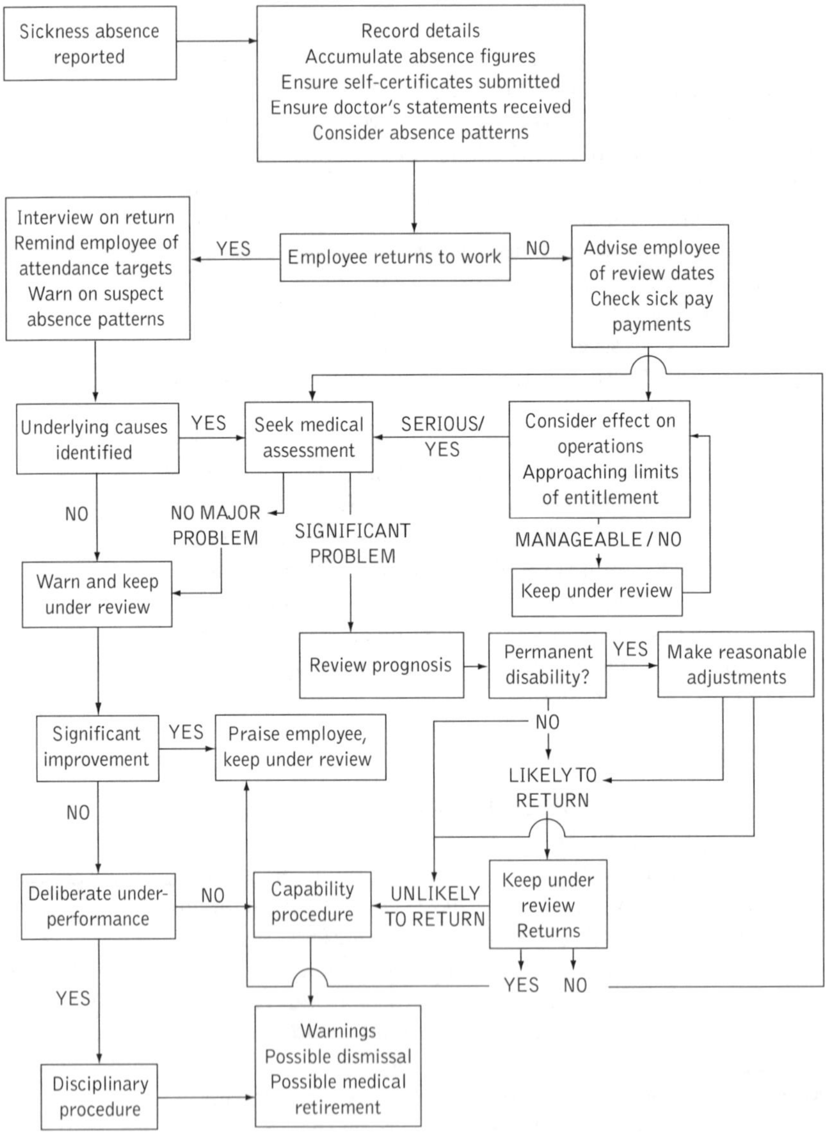

```
Sickness absence reported
    │
    ▼
Record details
Accumulate absence figures
Ensure self-certificates submitted
Ensure doctor's statements received
Consider absence patterns
    │
    ▼
Employee returns to work ──YES──► Interview on return
                                   Remind employee of
                                   attendance targets
                                   Warn on suspect
                                   absence patterns
    │
    NO
    ▼
Advise employee of review dates
Check sick pay payments
    │
    ▼
Consider effect on operations
Approaching limits of entitlement
    │
    SERIOUS/YES ──► Seek medical assessment
    MANAGEABLE/NO ──► Keep under review
```

- Underlying causes identified — YES → Seek medical assessment
  - NO → Warn and keep under review
- Seek medical assessment:
  - NO MAJOR PROBLEM → Warn and keep under review
  - SIGNIFICANT PROBLEM → Review prognosis
- Review prognosis → Permanent disability?
  - YES → Make reasonable adjustments
  - NO → LIKELY TO RETURN / UNLIKELY TO RETURN
- Likely to return → Keep under review — Returns? YES / NO
- Significant improvement — YES → Praise employee, keep under review
  - NO → Deliberate under-performance
- Deliberate under-performance:
  - NO → Capability procedure
  - YES → Disciplinary procedure
- Warnings / Possible dismissal / Possible medical retirement

MODEL 4.5 Capability procedure

1. *The Charity* recognises that in an organisation of its size, informal resolution of concerns about an employee's performance is usually the best way of maintaining effective working relationships. It is therefore incumbent upon the chief executive, who has full responsibility for all issues of quality management, to seek to resolve matters of minor underperformance quickly and without recourse to this procedure. *The Charity* also recognises that such matters of incapability are rarely the fault of the employee (where there is deliberate underperformance, that is a matter for the disciplinary process) and therefore seeks to deal with them in a non-pejorative manner.

2. It is however recognised that the more serious incidents of underachievement, or the continued failure to resolve minor concerns, may need to be dealt with under this formal procedure. Such matters are likely to be derived from a failure to achieve targets of output and quality determined through the annual appraisal process.

3. If in the chief executive's opinion there has been a significant underperformance serious enough to warrant formal action, then the employee shall be so advised in writing, setting out the grounds for concern, and indicating how the chief executive intends to proceed to substantiate them. In most cases, the chief executive shall conduct the capability hearing; for circumstances where continued poor performance could result in an employee's dismissal with notice, the chief executive will investigate the concerns and present findings to the staffing sub-committee of the trustee board.

4. At least three working days prior to any formal capability hearing, the full details of the concerns about the employee and of any evidence or witnesses that will be brought to substantiate them should be provided in writing to the employee and (if appropriate) the employee's representative. The employee should provide in writing at least 24 hours before the hearing details of any witnesses and evidence to be called to refute the allegations.

5. At the hearing the concerns, and evidence to support them, will be presented first; the employee's response to them will then be offered. Both sides may cross-examine evidence and witnesses. A decision on the substance of the concerns will then be made, sitting alone, by either the chief executive or the staffing sub-committee as appropriate, who may seek such advice in reaching their conclusions as may be necessary. The decision will be made on the balance of probability.

6. The decision will then be communicated to the employee. If the case has been found not proven, the matter will end there, and all reference to it will be expunged from *The Charity's* records. If the case has been found proven, the employee will be invited to make a statement in mitigation. A programme of support and training will then be developed jointly between the chief executive and the employee, including targets for improvement and anticipated

MODEL 4.5 Capability procedure [continued]

timescales. A formal decision will also be made on the outcome of the capability process, which may take one of the following forms:

- **First written capability warning** – when the concerns are relatively minor, and immediate improvement can be reasonably expected.
- **Further written capability warning** – where there has been a continuation of underperformance, despite previous support.
- **Final written capability warning** – where despite a significant effort to improve the employee's performance, it is still unacceptably poor and without immediate sustained improvement; dismissal is likely to be the result.
- **Dismissal with notice** – where the employee has consistently failed to remedy underperformance, and there is no reasonable expectation of targets being met.

7 Targets for performance improvement, including standards and timescales, will be determined in accordance with the circumstances of each case. At the end of the period set for improvement, the capability hearing will reconvene to evaluate performance and, as appropriate, set further targets and issue further warnings.

8 An employee may appeal against the outcome of a capability hearing on the grounds of its findings, the severity of the warning, the nature of the improvement targets or the proposed support to be given to achieve them. An appeal against a decision by the chief executive will be heard by the staffing sub-committee; an appeal against a decision of that body by the full trustee board, excluding members of the sub-committee. The same procedure will generally apply as at the original hearing, save that only evidence and findings in dispute will be considered. The appeal body may substitute any alternative outcome, or uphold the original decision.

9 All employees have the right to be represented by a trade union official at all formal stages of the capability process, although during investigations the chief executive has the right to discuss matters alone with them. Employees and their representatives have the right to a reasonable amount of time off with pay to prepare and present the defence to the allegations.

10 In the event of capability action against the chief executive, the procedure set out above will apply, save that the matter will be investigated and the hearing conducted or presented by the chair of the trustee board.

11 This procedure should generally be applied in the case of extended sickness absence, or ill-health resulting in underperformance by the employee. However, it may be appropriate to avoid some of the incremental stages set out in section 6 above, and *The Charity* will always seek to secure appropriate medical advice before any final managerial decision is taken.

the model offered on page 62, adapting it as appropriate to fit your own structures and to reflect the size of your charity. But before you do, there are a few points that are worth highlighting:

- Some grievances are obviously baseless and mischievous. If you want to avoid tying your management processes up for weeks, it may well be advisable to build in a veto, controlled by the charity itself, against further consideration of such frivolous or vexatious grievances. But then don't use it unless you really have to, or the credibility of the whole process may be seriously undermined.
- Grievances should always be heard by someone who has the authority to do something about the employee's concerns. Usually this is the line manager of the person against whom the grievance has been taken out, but this may not always be the case, and senior management should select very carefully the appropriate person to adjudicate. Additionally, if grievances are about sensitive matters such as alleged harassment, the aggrieved employee may wish for the matter to be taken out of the normal line management arrangements.
- There may be some areas where grievances are off limits. These can include matters about which the charity can do nothing, such as the state of the law and how it affects the employee, or taxation or national insurance matters (but normally, how the employer applies the law to the work situation may be a legitimate cause for concern). Or they may be about policy matters over which the employee may not see eye to eye with the charity, but which quite properly are for the employer to resolve.
- Some collective disputes, such as a pay claim, are not really a set of individual grievances, and it could become extremely messy if the charity sought to resolve all the grievances separately. That is more properly part of the industrial relations process, and however you go about resolving such collective matters, you would be well advised to avoid the grievance process for doing so.
- Finally, it has not been unknown for an employee, when faced with a disciplinary complaint, to seek to counter or neutralise it by slapping in a grievance, often against the very manager who has laid the disciplinary complaint. Many employers have faced this one at some time, and charities do need to have a clear line on it. In general, I would suggest that disciplinary hearings should take precedence, the employee should be told that the concerns in her/his grievance can be aired as part of her/his defence to the disciplinary complaint, and that if there are any outstanding issues once the disciplinary business has been disposed of, that can be the subject of a later grievance process. Without such a firm stand, you run the risk of losing control of the whole management process.

> **MODEL 4.6** Grievance procedure
>
> 1. *The Charity* and its staff believe that it is usually best to deal with concerns quickly and informally. In this way, small problems do not get bigger, and larger issues are properly and promptly confronted.
> 2. An employee who has a grievance arising from employment with *The Charity* shall first raise it informally with the person about whom or whose actions there is concern. In most cases, such a direct approach will resolve any difficulties and misunderstandings to the mutual benefit of all parties. Only if the matter cannot be resolved in this way should the employee then raise the concern with the next person up the management chain, who will seek to conciliate.
> 3. If, in the view of that manager, conciliation is neither possible nor appropriate, then the employee will be invited to submit a formal grievance, in writing, to that manager, who will be expected to arbitrate and respond within ten working days. If it is not possible to determine the issue within this timescale, the employee (and any other parties involved) will be so advised, and an anticipated timetable published.
> 4. If the manager is of the view that the grievance is frivolous and to pursue it would be an inappropriate use of *The Charity's* resources; or if it appears that the concerns raised can be more appropriately dealt with through collective consultative processes; or if they relate solely or principally to policy issues of *The Charity*; then the manager will refer the issue directly to the chief executive, who may rule that the grievance is invalid and may not be further pursued.

Let's hope you never need to cope with indiscipline or incapability, with grievances or gross misconduct. But just in case you do, you will at least now have something to guide you. And if you are still worried, do remember that it's almost always cheaper to take professional advice early than to pay for your mistakes in Employment Tribunal awards and ill-feeling later.

In summary ...

- Best practice in voluntary sector personnel management derives from an ethical application of the charity's cultural norms towards its staff, including acceptance of legal obligations, applications of codes of practice to all, consultation and involvement of staff, fair but not excessive salary levels and genuine equal opportunities.
- A strategic approach to the management of staff, creating a framework of personnel policies and practices, will be far more effective than a reactive and haphazard approach that reflects a charity's growth pattern.

5   If the employee is not satisfied with the arbitration decision of the manager, there is a right of appeal within five working days to the chief executive, with whom a meeting will be convened as soon as convenient, and whose decision is final. At that meeting, the manager will explain the arbitration, and the employee will explain the continuing concerns; both sides may cross-examine any evidence of witnesses presented.

6   There is a right to representation at all formal stages of this procedure.

7   In the event of a grievance against the chief executive, the chair of the trustee board will conduct all stages of the procedure beyond the initial informal approach described in paragraph 2 above.

8   The following exceptions apply to this procedure:

- Where there is an allegation of harassment or discrimination, the informal approach described in paragraph 2 above may be bypassed.
- Matters related to policy concerns, or to tax, National Insurance, Statutory Sick Pay, Statutory Maternity Pay or other issues outside the control of *The Charity* may not be the subject of a grievance about action taken unless the employee can show that *The Charity* has acted improperly.

9   Where an employee has invoked a grievance in response to disciplinary action, it will not be determined until after the disciplinary action has been resolved, but in so far as it is appropriate, aspects of the grievance may be considered in parallel with or as part of the disciplinary hearing.

- Charities are microcosms of society, and as such need rules to hold them together. For those rules to be effective, they must be understood by everyone involved and must be fairly applied.
- A charity's rules should reflect its culture; but most organisations will wish to include some basic references to serious matters such as dishonesty that would constitute gross misconduct.
- There should be clearly understood disciplinary procedures, based upon the principles of natural justice, that allow for the rules to be enforced. These must be applied fairly, with staff subject to them being told what they have done wrong and being given the opportunity to defend themselves and appeal against any findings.
- A parallel process for dealing with cases of incapability is both a useful management tool and an indication of fair employment practice. This can apply in all cases, including sickness, where an employee is no longer able to undertake her duties, but where she is not at fault.
- Staff should have access to a grievance procedure that enables them to air fully any legitimate concerns they may have about how they are being managed.

CHAPTER 5

Communication and staff involvement

INTRODUCTION

In later chapters this book will, quite rightly, turn its attention to issues of staff motivation and rewards beyond the basic contract of employment. However, it is worth stressing at this point that there will be very few employees who will respond to these approaches in the long run unless they get something out of their employment contracts and service conditions in the first place. Without having the basics in place, no end of good interpersonal skills will help avoid high staff turnover, low morale and unrest.

Accordingly, the next two chapters look at how these 'basics' can best be achieved. This chapter focuses on issues of communication and staff involvement and looks at possible approaches to managing the industrial relations process: whether you choose to take an individualist or collectivist approach, whether you recognise unions and how far your staff get involved in consultation and decision-making. Every charity, and every charity trustee, will have different views, and it is not the purpose of this book to be prescriptive on such matters. Good employment practice can operate in a variety of guises. The important thing is to establish and maintain arrangements that have the confidence of the trustees, the managers who have to operate them and most of all, the staff whose working lives are determined by them.

A framework to believe in

Voluntary sector managers are likely to argue that industrial relations in the charity world are more complex than elsewhere because, whilst staff want to enjoy better conditions, many of them are also driven by altruism. Of course, charities want to operate cost-effectively, but the needs of their service users will not always allow for that, and success will depend on the value put in by the employees, not on the surpluses they create. Of course, charities will want to rely on the goodwill of their staff, and most will want to be seen to be good employers, but they will still have to juggle with competing demands on their resources and will still be faced with painful choices between the needs of their clients and the legitimate demands of their staff. And those staff will also have to face painful choices, where their own altruism and particular skills and objectives on service delivery can be pushed to breaking point as they perceive themselves to be exploited rather than deployed, and possible choices between pay rises, redundancies and diminishing services.

No wonder voluntary sector industrial relations are complex. It's not a simple struggle of industrial Titans, any more than it's a straightforward 'let's all pull in the same direction' scenario. And with the increasing professionalisation of the sector, with more services being delivered by paid staff, and volunteers being relegated to support roles, the tensions are likely to increase. It is, in my view, no coincidence that voluntary sector employers are far more likely than their public or private sector counterparts to find themselves facing complaints to Employment Tribunals from aggrieved employees whose expectations have been dashed.

Interestingly, though, there seems to be a lower level of collective industrial action in the sector than elsewhere, which does suggest that, where staff are organised and unionised, good structures and relationships are generally well managed by both sides, and where they are not, management nevertheless listens sympathetically. You could, of course, equally argue that there is a largely passive workforce who don't react to the more extreme examples of managerial diktat. Whilst undoubtedly this is true in some circumstances, it seems to be a fairly unlikely proposition for the whole sector – after all, if people are passionate enough to work for charities in the first place, is it likely that they will be totally passive when it comes to their own circumstances? Those that like their situation manage well and respond to good management. Those that don't, walk – and there is some evidence that larger charities are experiencing high staff turnovers, probably more a reflection of their management style than the nature of the sector generally. Only a few remain to fight it out – and that goes as much for chief executives as it does for other staff.

Whatever your industrial relations arrangements, the system has to be seen to be fair, and to work. It has to be one that everyone – or nearly everyone – can believe in. Two key elements need to be present: equity and openness.

Equal opportunities employment

It is very easy to claim to be an equal opportunities employer. In some parts of the public and voluntary sectors it is very difficult if you don't do so. In some charities, it is still impossible to get people away from the idea that equal opportunities is about giving free homes to black one-legged single parent lesbians – and the tabloid press doesn't help. But that is not what equal opportunities is about. Of course, people who are disadvantaged by society should be treated properly – just as everyone else should. Of course, we should recognise the disadvantages they have had to face (and in many cases have successfully fought by themselves to overcome). But we should not be treating the disadvantage: true equality of opportunity is the development of strategies to neutralise those disadvantages, so that the real needs of every person, and their true abilities, can be given equal attention and worth.

Equal opportunities in employment is, equally, not about ensuring that everyone gets the same share of the cake or, put another way, everyone rises to the top. It is about giving everyone equal access to the opportunity to fulfil their potential, by removing artificial barriers, whilst recognising that everyone is different and will be able to contribute at a different level. Some examples of proper equal opportunities in employment in action are:

- Using unbiased aptitude tests to measure true ability and potential, not rejecting their use because some black candidates have done poorly on some bad tests in the past.
- Recognising that women are still the principal carers in our society, and therefore avoiding promotion criteria that depend on long unbroken service – a qualification that women, who are more likely to have career breaks to care for young children or elderly relatives, are not going to meet.
- Reorganising your office layout so that a wheelchair user can do her job on the ground floor, taking her work to her, rather than blocking her promotion because she can't get up to the top floor where the exciting jobs are and where the managers sit.

You will no doubt be able to think of countless other examples of good equal opportunities in practice, and may be wondering why I am stating what seems to be so obvious to you. At one level, of course, it is; but for many people, even these examples are a novelty, and even for the more sophisticated and aware managers, there is always more to learn, particularly around cultural sensitivity on issues such as sexuality, religion and disability. We are all learning all the time, because we all come from a particular personal perspective, and we won't always get it right when working with somebody who offers a different perspective.

There is probably more knowledge and experience of practical equal opportunity issues within the voluntary sector than anywhere else. The reason is quite simple. By their very nature, charities are dealing with people who, one way or another, are disadvantaged – otherwise they wouldn't be charities. Whether you are dealing with the relief of poverty, combating disease, promoting education, relieving unemployment, promoting urban or rural regeneration or capacity building (the areas which the law recognises for the definition of charitable objectives), you will, all the time, be coming across people who have missed out on the mainstream of life, and will be seeking to redress their disadvantage. You and your staff will have a unique understanding of issues surrounding particular areas of poverty, illness and ignorance. By working to reduce these people's disadvantage, to offer them parallel, albeit sometimes different, chances as the rest of society, you are practising equal opportunities.

That is why, in my view, it is so important that equal opportunities is also part of the mainstream thinking in your staff relations. Apart from the purely ethical stance, on which we all hold more or less strong views, any voluntary sector employer that seeks to combat disadvantage for its service users, but fails to do so for its staff, will run a severe risk of being accused of hypocrisy, and will certainly be giving out very contradictory and confusing messages to those people it relies on most – its staff and volunteers. Ultimately, that will square the circle, and its service users will get the same message – just as the large (nameless but thankfully now reformed) charity did twenty years ago, when it avoided employing black staff 'because our rather conservative members would not be able to relate to them'. Its main charitable object? Relieving poverty in Africa!

We will never get it completely right, but as long as we are prepared to learn by our mistakes and act promptly on them, we can develop. As long as we continue to measure equal opportunities in terms of outcomes – how the life of a service user was enhanced by more culturally sensitive provision, the blockages that were removed to enable a woman manager to secure a better job, or how junior staff made a greater contribution after they were empowered through more studied involvement – we will move towards that success.

But if we slip back to (or, in the case of some emerging charities, start for the first time) seeing equal opportunities in terms of process (you must all use the same application forms, everyone who applies gets an interview, all requests for assistance are treated in strict date order, and so on *ad nauseam)*, we will miss the point. Many of these things are necessary at certain times, but they certainly are not sufficient.

Equal opportunities is a theme that I have sought to maintain throughout this book, rather than to devote a specific chapter to the subject. That is because I fervently believe that it underpins everything that should be done in the name of personnel management, and to put it in a stand-alone section could marginalise it. But I have made the effort to emphasise it in the industrial relations context, because in my view an effective approach to true equality of opportunity is the key element to ensuring that the whole panoply of negotiation, consultation and communication works well. It helps managers and staff to focus on the core element – the proper recognition and realistic reward of every individual for their true worth.

All that, and openness too

You don't just have to be fair, you have to be seen to be fair. If your staff, volunteers, service users or donors are not clear about what you are doing and why, they may start to believe that you are doing something else. It takes a great deal of clever marketing and public relations to explain away and recover from unsavoury revelations. Some charities never recover. Very often, the sordid details would never have happened at all if information systems had been more open, people had more of a sense of sharing and felt more responsible for themselves and for each other's actions.

Of course, there will always be people who seek to buck the system, to exploit their position for their own ends, and the very nature of human frailty will always necessitate internal audit procedures, tight checks on people working in isolation with vulnerable clients and all the other managerial controls that are aimed to avoid charity nightmares. They won't always be successful, but they are more likely to be so in an open organisation where staff in particular are encouraged to share information and confidences.

But openness is not just about control mechanisms to cope with extremes of behaviour, however important they may be. It is far more about ownership of the organisation and its outcomes. If you share as much information as possible, people are more informed, and whilst they are also more likely to argue with you, they will do so from a more rational perspective, and in the end everyone will benefit.

Since the 1970s, trades unions have had the right of access to commercial information about the operation of employers. Whilst this was originally designed to strengthen their position in collective bargaining, and for that reason was fiercely resisted by unreconstructed employers, the practice of sharing with staff withered somewhat during the cutthroat 1980s when many commercial employers came to believe that they had to protect themselves from their competitors with curtains of secrecy. Even their own staff were suspect, and many executives found themselves shackled with 'golden handcuffs', which either prevented them leaving or made them ineffective if they did. Some of these views spilled over into the voluntary sector, although here there has at least always been a greater understanding of the need to share ideas and information as a precursor to sharing attitudes, irrespective of whether you do it with a union.

With the advent of a Labour government and a generally more union friendly environment, the pendulum is swinging back. Progressive management is now recognising that the advantages of openness outweigh the problems of leaks (indeed, they have found that being open with their staff is more likely to get them on their side and diminish the chances of such leaks), and EU legislation, particularly on Works Councils, means that employers are encouraged to get their staff involved – some enthusiastically, some more reluctantly, but all within the context of the adoption of the Social Chapter, which among other things, obliges employers to accept some degree of employee participation – and places a fairly strong obligation on employees and their unions to do so. How such involvement can actually be done is the subject of the later part of this chapter.

There are, of course, some things that do need to remain confidential. Employees' individual personal details should be confined to those who need to know them. That includes their home addresses, details of partners and dependants, personal finance matters such as tax codes and national insurance status, records of appraisals and personal development. Similar information on clients, service users and donors (unless they are corporate ones, in which case their donations should be recorded in their own accounts) can also be personal and therefore confidential.

More difficult is the question of individual salaries. It is straightforward enough if everyone is paid on established scales – they can be published. If chief executives and other senior managers are on individual salaries and their staff are on published scales, then I would suggest that there is a strong argument for those details to be published too. But what about performance bonuses? By publishing how much people get, you are revealing how well (or badly) they are doing, and that is an issue for them and their managers through the appraisal process – which depends on confidentiality for managers and staff to be honest with each other. I would therefore propose that the details of what is available in the reward scheme are made public, but that the actual payments are not.

There is, finally, the issue of commercially sensitive information. It does exist in the voluntary sector, particularly as more and more charities are being drawn into the contract culture and need to win deals with local authorities and the health service if they are to survive. There can be no hard and fast rules, but an appropriate guideline would be to keep the secrets to a minimum and reveal their details as soon as you think it appropriate to do so.

Communication, consultation and negotiation

Sharing information does not necessarily mean sharing control. Every organisation will think differently about how its decisions are made, and by whom. The balance will be determined by its culture, the nature of its operations and the views of its key players, and will vary over time.

Organisations with a strong degree of managerial control are likely to make most of their decisions at the top. The better ones will then communicate their decisions, working on the premise that if staff are informed about decisions and the reasons for them, they will be able to understand and accept them. This calls for effective systems of information sharing, whether this is done through staff newsletters (nowadays increasingly done electronically) or through management briefing chains, where the same message is promulgated throughout the organisation, with local additions by local managers offering information relevant to their particular work areas.

As well as communicating key decisions effectively, many organisations go a step further and seek views of staff before those decisions are made. They recognise that the full wealth of knowledge does not necessarily lie simply with the decision-makers, and that the talent, understanding and views of staff are resources to draw upon to make their decisions that much better. This is the process of consultation; it means that staff can have an input, but that the decisions still ultimately lie with management. And the more management consults, the more likely it is that their decisions will be sensible and acceptable.

The more open an organisation, the more likely it is to be ready to negotiate on key issues that affect its staff. The fundamental difference between negotiation and other forms of sharing is that both sides have a veto – until there is agreement, no progress can be made. Many will argue that staff can therefore hold the charity to ransom; whilst others will counter with the line that unless staff do agree, they are going to be pretty disgruntled if they have changes imposed on them, and those changes will not happen.

Clearly, it does not make sense to negotiate about everything – your charity would simply grind to a halt if you had to have an eyeball-to-eyeball meeting every time you needed to repaint the front door. But well-managed organisations do have a clear industrial relations strategy that determines which matters will be the subject of consultation, what will be negotiated before changes happen, and how decisions will be communicated. This strategy is often encompassed within a procedural agreement; this sets out different issues to be treated in different ways, and the processes whereby that will happen. Every charity will have a different combination, to be determined according to its circumstances, and I offer overleaf a model that can be used as a basis for your own thinking. It has deliberately been written in general terms, since you may or may not wish to offer formal union recognition within it, and you may well draw the boundaries between what is and is not included in areas for negotiation differently, but for all that it should provide a framework to be developed to suit your own charity's circumstances and approach to how it views its staff. You may notice that some degree of managerial control remains through the use of 'normally' when offering a commitment to negotiate prior to implementing change, and through the right of the charity to withdraw from the agreement by giving notice of its wish to do so. These backstop clauses should however be used sparingly, or the credibility of your intention to negotiate will be seriously damaged and it will be that much more difficult to enter into discussions with your staff next time.

To recognise or not to recognise ...

In organisations with twenty-one or more employees, trades unions in the UK now have a statutory right to be recognised as representing collectively their members who are employees with any particular employer, provided they can demonstrate that they can secure membership amongst a significant proportion of the workforce and a majority in any recognition ballot. However, the idea of a recognition ballot often suggests that an employer is reluctant to accept that a union has a role, albeit that the employer may ultimately be dragged to the negotiating table. In most cases, pragmatic employers have been prepared to recognise unions voluntarily, often persuaded in this by the unions demonstrating the advantages – either by force through the threat of industrial action if they don't or, better, through the argument that dealing collectively on a range of issues is preferable to negotiating them with each individual employee.

Recognition does not directly afford a union many specific statutory rights; unions' powers have been significantly eroded in recent years, and in any case these have always only been available to certified independent unions that are free from any direct or indirect control of the employer. The rights that remain are:

- Consultation on redundancy.
- Consultation on the effect of a transfer of undertakings.

> **MODEL 5.1** Arrangements for staff involvement
>
> 1. *The XYZ Charity* recognises the value to its work contributed by its employees, and that their knowledge and understanding of its operations is a major factor in its success. Accordingly, it will, as far as practicable and reasonable, seek to inform staff of decisions that affect their working lives, and offer them an opportunity to be involved in the decision-making process.
>
> 2. To this end, it has established a Joint Consultative Committee, on which both management and staff representatives sit, and which will be the forum for discussion of matters affecting staff's employment conditions.
>
> 3. It has also introduced a mechanism whereby all managerial decisions are swiftly and accurately communicated to all staff affected by them, through a weekly staff briefing.
>
> 4. *The XYZ Charity* reserves the right to determine the following matters, and undertakes to communicate and explain its decisions to staff at the earliest appropriate opportunity:
>   4.1 Major policy issues determining the areas of work in which the charity will be involved.
>   4.2 Financial and budgetary management.
>   4.3 Contracts with suppliers, clients and partner organisations.
>   4.4 Appointment of all staff members.
>   4.5 Legal matters and the discharge of the charity's liabilities.
>
> 5. *The XYZ Charity* will consult with staff through their representatives on the following matters before determining its policy:
>   5.1 Management of health and safety.
>   5.2 Equal opportunities policy and practice.
>   5.3 Restructuring, redundancies and staffing levels.
>   5.4 Work locations.
>   5.5 Remuneration policy.
>   5.6 Grading structure.
>   5.7 Recruitment and selection procedures.
>   5.8 Disciplinary, capability and grievance arrangements.
>   5.9 Staff training and development programmes.
>   5.10 Other significant personnel policy matters.
>
> 6. *The XYZ Charity* is prepared to negotiate with its staff over the following matters, and will not normally implement decisions relating to them until agreement is reached:
>   6.1 Pay levels, bonus schemes and other additions to basic salaries.
>   6.2 Pensions.
>   6.3 Other financial benefits, in particular travel allowances, childcare arrangements, subsistence payments, overtime rates.
>   6.4 Non-pecuniary service conditions, in particular leave, hours, flexible working.
>
> 7. The Joint Consultative Committee will meet for one hour every month, and more frequently if there are urgent matters to discuss. It will be the responsibility of management to publicise the outcome of its discussions.
>
> 8. *The XYZ Charity* reserves the right to terminate or amend this agreement by giving at least one month's notice of its intention to do so.

- Limited disclosure of information for the purposes of collective bargaining.
- Protection for members against discrimination for membership or involvement in appropriate union activities.
- Appointment of safety representatives.
- Reasonable time off with pay for union officials, for union duties and relevant training.

Recent EU legislation and case law has tended to extend these rights to all employee groups, not just recognised independent trades unions; this is particularly true over consultation on proposed redundancy and other one-off matters. The point about union recognition, however, is how the bargaining process is then conducted. Once a union is recognised, it will seek to agree procedures for consultation and negotiation, and these will include what is available for negotiation. Once a union is recognised, the employer will normally find that unscrutinised managerial decision-making is a thing of the past. Subsequent derecognition can be very painful.

It is not for me to tell you whether to concede recognition. You can consult with your staff perfectly well without it – a staff association or even a staff meeting can appoint its negotiators, and you can write your contracts and procedures in such a way as to include reference to them and to their deliberations with management. Equally, if there is a strong feeling for union representation (perhaps amongst a third of your workforce in the first instance), then to seek to avoid recognition and establish other channels may be a recipe for discontent and loss of face if and when you do finally concede it.

Some charities feel that it is better to discuss matters solely in-house with their own staff, partly because secretly they believe they can get away with more when there aren't professional negotiators around, but mainly because they feel trade union officials from outside will not really understand what their business is about. This was certainly the case a few years ago, and there may still be pockets of this kind of poor communication, particularly where a charity works closely with statutory bodies and the unions there have a tendency to consider them as an adjunct of, say, a local authority housing department. However, that situation is changing. Several unions now organise their members in voluntary sector branches, with local shops in each charity, and have full-time officials with a specialist knowledge of the sector. In any case, full-time union staff are thin on the ground, and it is in their interest to ensure that most union activity is carried out by local representatives and only backed up by them – they will come in personally only for the more serious or contentious matters. Fears about external influence are therefore largely unfounded.

Some other charities feel that by recognising a union they will be undermining the family atmosphere that has been the hallmark of their operations. This is very often the case with smaller organisations and the rather more traditional and long-founded bodies. If your charity is like that, I am not suggesting that you should recognise an independent union for the sake of it, but you do need to keep the lines of communication with your staff open in a different way, recognise the signs of concern and be ready to respond. After all, employees are people with aspirations, whether or not they are in a union – it's just that those aspirations may be expressed in different ways, at a different pace and at different times.

If you do recognise a union, you may well be asked to arrange check-off facilities for members. That is, union subscriptions are collected through the payroll and passed on, for which service the employer can levy a reasonable charge. This is an eminently sensible administrative arrangement – it stops your employees who are union officials from wasting their time collecting the subs, and enables you as an employer to know who is in the union, and therefore how strong and representative it is. Whilst most employers who recognise unions, and certainly those in the voluntary sector that do, support check-off, current legislation means that individual union members have to confirm every three years that they wish the arrangement to continue, otherwise you will be making illegal deductions from salaries – a case for joint management-union co-operation to ensure that people stay signed up to the arrangement.

Whether or not you choose to recognise a union for collective purposes, every employee has a right individually to join one and be represented by the union wherever your procedures allow for external assistance, for example in a disciplinary hearing. It would be inappropriate for management to dictate who may represent individuals, provided that you allow external representation at all; some staff bring their solicitor along (you need to ensure that they do not act over-legalistically), others a friend or a union rep. If you are really determined to avoid any union involvement, you can only really do it by making clear in your procedures that the only representation allowed has to come from within your charity – and even then, there might be another of your employees who is also in the union who could play the part.

... Management is still responsible

The role of trades unions – or staff associations – is to represent the interests of staff; it is not to do management's job of communicating or implementing decisions. Management is about making things happen, with the available resources and within determined constraints. Those resources and constraints will have been influenced by the industrial relations process, but there it stops.

So, however you get to your decisions, whether they are on policy-making, operational matters or employment conditions, it is up to you as a charity manager to make sure that everyone affected by them clearly understands what the decisions are and what is required of them. It is not for your staff representatives to tell everyone what has been decided – they will inevitably put their own perspective on the issue, when what you want is for the charity's view to prevail and be clearly communicated. It is not for the unions to take responsibility for implementing the decisions, even though as employees individual union members may well have specific responsibilities in this regard.

There was never much of a tendency in the voluntary sector to reflect some of the worst aspects of the old British industrial relations scene. There were few examples of staff refusing to be told anything by anyone other than their shop steward, or of the works convenor deciding who would get the next vacant job. But there are some cases amongst charities where managers, and more particularly trustees, in one sense or another seem to seek staff permission before they implement a decision, or seek to distribute information through the union network. If you have to ask permission, you haven't completed the consultative or negotiating process, and if you use someone else's lines of communication, how can you be sure that the right message has been conveyed? No, the buck and the responsibility remains with management – charities that are run as workers' co-operatives tend to fail very quickly.

Coping with industrial disputes

In an ideal world, of course, there wouldn't be any disputes, because you had managed so well and presented your case so effectively that negotiation and consultation resulted in consensus every time. Unfortunately, it isn't always like that and there will be times when legitimate expectations of staff will collide with understandable concerns of your charity. For example:

- The rate of inflation may be rising, staff will want to protect their standard of living with a decent pay rise, but your income is falling because of a squeeze on your principal source of income – the local authority.
- Staff may see people in similar organisations working shorter hours, but you need them to do more for the same money if you are going to meet all your service users' needs.

- You need to relocate your operations to meet the needs of your clients, but all your key staff have settled homes and cannot afford to move.

All these are perfectly genuine reasons where conflicts become inevitable, and doubtless you will think of many more from your own experience. In one way or another, they all lead to industrial conflict, and the skill of the manager is then to pick a way through the maze to a resolution that at best satisfies everyone, or at least minimises dissatisfaction on all sides.

I do not propose offering ready solutions to industrial disputes, either those that I have cited as examples above, or others that may arise in the course of your career as a charity manager. There are never any easy fixes, because the personalities and subtle nuances involved change on every occasion. Anyone who offers simple solutions to such matters is almost certainly a charlatan or a politician playing to the gallery – it needs immense sensitivity and people skills to resolve disputes. But there are a few guidelines to successful negotiations always worth bearing in mind:

- Never lose sight of your objective, and be aware of how far you are prepared to compromise on it – remember where your bottom line lies.
- Judge very carefully how much you offer in any negotiation – if you are too generous too early and offer your real bottom line, the other side may think that there's more to come, and you may never obtain a meeting of minds.
- Never say 'this is my final offer' unless you mean it.
- Always respect where the other side is coming from – you may not agree with them, but they have just as much right to a view as you do, and hold it equally passionately. As a negotiator, your job is to find a middle-ground, win-win solution.
- Don't say that something is a principle when it isn't – the moment you concede on a principle, you lose your credibility as a person of integrity.
- Avoid the temptation of resorting to dirty tricks, ridiculing the other side, scoring points and otherwise demeaning what should be a constructive attempt at resolving differences – however frustrated you may be by others' intransigence. One nasty remark now can cause ages of resentment later.
- Always look for the positive sides of your 'opponent's' case, building up rather than casting down – these will enhance the chances of some form of joint ownership of the eventual outcome.

Whilst you are applying these and other sensible management techniques to resolving your differences, there may be formal industrial action going on, although with the current severe restrictions on union rights in this field that is increasingly rare. However, it can be intense when it does happen, and liable to spin out of control if you are not unionised and hence with access to experienced union officials to offer moderating counsel. Whether or not there is such formal action, you are still in dispute with your staff, and you will doubtless wish to resolve that so that you can all get on with the business of the charity. If you are in formal dispute, it is worth being aware of at least the basic elements of industrial relations law:

- Industrial action does not have to be a strike – it can be any action that involves a breach in an employee's contract, such as a refusal to work overtime or to carry out duties in a particular way.
- Before any industrial action can start, the staff involved have to indicate their agreement to it in a secret ballot, whose terms must comply with certain guidelines and must be made available to the employer, together with the result. If the action is not started within thirty days of the ballot, a new vote must be held, and if the employees want to change the nature of the industrial action, they may have to hold another ballot.
- Staff can only take industrial action against the employer, not against suppliers, customers or associated organisations, and then only at their own workplaces, picketing in small numbers – no flying pickets, no secondary action and no mass demonstrations are allowed, at pain of injunctions.
- Unless unions follow these rules carefully – and they are responsible for the actions of their members who do not – they are liable in law for any damages the employer may incur, and union officials may find themselves in court.
- Any employee who takes industrial action and is in breach of the contract of employment can be sacked without any right of appeal to an Employment Tribunal for unfair dismissal – unless it can be shown that only some people taking the action were treated in this way. So if you sack the entire workforce, your action will be fair, but not if you only get rid of the 'ring-leaders' (usually the union officials). It is however automatically unfair to dismiss someone just because they are a member of a union, recognised or not.

Whether as an employer you choose to use the law to restrict your staff's scope for industrial action is a decision that you can only make in the light of all the circumstances. Suffice to say that on the few occasions in the voluntary sector when employers have followed this route they have found themselves faced with an even more determined workforce and a bitterness after the dispute was resolved that lasted for a very long time.

Do trustees have a role?

Thus far, I have spoken in terms of managers rather than trustees dealing with all industrial relations work. That is because in most charities the management of staff is sensibly left to the professional executives who are employed to perform that task. In the private sector, this is not an issue, since the board at the top of the organisation is both its policy-making body and its paid executive. In the public and voluntary sectors, however, there is the added complication of the overall control of the organisation being vested in unpaid (and in the best sense of the word, amateur) councillors in local government and trustees in charities.

There is regrettably a tendency on occasion for trustees to get involved where it is probably inappropriate for them to do so. Individual employees may take individual concerns to them; they may engage in debate over policy with members of staff; or they may wish to tell the chief executive how to manage a particular staffing situation. All these circumstances can create havoc, as policy is made or amended on the hoof, individuals feel they have been given differential treatment, and carefully worked out long-term strategies lie in tatters.

Clearly there is a role for trustees in the management of staff, just as there is when they come to deal with finance and all other key assets. But as with those other assets, they can make the most effective contribution at a strategic level, agreeing overall personnel policies, implementation strategies and priorities, all for the chief executive and other managers to introduce and operate. This is easier in a larger charity, where there is sufficient depth of management experience to do all these things; in the typically smaller organisation, where there is one chief executive and perhaps not more than a dozen staff, that chief executive may need to rely rather more on the expertise of trustees to offer advice on how to carry out some of the personnel basics effectively, just as she would turn to them for, say, fundraising, finance or computing expertise. The point, then, is for the trustees to support her in getting it right, rather than do it themselves.

As ever with personnel matters, it is not quite as simple as that. Unlike the charity's finances, its staff have feelings and a sense of commitment to the organisation and its goals, and they rightly see these being fundamentally affected by the activities and decisions of the trustees. They will want a channel through which to express their legitimately held views, and I would suggest that an occasional forum where staff representatives can meet informally with the trustees and exchange ideas is a useful safety valve. It must, however, be clear that such a forum is not a negotiating or decision-making body – that should be delegated, within an established framework and policy guidelines, to the chief executive.

Indeed, any sensible chief executive, although empowered to lead on all personnel matters, will wish to seek guidance on the principles from her trustees. Major issues could well be at stake and the trustees will want, at the very least, to be kept informed. Sensible trustees will also recognise that unless they do empower their chief executive in this way, and avoid being seen as too involved in the day-to-day processes, effective management of staff will become extremely difficult and eventually impossible.

There are two – and only two – exceptions, to this principle. First, the trustees themselves must assume the responsibility of employing the chief executive, of setting her terms and conditions and of monitoring her performance. In a small charity, this can be done relatively informally, although the chief executive herself must have confidence in the process. The whole trustee board may wish to be involved, although it is more usual, and normally preferable, for the responsibility to be delegated to the chair, sometimes working closely with another trustee such as the vice-chair. If the trustees do not have much personnel management experience (after all, they are probably there because of their expertise in or commitment to the charity's prime objectives, which are not usually the employment of staff), then external consultancy assistance may be useful. And if the chief executive herself feels isolated, as many do, the wise trustee board may well agree to offering her external mentoring support.

The other exception is the role of trustees as a final point of appeal in any disciplinary, capability or grievance process. If it is accepted that the chief executive has full responsibility for personnel matters, this may well include, particularly in smaller charities, the power to deal with dismissals and other serious outcomes. Fair employment practice requires that there should be a possibility of appeal, especially when an employee has been dismissed, and if the chief executive has taken the sacking decision, where else can the appellant fairly turn to appeal against that decision but to the trustees? In these circumstances, however, trustees would be acting not so much as another level of management than in a quasi-judicial capacity. It would, in order to maintain the chief executive's own morale and the staff's confidence in her management skills, always be necessary to ensure that her position was not undermined by any subsequent decisions of the trustees or a group of them sitting as an appeal panel. For this reason, I would always counsel that any appeal process is not a rehearing, but only tests the reasonableness of the original decision in all its circumstances.

In summary ...

Voluntary sector personnel management is both like, and very different from, employment in other parts of the economy. The similarities lie in the facts that the framework of legislation and best practice applies equally to charities as it does to any other employer, and that all employees come to work to be paid. The differences are, basically, that they also come to work because they believe in the cause, and this results in conflicts of loyalty not normally experienced outside the voluntary and to some extent the public sector; and that as a consequence expectations, and the processes to deal with them, are that much more complex. In summary, the key points are:

- To be a successful employer, you always have to meet your staff's basic needs for a reasonable wage and other benefits. Everything else is marginal and will be of little benefit if you don't get the basics right.
- Industrial relations in the voluntary sector is particularly complex, primarily because not only will staff have needs like every other employee, they are also likely to have mixed feelings about pressing for those needs when they share the altruistic objectives of the charity for which they work.
- Equal opportunities in the sector is particularly important, as it reflects the goals of the charity itself, and a failure to be seen to be fair in staffing processes will quickly reflect on the image of the employer.
- With at least partially shared objectives, openness is especially important within the voluntary sector; staff will quickly become suspicious and demotivated if they believe that there is a hidden agenda. They will be inspired to make that extra effort if they know to what use it will be put.
- Every charity will operate differently, and decision-making power will lie in different places at different times, with differing matters open for communication, consultation and negotiation. The balance, and decisions on whom to negotiate with, can only be determined by the culture of the individual charity, but wherever the balance lies, staff management skills of the highest order are needed in order to achieve continuing success, to minimise the risk of conflict, and to resolve satisfactorily those conflicts that do inevitably arise, whether or not unions are recognised.
- The lead on managing the employment process should normally be delegated, with appropriate guidelines and safeguards, to the head of the paid staff; trustees should avoid getting involved in detail apart from in specific circumstances.

Staff conditions – what you have to do

CHAPTER 6

INTRODUCTION

British employment law affords employees relatively few absolute rights, but rather provides a framework within which employers and their staff are expected to come to mutually satisfactory arrangements (see chapter 3 for more details). There are, for example, very few indicators in either statute or case law on the level of sickness entitlement, but there is an insistence that in every employment contract there should be reference made as to what entitlement does exist.

Where the law is more prescriptive, this is largely because of requirements imposed on employers, either through the courts or via secondary legislation from Europe in the form of health and safety measures, equal opportunities legislation and case law. This chapter outlines the key terms and conditions of employment that will form the basis of any formal agreement between employer and employee.

A raft of rights

Employment rights can be summarised as follows:

- To be told what your terms and conditions are (*see below*).
- To be paid in accordance with your contract, and not to have any unreasonable deduction, within or beyond the contract (*in accordance with the Employment Rights Act*).
- Not to be unfairly dismissed (see also chapters 3 and 12).
- Not to be discriminated against (*in accordance with the Sex Discrimination, Race Relations and Disability Discrimination Acts* and secondary legislation or victimised because of actions under these Acts.

- To have a specified amount of maternity leave and pay, annual leave and time off for public duties (*see below*).
- To be provided with a safe place of work (*in accordance with the Health and Safety at Work Act and associated legislation*).
- To belong – or not to belong to a trade union (see below).
- To Statutory Sick Pay if eligible (see below).

CASE STUDY 6.1   The case of the overgenerous employer

A large voluntary organisation in a rather unpopular branch of the social welfare field undertook a range of different activities, including research and development into best practice in the organisation's subject, a great deal of political lobbying, and a large number of direct service delivery projects on behalf of the health service. The management structure of the charity was such that each part of it tended to keep to itself, and the whole organisation was led by a charismatic chief executive. It was his public image that ensured it stayed in the limelight and secured work from other providers, but he did not care too much about the day-to-day workings and, as is often the case in these circumstances, few resources were put into infrastructure support.

Because of their high reputation, the researchers were in considerable demand from partner organisations, both to undertake joint projects and, on occasion, to be seconded. One such secondment was for six months to an umbrella organisation of which the charity was a participating member.

The employee concerned entered into a complicated arrangement between the original employer, the umbrella organisation and herself, whereby the new organisation would be responsible for her salary, but that this would be under her old terms and conditions, and she would remain an employee of the original charity, with the intention of returning at the end of the secondment.

After the first month, she was surprised to discover that she got a pay cheque from both charities. She queried this with her old employer, only to be told that it would be sorted out. In the meanwhile, she put the extra money in the building society. The next month, the same thing happened, and the building society account got bigger. She asked for an explanation, but got none, and suggested to the old employer that, for some reason, it intended to pay her, so could she please keep the money? There was no reply. Then Christmas came, and she used some of the extra money to buy her family presents.

The double salary kept on accumulating, each month she was told it would be sorted out between personnel and finance, and then a cashflow crisis hit the original employer, and redundancies were mooted. In the meantime, the umbrella organisation had some vacancies and offered her permanent employment. She accepted, and immediately claimed rights under TUPE to her old conditions, even though the position offered was at a lower salary, because she claimed the work she would be doing was the equivalent to what she had been doing with the original employer and for which she had been seconded in the first place.

The original employer then declared her redundant and asked for its money back – by this time amounting to six months'

Everything else is, for the moment, negotiable, but of course, once it has been negotiated, every party to any employment contract has the right to seek redress in the courts either to enforce it or to secure damages for its breach.

Before we go any further, consider case study 6.1 on how *not* to do it.

salary. She refused, and in the end it had to write the money off as a huge redundancy lump sum, far greater than what she would strictly have been entitled to under her old contract. And the new employer had to accept her on protected terms, thereby disrupting its own salary differentials.

Both organisations learnt a great deal from this mess:

- You need good records and good communications between different departments, particularly between personnel and finance, and you must have systems to check that actions have actually been carried out. Bureaucracy does have some uses.

- Secondments must be clearly underpinned by agreements setting out the rights of both employers and the employee, particularly her employment status and right to return. In this case, nobody was sure from the outset who the employer was.

- If you make overpayments, you must act swiftly to recover them, or the employee may have a justified claim to the money, particularly if it had not been made clear to her that she must not spend it – if she reasonably (even if mistakenly) believes she is entitled to the overpayment, it will be gone forever. The Employment Rights Act, and precedents stemming from it, has been very tough on employers in such cases.

- Confusion is likely to reign in transfer situations of this kind, and secondments can easily get confused with alternative employment. It is usually better for the original employer to continue to pay the employee, and for the receiving organisation to make a payment to the employer. That way, issues around TUPE are less likely to arise.

- If you do appoint someone who was previously seconded to you, you may well find yourself faced with a TUPE claim. It is probably better to create a break between the secondment and the appointment, to avoid any suggestion of a continuous contract and a seamless transfer.

- Even trying to keep to basic statutory entitlements can be expensive if you don't understand their detail and what their implementation implies.

- Bad administration and lack of foresight can be very expensive – in this case, huge and unrecoverable overpayments that may well have been in breach of charity law, and an employee on service conditions nobody wants. It really is a false economy not to spend time in advance dealing with the detailed consideration and planning of handling such complex issues. Remember the old adage – if it can go wrong, it will. Planning ahead can avoid that eventuality.

Statement of particulars

Within two months of their starting work, you must provide anyone employed for more than one month with a statement setting out the principal terms and conditions under which they are employed. Since most if not all of these details will have been discussed with prospective employees beforehand (how else would they know whether the package you were offering was good enough to make them want to join you?), it makes good managerial sense for you to provide a draft of this document before the start date, and get the formal version signed on the first day. If you do fail to provide such a statement – or indeed any other details of what forms the contract of employment – then your employee can go to an Employment Tribunal and ask them to determine the contract; that is, they will decide what the terms of it are, and impose them on you. This could potentially be a very expensive outcome for what is administrative laziness.

If any of the terms of employment change, you are obliged to notify the employees concerned of the details of the changes within one month of them taking effect. So, for example, if they get a pay rise, you will need to let them know what the new salary is. You do not have to issue a new statement of particulars each time, but it is sensible to make clear in any letter that you do issue that it is amending the statement that the employee holds. Whilst this is not so much of a problem with matters such as salary details, there can be difficulties where there are amendments to items such as a disciplinary procedure. This is why such matters are dealt with as *implied terms* in the contract – reference is made to where they can be found elsewhere, and you do not then need to spell out in absolute detail every single dot and comma change when they are invoked.

Employer

Your charity must identify itself as the employer; if the employee works for a separate entity, such as a trading concern, then this can be shown as the employer, provided it is independent of the main organisation. If you are dealing with the staffing matters on behalf of another charity, it is it, not you, who is the employer, and its details must be shown.

Employee

A full name by which the employee can be identified is required. If there is any doubt, a home address or other identifying data should be included.

Job title

Many organisations tend to have rather bureaucratic job titles, such as senior principal assistant administrative officer, which sound grand but don't always mean very much to people outside such rarefied atmospheres. It is better to include here something that briefly describes what the postholder actually does and which is unambiguous, such as chief executive, director of finance, personnel manager, housing officer, fundraising assistant, night care manager, and so on. The important thing is that it can relate to a job description or a set of duties that both employer and employee understand and agree. But I would suggest that it is not a good idea to include the job description in the statement of particulars, or even make direct or oblique reference to it. If you do, there is always the increased risk of the courts viewing it as part of the contract of employment. They have a tendency to do this anyway (which is why it is I have suggested in the model in chapter 8 to include a specific disclaimer against this), and you don't want to encourage them!

Employment dates

These two dates (see model 6.1) will normally be the same if an employee is new to both the organisation and the job. The start date for employment purposes is usually the first day on which they work and are paid (including if they are off sick on the first day), but be careful if you start paying someone on a rest day. However, if the employee is promoted within your organisation or otherwise moves jobs, you need to issue a new statement showing the start date in the new job, and the old start date as well.

This also applies if the employee has transferred to you under TUPE (see chapter 3) – the date for continuous employment is when they started with the transferring employer, and it would be a good idea to make this clear at this point in the document. And remember, if the employee has continuous service that offers employment protection and you promote them, a probationary period, whilst useful to monitor progress, will not protect the employer if the person fails the probation and is sacked. Better if you can to revert them back to their old job or, at worst, use your capability procedure to show they have been dismissed fairly.

Place of work

You should include the normal or principal place of work. If the employee works from home, or is always on the road (for example, a regional fundraiser without a local office), then give the place

MODEL 6.1 Statement of particulars

The XYZ Charity
Statement of particulars of terms and conditions of employment

Employer

XYZ, currently of 123, Outer Reaches High Street, London N28 9ZZ

Employee

Job title of employee

Date of start of employment in this post

Date of start of continuous employment with XYZ

Place of work

At the XYZ offices, currently 123, Outer Reaches High Street, London N28 9ZZ. You may be required from time to time to undertake duties at other locations. Should the office be moved, you will be required to relocate.

Remuneration

This post is paid at the XX grade, which at the time of the start of your employment is set at £XX,XXX. An annual cost-of-living award may be made at the discretion of the management committee.

A performance-related award, based on your annual appraisal, may be payable in addition.

You will be paid one twelfth of the annual salary on the seventeenth day of each month by direct transfer into your bank account.

Working hours

You are required to work 35 hours per week, in accordance with XYZ's arrangements as set out in the Staff Handbook, normally within the general band of 9.00 a.m. to 5.30 p.m., Mondays to Thursdays, and 9.00 a.m. to 5.00 p.m. on Fridays. Up to one hour may be taken each day for lunch, and flexible working hours within and beyond these parameters may be worked with the approval of the chief executive. Overtime is not payable, but time off in lieu may be taken, subject to the approval of the chief executive.

Holiday and other leave entitlement

You are entitled to time off with pay for all public holidays, together with an additional three days to be taken immediately prior to or after certain bank holidays, as notified to you by the chief executive.

You are entitled to 25 days' paid annual leave per completed year starting on 1 April each year. In exceptional circumstances, and with the approval of the chief executive, up to five days' outstanding leave may be carried over to the next leave year.

You may in addition be entitled to various special leave rights, including maternity, carer's and paternity leave and associated benefits, in accordance with XYZ's

---

to which she normally reports or the head office, and explain this.

Whilst it is a good idea to include the 'you must move anywhere' clause, you cannot entirely rely on it, if the courts think that such a requirement is unreasonable in all the circumstances. They will look at each case on the facts, and may conclude that you have constructively dismissed, or made redundant someone who refused to move. So be ready with convincing explanations

arrangements as set out in the Staff Handbook.

Notice

You are required to give one/three months' notice of your resignation from this post.

You are entitled to four weeks' notice of termination of employment for the first four years of your continuous employment with *XYZ*; thereafter you are entitled to one additional week's notice per completed year of service, subject to a maximum of twelve weeks.

Sickness and injury

If you are ill or injured whilst at work, you are required to abide by *XYZ*'s sickness procedures as set out in the Staff Handbook.

You will be entitled to sick pay in accordance with *XYZ*'s arrangements as set out in the Staff Handbook.

Pensions and retirement

These are in accordance with *XYZ*'s arrangements as set out in the Staff Handbook.

Disciplinary, grievance and capability procedures

These are set out in the Staff Handbook.

Probation

Confirmation of your appointment is subject to a probationary period of six months, which may be extended by *XYZ* by a further three months.

Collective agreements and determination of service conditions

XYZ does not recognise any trade union to negotiate terms and conditions on behalf of all staff, although it respects the right of any individual employee to belong, or not to belong, to a trade union of their choice. Conditions of service will be as determined by the management committee and as set out in the Staff Handbook, or as otherwise notified to you from time to time.

All staff are bound by the service conditions, rules and procedures as set out in the Staff Handbook, except where specifically indicated to the contrary.

Amendments

XYZ will provide you, in writing, details of any changes to these particulars or to any implied terms of your contract of employment within one month of their implementation.

I accept employment on the basis of these terms and conditions

signature of employee:

.... date: ....

signed on behalf of *XYZ*:

.... date: ....

---

for the need for any move, and consult at length with the staff affected beforehand.

Remuneration

It is easier to include a scale here rather than a detailed salary, since scales change all the time. This is one of the good examples where an explanatory letter about any changes avoids the need to reissue the statement of particulars. If there are additional payments, such as individual performance pay, profit-related schemes, output bonuses, Christmas bonuses, etc., which, provided certain criteria are met, are automatically available, these form part of the contract and reference to them should be included here. You are obliged to tell your employees how they will be paid, and when.

Working hours

The Working Time Regulations (see chapter 3) now mean that there are fairly strict limits on the time that employees can work and the breaks to which they are entitled. For most charities, abiding by the forty-eight hours per week limit, with at least one day off and a break after a maximum of eleven hours, should not pose any problem. In any case, it is possible, at least for senior staff, to opt out if they want to. But where you may be operating on a twenty-four-hour basis, say in a care home, then you will need to organise shift patterns carefully. The Department for Education and Employment (see Directory) publishes detailed advice on the application of the Regulations, and you should make sure that you understand and apply this in your own situation.

Holidays

There is now an absolute right to four weeks' paid holiday, reflecting the minimum practice that has existed in most of the voluntary sector for years. However, there is no right to time off, with or without pay, for public holidays unless the contract allows for it. However, where there is such a right, the level of entitlement must be spelt out. There is a right to 'reasonable' time off (it does not have to be with pay) to carry out public duties, such as jury service, work as a councillor or as a school governor. Any arrangements for the protection of outstanding leave entitlements and for booking leave, are entirely contractual rather than statutory matters, although, again, it would be wise to include reference to them where they exist.

Maternity

Maternity leave entitlements are horribly complicated, and maternity pay and regulations surrounding other maternity-related benefits are equally complex. Rights start even before the maternity leave begins, with an absolute right to time off with pay for ante-natal care. All calculations for which entitlements and benefits are available flow from the assumption that a woman could not actually know she was pregnant when she started with you; so for example the six month qualifying period for full Statutory Maternity Pay (see below) requires those six months to be at a qualifying date eleven weeks before the expected date of confinement (i.e. thirty-seven weeks altogether).

The minima for maternity leave (which can be extended by any contractual agreements that are then in effect statutorily protected) are that any woman may have up to eighteen weeks off. A woman with one or more years' service at the beginning of the 11th week before the expected date of confinement can have up to twenty-nine weeks.

The pregnant woman is expected to give twenty-one days' notice of her intention to take maternity leave; she may postpone her return for up to four weeks for medical reasons and, if she is on a longer period of maternity leave, the employer can postpone it too. But women on short ('ordinary') maternity leave do not need to give any notice of their intention to return, they can just turn up on the originally planned date – or, if they want to come back early, give twenty-one days' notice; as do women on longer ('additional') leave to return early. For the employer's part, he can write to the woman from seven weeks after the expected date of confinement, asking her if she is coming back at all. If she doesn't reply, then technically her right to return is lost, but it would be a brave employer indeed who risked the wrath of the equal treatment lobby in enforcing that one!

Rights during maternity leave are also complex. Women enjoying any length of maternity leave period have all their rights preserved (seniority, leave entitlements, etc.) apart from pay. This includes the right to be consulted, just like every other employee, on potential redundancy. And if you do make her redundant, it will be probably very difficult to prove that you have done so for a reason that is not connected with her pregnancy. Result: an automatically unfair dismissal.

If she does come back, she has a right to return to the same job. So if it is not practicable to keep the job open during her absence, you need to find a suitable alternative, just as you would with any other redundancy. If it's not suitable, or if she refuses it, a dismissal arises around the ensuing redundancy, to which there may or may not be entitlement to compensation – or, at the worst, another opportunity for unfair dismissal allegations. And if she asks to be allowed to return on a part time basis, then you need to think very hard before you refuse, as this could well be considered to be discriminatory. Occasionally, it may be impractical, but you should try to accommodate such requests; a trial period or agreement for part-time working to last only for a specified time might be a way forward.

And while she's away, there is usually a statutory entitlement to Statutory Maternity Pay (SMP) or, at the very least, the reduced

Maternity Allowance, irrespective of the number of hours worked, provided she has worked for you for at least six months up to and including the 15th week before the baby is due and has earnings at the prevailing national insurance lower limit. SMP is payable for six weeks at the higher rate, and twelve at the lower; the higher is 90 per cent of normal pay, the lower the same as the Statutory Sick Pay (SSP) award. But there are limits to when it can be paid, and these do not necessarily coincide with when the woman takes her maternity leave.

Finally, for women who (usually because of lack of service) do not qualify for SMP, there is a payment of Maternity Allowance, which is a DSS funded benefit – but you need to know about it, so that you can advise your staff to claim.

And what do you do to cover her work while she is away? Some employers share the work out, others promote staff temporarily, some recruit a temp. All are possible, but all are likely to involve you in some direct or indirect additional cost. It's difficult to budget for this, unless you are large enough to set up a contingency fund (and have a young female workforce likely to prompt its use!). A few (and rare) generous local authorities have set up a maternity fund to help out smaller charities to cover these costs, but they are also strapped for cash, so that is unlikely to be a runner. You may just need to reorganise your workload in the short term, delay filling other posts or make savings on non-staff costs. And maybe maternity is the time to call in a few favours from volunteers.

If you do recruit a temporary employee, make sure that it is clear that the length of their service is dependent on the pregnancy of the specified employee they are covering; that way, it's fair to dismiss them when she returns. If she doesn't return, you could well find yourself with a fully trained person who can take over the job on a permanent basis. But beware: on the basis of Sod's Law (things that can go wrong will), it could be just your luck that the temp you have recruited to cover the maternity leave falls pregnant herself! Then it *really* gets complicated!

That's just a summary of the position – I said that it was horribly complex, and there is a range of other hidden rocks on which the unwary employer may founder. In general I would advise: if in doubt, be generous, and include all maternity arrangements in a separate, all-encompassing policy and procedure statement that can be referred to from the statement of particulars, and which can be regularly updated as the allowance levels change and the state of the law develops. A model policy, which goes well beyond your statutory obligations, is shown as model 6.2 (page 92). This is perhaps suitable for consideration only by larger charities that can afford to cover the overheads; smaller ones may feel it necessary to be considerably less generous. I have taken the opportunity in this model not only to include the specific maternity aspects, but also to address issues of new statutory rights in relation to caring for dependants.

Notice

After one month and up to two years' service an employee is entitled to one week's notice of termination of the contract, and then one week's notice per completed year of service, up to a maximum of twelve weeks. An employee must give one week's notice after one month's service. These are minima, and it is entirely a matter of contract whether more generous arrangements are sought on either side. Suffice to say that it is very difficult to hold an employee to a long notice period if she is determined to go early, and whilst she normally has a redress against you for wrongful dismissal if you fail to give her, or pay for her contractual notice entitlement, it is not worth suing her for breach of contract if she just ups and leaves (although you might amend what you say in your reference about her as a result).

Sickness and injury

There is no absolute entitlement to sick pay provided by the employer, although provided the employee qualifies, the employer is obliged to pay Statutory Sick Pay (SSP). Most charities do however have some form of occupational sick pay for a given period that tops up SSP. Be warned, however. Where employers have failed to mention anything at all about sick pay in their documentation (even failing to say there isn't any), the courts have ruled that, when an employee does go off sick, provided the employment contract continues, they are entitled to full pay without any deductions.

Pensions and retirement

If you do not make any employer provision, you and your employees are likely to have to pay higher national insurance rates to cover contributions to SERPS (the State Earnings Related Pension Scheme). In any case, if you have five or more employees you are obliged to make provision for your employees to have access to some form of stakeholder pension, although there is no obligation on the employer to contribute to it or for the employee to take up the offer.

If you do make any provision for a pension scheme, you are obliged to provide information to your staff about it in accordance with the current regulations of the pensions authorities (and even if you don't, you still have to tell staff that in their statements of particulars). These tend to be complicated, and will

MODEL 6.2

XYZ Charity
Maternity and Carers' Leave Policy

1. As a responsible employer in the voluntary sector, and one which takes its wider social responsibilities seriously, the *XYZ Charity* is committed to supporting its staff in their responsibilities beyond the workplace, confident that such support will be reciprocated through their dedication to the work of the charity. Accordingly, it has adopted the following policies, which include all employees' statutory rights but which go beyond these basic obligations. Procedures for the administration of these benefits will be explained by the charity's personnel department as appropriate.

2. Maternity

    2.1 All staff are entitled to the prevailing levels of statutory maternity leave and pay, according to their length of service. These entitlements will be incorporated into *XYZ*'s scheme of entitlements as follows:

    2.2 *Staff with less than six months' service prior to their expected date of confinement*: Maternity Allowance should be claimed from the Benefits Agency. In addition, they will be entitled to the statutory eighteen weeks' maternity leave, of which six weeks will be paid at half pay by *XYZ Charity*, less the value of Maternity Allowance available.

    2.3 *Staff with at least six but less than twelve months' service prior to their expected date of confinement*: Statutory Maternity Pay (SMP) will be paid, plus a further six weeks on half pay. In addition, they will be entitled to the statutory eighteen weeks' maternity leave, which with agreement may be extended to twenty-nine weeks.

    2.4 *Staff with at least twelve months' service prior to their expected date of confinement*: There will be an absolute entitlement to the full twenty-nine weeks of statutory maternity leave, which will be paid at the upper SMP rate of 90% of their normal salary for six weeks, plus a top up by *XYZ Charity* of the additional 10% and a further four weeks at half pay, following which twelve weeks of the lower SMP rate will be paid. In addition, staff may with agreement extend their maternity absence for a period amounting to forty weeks in total.

    2.5 *Staff with two or more years' service prior to their expected date of confinement*: In addition to the benefits set out in 2.4 above, maternity pay funded by *XYZ Charity* will be extended to three months on full pay and three months on half pay, these figures including the upper and lower rate SMP entitlements. The payment of

differ in every case, so I would suggest that you agree with the organisation running your scheme for you exactly what you need to say, and set it out it in a separate document to the statement of particulars. Note that the law on equal treatment is developing rapidly, and whilst pensions used to be excluded under the legis-

the three months on half pay will be conditional upon the employee returning to work following maternity leave for a period of at least three months of equivalent hours prior to the leave (i.e. if she chooses to return half time, she will be required to work for six months for this benefit to be available). Failure to fulfil this obligation will normally result in recovery of the additional payments. There will be an absolute right to take maternity leave for up to forty weeks.

3 Paternity

An employee who is the partner of a pregnant woman shall be entitled to up to two weeks' time off at or around the time of the birth, as follows:

3.1 *Employees with less than twelve months' service*: one week unpaid, one week at the prevailing SMP rate.

3.2 *Employees with between one and two years' service*: one week at full pay, one week unpaid.

3.3 *Employees with more than two years' service*: two weeks' full pay.

4 Carers' leave

4.1 Employees are entitled to a reasonable amount of time off to care for their children in accordance with their statutory rights. Additionally, *XYZ Charity* will extend this right to cover the care of any other person whose principal carer is the employee. The overall level of time off available will be thirteen weeks in any five year period.

4.2 *Employees with less than one year's service*: There is no statutory right to such leave, but *XYZ Charity* will at its discretion grant up to four weeks' unpaid leave in any one year.

4.3 *Employees with twelve or more months' service*: The thirteen week period may be taken at any time during the five year period. In any one year, up to one week of this leave will be on full pay, and one on half pay.

5 Adoption

An employee who is the adopter of a child under the age of five (or, in the case of a child with special needs, under the age of eighteen) will be entitled to the following adoption leave and pay entitlements:

5.1 If the employee is the principal carer of the child, the range of maternity benefits set out above in para 2 shall apply.

5.2 If the employee is the partner of the principal carer, the range of paternity benefits set out above in para 3 shall apply.

Adopters of children who fall outside these categories shall be granted time off, with or without pay, at the discretion of *XYZ Charity*.

lation, this may no longer be the case, so you will need to review carefully both what you say and what is provided.

A great deal of employment legislation, and in particular whether a claim against you may succeed, depends on what your normal retirement age for staff may be. So, for example, if people normally retire at 60, then the exceptional cases staying on until, say, 64 would have problems arguing that they had a case for claiming unfair dismissal. But even then it's not that straightforward: if you normally have different retirement ages for different groups of employees, one may seek to bring an equal value claim against you, citing different treatment on gender grounds with the other; and your situation could be even worse if you have one retirement age for men and another for women (yes, a lot of charities still do, even though it is illegal). The safe way is either to have one age which you rigidly enforce, or a range of possibilities within which you make absolutely sure you do not treat men and women differently.

Disciplinary issues and grievances

Assuming that you have these (and although the law says that it is not strictly necessary for organisations with fewer than twenty employees to tell anybody about them, I would suggest that there is no mileage to be gained in keeping quiet), then you must tell your employees about them. This can be done as a separate document referred to in the statement of particulars, a far more convenient arrangement than including what is often a series of substantial documents within what should be a crisp statement of rights and obligations. Although the Employment Rights Act makes no reference of an obligation to publicise a capability procedure, the ACAS Code of Conduct on Disciplinary Practice and Procedures does recommend that separate arrangements should be established to deal with these matters, and if you are making reference to the two other documents, you might as well include this one.

Probation

The law does not directly recognise the concept of probation, except that the exemption period related to unfair dismissal is generally deemed to have been provided to cover the period when an employer is testing a new employee's suitability. However, as noted above, with the arrangements for continuous service, probation in a new role with an old employer does not protect against unfair dismissal.

What you can quite legally do is have separate contractual arrangements during such a probationary period, for example, on salary arrangements or operative notice periods – provided all parties sign up to it. But since probation is not a legally recognised concept, there is no obligation to make any reference to it in the statement of particulars.

Collective agreements and amendments

If you recognise a trade union and your agreements with it form part of your employees' contracts of employment, you need to include reference to these processes in the statement of particulars. It is very often the case that many of the items discussed above – disciplinary procedures, pension arrangements, maternity pay, and so on – which are too cumbersome to be included in the main document, are the subject of some form of collective discussion. For other charities, they are still determined solely by management. Whichever way you determine your staff's service conditions, if these are derived from any collective agreements or are external to the statement of particulars, it is always prudent to make reference to them and how the employee can be aware of them ('a copy of which can be inspected in the chief executive's office').

Signatures

It is not strictly necessary for the parties to sign the document for it to have legal status – if the employer is providing the pay and conditions set out in it, and the employee is doing her job, the contract exists. But it does make it much easier to demonstrate that there is good will on both sides if both have put their names to the document.

Other points

There are a few less usual points that may occasionally crop up in agreeing employment contracts of which you should be aware:

- If the contract is a fixed-term one, you need to say when it will expire.
- Conversely, if it is a temporary one, you need to indicate its likely duration – but don't tie yourself into employing the temp until then.
- If the contract is, directly or indirectly, to cover maternity leave, it is a good idea to tie it in by naming the pregnant employee, thus making the duration dependent upon her confinement and absence.
- If there are no particular entitlements to holidays beyond the statutory minimum, sick pay apart from Statutory Sick Pay, pensions or salary, then you need to say so – if you don't, an Employment Tribunal may impose them on you.
- If staff transfer to you under the TUPE regulations, you do not need to issue a new statement of particulars, as the transferring staff will bring their existing rights with them – but you

do need to give them a written note of the details of you as the new employer.

Making payments

Much of what is described above was derived from the Wages Act, now incorporated into the Employment Rights Act. It is, in addition, worth noting the following provisions.

You can decide how you are going to pay your employees – they do not have a right to demand cash payments, for example – but if they were paid in a particular way before the Act was introduced, you cannot change that unilaterally.

You may not make deductions from your employees' salary that are not covered by either statutory or contractual provision. Whilst tax, national insurance and Attachment of Earnings are permissible, you will fall foul of the law if you deduct union subscriptions without an affirmative instruction to do so, repayments for a loan without an agreement, or adjustments for till losses unless there is provision within the employment contract to do so (and even then, not more than 10 per cent of the salary). So no fines for misbehaviour, unless they are spelt out in the disciplinary procedure, and that is clearly spelt out as an implied or express term in the employment contract (and who's going to agree to that?)

If you make erroneous or overpayments to an employee, you may only recover them if you explain the error – and even then, if he has already spent the money, reasonably believing he was entitled to it, you may not be able to get it back.

The lesson in all these is quite simple but demanding: keep accurate records, take care in what you do, particularly in your documentation, take advice on complex issues to keep up to date with the state of the law, admit and rectify mistakes quickly. But if you are in doubt, hold back on payments or the granting of benefits – it is far easier for you to make amends afterwards than for you to get back from an employee (often, an ex-employee) something to which she may not have been entitled.

Which rather brings us on to the next chapter. In this one, I have set out the main things that as a responsible voluntary sector employer, wishing to keep within the law, you must do. But this is no more than a basic minimum, not the basis for a personnel strategy. You can and will want to build on this, to develop arrangements and entitlements that suit your charity's needs, and those of its staff. In the next chapter, I shall explore how you can go about this, identifying the choices you may face in determining what is best practice and what you can afford to do, and equally, what you cannot afford to ignore.

In summary ...

- British employment has few fundamental rights, particularly related to service conditions. Such as do exist are largely founded upon ideas from Europe.
- Where rights do exist, such as the right not to be unfairly dismissed, they are usually open to evaluation by the courts as to what is reasonable in all the circumstances.
- Whilst staff do not in general have any service conditions specified by law, they do have the right to be told what their entitlements are, where these exist, and this is largely enshrined within the requirements to prove a statement of particulars.
- Other entitlements stem from associated legislation such as the Employment Rights Act and anti-discrimination legislation.

CHAPTER 7

Staff conditions – what you may want to do

INTRODUCTION

Whatever your views on how far the state – whether it is the British government or the EU – should direct what goes on in the workplace, agreement between employers and their staff is the most effective way of securing the service objectives shared by all parties to employment contracts.

We have a bedrock of legislation on employment conditions and rights, and may argue for ever about how far that should go. But what really counts is how you build on the legislation to ensure that your organisation is one that can honestly describe itself as operating good employment practices and, in particular, decent service conditions. This chapter gives a summary of the kinds of policies and practices you might consider to help take you beyond the basics.

Towards good practice

There is no single prescription to what constitutes good practice. It depends on a variety of factors, including your organisation's culture, your staff's expectations, what you can afford and what accords with the end-product – your services. I have assumed that any employer in the voluntary sector will at least want to subscribe to the minimum requirements of the law – if you don't, this book isn't for you.

But I also assume that, to a lesser or greater extent, you will want to go beyond the basics, and this chapter offers a guide to the issues you may wish to consider in doing so, whether you are developing a salary policy, designing a job evaluation scheme, determining appropriate levels of annual and special leave, considering what hours staff should work (and when), proposing non-salary benefits such as pensions and a retirement policy, negotiating procedural arrangements to cover redundancy, or sorting out what car allowances to pay.

These and other matters all fall within the broad description of 'remuneration policy', and I place the emphasis on 'policy'. Any organisation can grant a concession here, withhold a benefit there, resist a change or promote an individual development. The point, however, is to try to bring it all together so that a series of ideas becomes a policy, and a comprehensive approach to your policies becomes a personnel strategy. That is why I stress throughout this book the interconnectedness of everything you do in the name of managing people in charities; it all, in the end, locks together, but unless you have the key to that lock, you will be in danger of failing to relate inputs (donations and staff effort) to outputs (rewards and services). This chapter, therefore, offers a further perspective on the process of strategic development, by considering the range of options facing charity managers in terms of motivating and rewarding their staff.

Developing a salary policy

Many smaller charities feel that they do not have the time, the resources or the expertise to manage their own salary arrangements. Frequently, they will seek to follow arrangements determined elsewhere. Those providing medical services, for example, may seek to follow pay arrangements operated in the Health Service (an increasingly difficult task with the move towards local wage determination). Research-based charities often follow university scales, whilst those involved in education have tended to reflect teachers' pay arrangements. Many smaller charities, especially those whose members or managers have either a local government background or local campaigning roots, will look to local authority settlements to determine their pay levels.

Whilst this approach has much to commend it to those organisations that are unable or unwilling to devote many resources to personnel management, there are some considerations worth taking on board if you are about to embark upon such a course for the first time, or have already started to use someone else's industrial relations processes as your benchmark:

- Public sector pay over the past few years has been used as an instrument of fiscal policy and as a political football, with the result that it may no longer reflect the true worth of the job done. If your staff are paid in the same way, is their true worth reflected?

- The national negotiating machinery established mainly in the 1960s and 1970s is slowly but surely breaking up, so it is becoming increasingly difficult to secure an appropriate comparator, particularly as some organisations now see themselves in a competitive market and are less willing to make their salary information available.
- Changes in policy, or the effect of a particularly successful union campaign could, on the other hand, distort the pay settlement figures and produce an outcome your charity cannot afford. Do you slavishly follow a particular settlement, or have you built in a safety valve ('The *XYZ Charity* will seek to follow the awards of the Higher Education Negotiating Board, but will only agree pay increases as resources allow)?
- Budgeting can be rather more difficult when you are dependent on others for an input to one of your key components, particularly if their pay settlement timetable does not fit in with your budget development year. Some charities get round this by agreeing to implement someone else's pay settlement, but on a delayed basis – but even that can have its own problems, particularly at times of high inflation.
- Even if they do manage to follow the pay settlements of the benchmarked system, most models relate to organisations with structures far more complex than even the largest charities, and certainly more involved that those of the typical ten or twenty member staff team. There is therefore a tendency simply to adopt the percentage increase offered, which only really works when it is across the board; when, for example, it is bottom-loaded, it is more difficult to translate that into the charity's own circumstances. And most of the time, non-salary benefits that are part of the national settlements are ignored altogether.

Whilst following other settlements has had its strengths in the past, I do believe that its value will become increasingly limited in the future, especially as charities become more competitive and need to be more sensitive to their markets. I would therefore strongly counsel you to consider very carefully whether you should in fact develop your own salary policy and, within that, remuneration determination mechanisms. Even some of the smallest charities, with less than ten staff, are beginning to do so, and the really large ones have been doing it for years.

Model 7.1 highlights several points:

- The need to get the timing of the settlement, and its implementation, in line with your budget-making processes, and the ability to avoid paying in extreme circumstances.
- Even where salaries are set with reference to another process, the need to keep an eye on the market, both overall and in respect of individual posts.

> **MODEL 7.1** Salary policy using external determinants
>
> 1. *The XYZ Charity* normally sets its salary levels for paid staff by following the pay settlement of the local authorities' National Joint Council (NJC) for Administrative, Professional, Technical and Professional Services (APT&C 'Purple Book'). Additionally, it will regularly review pay arrangements elsewhere in the voluntary sector, and will seek regular advice as to the continued appropriateness of its salary policy.
>
> 2. An annual cost of living increase will be awarded six months after the due date of the APT&C settlement. In extreme financial circumstances, the management committee reserves the right not to award this increase as an alternative to declaring redundancies. In such circumstances, backdating of the pay award will take first priority for *The XYZ Charity* once finances have been secured.
>
> 3. Grades will be determined by the director, following consultation with the chair of the management committee, and will take account of:
>   - salaries paid elsewhere in appropriate comparator organisations within the voluntary sector
>   - relativities within *The XYZ Charity*
>   - affordability
>   - equal value considerations.
>
>   The salary grade of the director will be determined by the management committee.
>
> 4. Salary grade bands will follow the arrangements pertaining under the national scheme, with three to five incremental points. Newly appointed staff will normally start at the bottom of the band, unless there are exceptional circumstances, determined by the director and confirmed by the chair.
>
> 5. One incremental point increase will be awarded in the month following each anniversary of the employee's start in post, until the top of the grade is reached. Where the employee has demonstrated an exceptional and sustained performance in post, an additional increment may, at the discretion of the director, be awarded. Conversely, where there is continued and substantial underperformance, the director may withhold the granting of an increment.
>
> 6. Staff promoted from one salary grade to another will start on the bottom of the new band, or at the first point above the existing salary point if bands overlap.
>
> 7. Staff whose grade has been reduced as a result of restructuring will enjoy personal protection of their existing salary until such time as cost of living and incremental awards bring them back in line with their new substantive salary.
>
> 8. All posts are also paid the agreed NJC London weighting supplement.

- The need to have some system of setting grades within the overall salary policy framework, which can be a simple determination by the chief executive, or may be determined by a more complex though arguably more equitable job evaluation approach.

- The need at least to consider how staff are appointed to, and advance within, their grades – if you have increments, do they always start on the bottom, should they progress upwards automatically, can you accelerate or withhold increments, what do you do about personal protection, and so on.

The model is but one of many possible permutations, all of which will be dependent on your own charity's needs. An alternative approach is offered in model 7.2.

MODEL 7.2 Do-it-yourself salary-setting

1 *The XYZ Charity* believes that its staff should be appropriately remunerated to reflect the degree of their responsibilities and the extent of their successful contribution to its key objectives. As a responsible employer, it will also seek to protect staff against erosion of their standard of living.

2 There are five grades that can be applied to posts within the organisation, apart from those of the director, for whom alternative arrangements operate. It is for the director to determine, through the application of the job evaluation scheme, which grade is appropriate to which post, subject to considerations of internal relativities and budgetary constraints. Posts may be regraded at the discretion of the director. Salary upgrades will bring with them all the benefits associated with the enhanced salary; staff subjected to downgrading will enjoy personal protection of their salary for a period of two years, thereafter reverting to the substantive salary and conditions of the post.

3 The management committee will review all salaries for grades annually and, whenever it is financially expedient to do so and after consultation with the staff, make adjustments with effect from 1 September (or at any other date as may be acceptable) to reflect any changes in the retail price index or in response to any other benchmark agreed as appropriate.

4 All employees will have their performance evaluated as part of the annual appraisal process, against the following standards:
   - **Excellent** – has met all possible targets and considerably exceeded quality performance standards.
   - **Good** – has met all possible targets, on occasion exceeding standards.
   - **Satisfactory** – has met all possible targets to an acceptable standard.
   - **Less than satisfactory** – has failed to meet some possible targets, and/or has not always worked to a satisfactory standard.
   - **Poor** – has significantly underachieved on many targets and has generally worked at an unsatisfactory standard.

5 Staff not satisfied with their assessment may appeal against any decision, using the grievance procedure.

6 Performance rewards will, subject to financial resources being available, be made as follows. They will be paid as single taxable lump sums in the month following completion of the annual appraisal process, and will not be consolidated into any subsequent base salary.

Again, I have used this model to highlight several points:

- Salaries, or part of them, can be related to performance, but it is a good idea to provide staff with an acceptable base salary and offer reasonable incentives on top. The efficacy of this and other ways of relating pay to outputs is discussed below.
- Performance pay can be determined by the outcome of the appraisal process, as in this model, or the reward setting exercise may be undertaken separately. Either way, it is good prac-

Performance assessment	Type of award	% of basic salary*
Excellent	maximum	20%
Good	advanced	12%
Satisfactory	basic	6%
Less than satisfactory	none	–
Poor	none, remedial action	–

*Resultant figures to be rounded

The XYZ Charity
2001/2002 SALARY POINTS

All salaries are in £ sterling (actual performance awards shown in brackets)

Salary band	Base salary	Basic	Advanced	Maximum
		With performance awards:		
1	14,500	15,375 (875)	16,250 (1,750)	17,500 (3,000)
2	17,000	18,000 (1000)	19,000 (2,000)	20,500 (3,500)
3	19,500	20,750 (1,250)	21,875 (2,375)	23,500 (4,000)
4	22,000	23,250 (1,250)	24,750 (2,750)	26,500 (4,500)
5	25,000	26,500 (1,500)	28,000 (3,000)	30,000 (5,000)

Adjustments to base salaries will be determined by the management committee following a review of the annual retail price index movement.

Consequent adjustments to performance rewards will be determined by the director, in accordance with the formula contained within *The XYZ Charity* salaries' policy, and following consultation with the chair.

tice for staff to know the criteria by which they are assessed, and for them to have a route to challenge the application of those criteria – whether they are applied to them as individual employees, or relate to some form of team award (an approach that has not yet taken root in the voluntary sector).
- In this model, I have put all the responsibility on the shoulders of the director; in larger charities, this may not always be practicable. The key point is that there needs to be consistency for the system to be fair, and to be seen to be fair. How you achieve that will be determined by your organisational structure.
- Performance awards are an addition to base salaries and should not normally be consolidated into them. If you do that, good performance in one year is rewarded forever more, whatever quality the subsequent performance may be.
- Salary bands can be determined either exclusively by management, or via a job evaluation scheme, with or without managerial constraints on its operation.
- Determination of salary rises remains the responsibility of the charity. This can be done either by tying levels to an external and objective factor such as the retail price index, or through the negotiation process if there is a system for staff representation, or in response to the need to reflect the norms of the organisation – always subject to the overriding consideration of affordability.
- The implementation date can and should relate to your budget cycle, with the possibility of putting it off if you need to. However, if you have too many such caveats, what you have ceases to be a policy, and becomes pragmatic management (sometimes known as knee-jerk flying by the seat of your pants!). So do try to develop a policy that stands a good chance of being applied consistently for a reasonable period – at least three years seems to have been a reflection of successful experience.

Rewarding performance

Traditional salary policies have concentrated on paying the rate for the job, determined by a combination of market factors, affordability and relativities.

In times when process and product were paramount, such systems served organisations well, particularly when most employees were expected to do roughly the same thing and to roughly the same standard. They also had the advantage of being easy to operate, with few disagreements about what was fair and appropriate and, indeed, few managerial decisions to challenge.

Working life is not as straightforward now – if indeed it ever was for the majority of voluntary sector organisations. Job tasks tend to be far more varied processes, are changing all the time and quality output is king. In a well-managed organisation, every employee will have different objectives and, implicit in that, different targets to aim at and different standards to reach. Hence the change of emphasis towards individual reward.

How far your charity should go in recognising this is a matter for you. You may feel that it is divisive and inappropriate for you to give potentially different financial awards to members of the same team, and you may well be concerned about rewarding effort when you cannot be sure either that the effort resulted in improved output, or that improved output was solely attributable to an employee's input. You may feel that some form of team bonus would be preferred, where at least there is a chance of evening out the individual performances to reflect the success of the team (and where peer pressure may be more effective than management supervision to raise the standards of the weaker members).

On the other hand, your charity may not have such a collectivist approach, and it and its staff will feel reasonably comfortable with the idea of rewarding success rather than just the ability to stay in the job. In those circumstances, an individual performance-related pay (PRP) scheme may be right for you – if so, you are joining upwards of a third of charities with employees who have gone down the same route. Each scheme needs to be designed sensitively and uniquely, but some pointers are:

- PRP needs to be an addition to, not a substitute for, basic salary; it can work well as a substitute for increments but, except at times of very low inflation, not for the annual cost-of-living pay round.
- There is a limit to how much PRP can fairly be part of the total salary package; whilst this varies from job to job, and indeed from charity to charity (fundraisers and marketing people usually expect to get more in performance pay than their colleagues, for example), anything much above twenty per cent on top of the basic pay and you may be storing up problems for the future.
- On the other hand, PRP levels need to be sufficiently high to work as an incentive – few staff are going to work hard to increase their performance significantly if the only reward they get is one or two per cent, which they might well get as an annual review anyway.
- It is often difficult to agree objective measures of performance – and when you do find some to introduce, there is a danger of their becoming mechanistic (such as how many visits a social worker achieved, rather than the quality of those visits). Provided there is confidence in management's ability to be

fair, an assessment by your supervisor on how well you met the real purpose of the job is probably the best you can achieve. If you are a really confident charity, part of that assessment may include feedback from service users.

- There is a growing body of evidence that PRP, in the longer run, encourages most staff to settle into a performance level that secures an income level sufficient for their needs; few will ultimately risk the high effort to secure the further marginal increase, but rather will play it safe to ensure that they don't slip back. So any scheme needs to be reviewed regularly, and its operation and the work of the staff involved in it closely monitored.
- Above all, the staff involved have to believe that the system is fair, and that they individually are fairly treated. If, after a year or two of operation, it is still viewed with suspicion, the belief still abounds that it is biased or inconsistent, and appeals occur every other week, there's something fundamentally wrong. Either the staff are right, or you sold it badly to them. But if staff are genuinely being assessed as above average, and the appeals mechanism is not being used, you've probably got it right – albeit that you still need to keep it under review.
- However you operate the system, you still have to face the issue of confidentiality. Whilst the parameters of the scheme can – and indeed, should – be well publicised, just like your salary structures, individual performance within them is, for most charities, a matter between the employee and her manager. After all, you would not like the details of your appraisal blazoned across the staff newsletter, particularly if a summary was 'could do better', any more than you would publicise the intimate details of an employee's capability hearing.

One theme that is currently developing, particularly in those voluntary sector organisations that are unhappy about introducing PRP or that are becoming disenchanted with it because of some of the concerns outlined above, is the development of a pay structure that rewards the possession of 'competencies'. Superficially similar to PRP, what this system attempts to do is to pay staff more the more they can demonstrate that they possess the key competencies needed to do a job well. This avoids the problem of their being unable to perform well (and hence lose pay) because of external factors beyond their control, but rather seeks to recognise and reward them for their real worth and the potential contribution they can therefore bring. Typically, a scheme would have a benchmark of a normally acceptable standard for the competent employee, set at 100 per cent, staff not yet at that level might be paid only ninety per cent, while those significantly exceeding it might get 110 per cent. The main problem with it is that staff are rewarded for high technical proficiency, whether or not they use all their skills, and hence pay is only loosely related to output. It is therefore necessary to keep the system under constant review, to ensure that the competencies being measured and rewarded really do relate to organisational core values.

If you are keen to recognise effort, but are against the idea of individual rewards, however they are determined, then some form of charity-wide bonuses may be the appropriate route to follow. Whilst for most voluntary organisations the idea of a profit sits strangely with their objectives (and in any case may well conflict with their legal charitable status), nevertheless they will still be aware that a department, a team or the whole charity has had a good year and will want to reward that. And whilst there is no profit as such to be distributed to shareholders, there will often be a surplus; indeed, every charity finance director will seek to generate one, if only to support expansion of the charity's work. So corporate bonus schemes, financed from accumulated surpluses (to which the staff have, after all, contributed through their efforts) may well be your right choice. If you have adopted a profit-related pay scheme (however you choose to describe it), then you and your staff may also benefit from considerable tax advantages – which may be a key element in your overall salary strategy to generate maximum reward at minimum net cost.

Job evaluation

There are two main strands to any salary policy. The first is how the overall levels are determined, which, with their add-ons, I have discussed above. The other is how, within that overall framework, relativities are established, that is, how the value of one job relates to another. Not surprisingly, that is called job evaluation, and, equally unsurprising, if it is to be a success in your charity, it will have to be driven by the key elements of what you are about. Unless your charity has developed a policy of setting separate salaries for each employee, and then keeping very quiet about what each employee gets, you will need some kind of system to show that the relative salaries, and the differences between them, are appropriate and fair.

There have been whole textbooks written on job evaluation. Most of them spend considerable time describing systems that, largely for equal value reasons, have in the main fallen by the wayside. I shall therefore deal with only two here, and one of them only in passing.

The latter is what I would describe as the 'internal ranking system', which, I would suggest, is only appropriate in very small charities, where it is not necessary to have a significant number of grades, and where all salaries can be (relatively) objectively determined by one person, usually the director. In such a system the charity will, typically, decide how much it can afford to spend on salaries, and then divide this cake up in differing proportions, with senior staff getting the most; how much less the others get will depend on how differently the charity perceives the value of their contribution. The whole process is often informed by external salary comparisons ('if the chief executive of a similar charity with twice the number of staff is getting X, how much should ours earn?'), and this is done either informally or through the application of salary survey data, often incorporating a formal salary review.

Such a system can work well with a small charity when the operations are relatively straightforward, narrowly focused and everyone knows everyone else, their work and their worth. But as soon as a voluntary sector body starts to diversify, to develop tiers of management and get much beyond the size where all staff can work comfortably in one team (typically, any number from ten upwards), a degree of remoteness begins to creep in, and the relative value of different contributions may not be so precisely identifiable. For many years, the voluntary sector drifted on like this, with many anomalies arising in salary relativities as managers made it up as they went along, which was fine as long as nobody questioned it.

But, quite rightly, many charity trustees, and their staff, have concluded that a more demonstrably fair system is needed. This move is driven on both management and equity grounds: management, because charities need to know whether they are getting value for money; and equity, because that underpins a great deal of what the sector is about, and few charities would wish to be accused of unfairness and bias. Added to that has been, in recent years, considerable pressure from the equal value legislation which, in essence, has meant that work of equal value should be equally rewarded. Since, even in the voluntary sector, the average female salary is below the male average, there is always a danger of losing cases of sex discrimination if you cannot demonstrate that the work your female employees are doing is of less value than that of your males. Sex discrimination can cost you, quite literally, hundreds of thousands of pounds.

It is an accepted fact of life that some jobs are more valuable than others. It is an equally accepted, though regrettable, fact of life that women tend to get the lower paid jobs, although that is slowly changing. Your charity is likely to reflect both strands – and your only defence against sex discrimination on pay grounds is that women are in jobs that genuinely are worth less. Your only action, once you have determined that, is to review your recruitment, training and promotion procedures to find out why women are not rising to the top, and do something about removing the blockages to their advancement.

But to return to job evaluation. It is now generally held that, in Britain at least, the only acceptable (although by no means completely watertight) way to defend against an equal value claim is to have a 'factor analysis' job evaluation scheme, i.e. one that values jobs in terms of the key values of your charity and does not measure them by any other criterion. Usually, this measurement is in terms of the level of skill, knowledge, experience, and so on required, although some practitioners now argue for a competencies approach – the ability an employee may potentially need to do the job. The construction of such a scheme takes a lot of time and effort, and you may well need outside assistance to achieve an outcome that fairly reflects the value of your employees' work, relates them one to another and to a salary system, and successfully defends you against accusations of discrimination. As I said, whole books have been written about the process – although it is, essentially, a practical rather than academic one. It would be inappropriate to go into too much detail here, but the key steps are given below.

Checklist 7.1 Job evaluation

- [✓] Determine from the outset who is going to own the job evaluation scheme. The charity, of course, but how far will the staff whose salaries are determined by it have a say in how it is run, and how far will they be given explanations on how it works? Generally, the more staff are involved, either individually or through a representative structure, the more likely are you to achieve success.

- [✓] Identify the key values of your voluntary organisation, both in terms of its objectives and how it views the work of its staff. This can be done through staff questionnaires, focus groups, discussions with management members, evaluation of your own literature and even asking people outside – for example donors, partners and users – what they think of you.

- [✓] Group these key values into sensible categories and retain only those that can be managed. These are the factors that constitute the body of your factor analysis scheme; and you should develop a definition of each that will be easily understood within your charity.

- [✓] Identify different levels within each factor and how much of that factor each job contains. Seek to describe what each level means. Whatever you come up with, you will need a concise but clear description for each level which, together with factor definitions, comprise the body of the scheme notes.

- ☑ Then – and, I would argue, only then – agree the relative value of each factor, and the relative strength of each level. This is probably the hardest part of the exercise, as individuals will have differing views, often prompted by the nature of their own roles; you will want to aim for a consensus, but may have to settle for something short of that.

- ☑ Conduct a separate exercise, ranking all (or a sample) of the jobs in the charity according to what is considered the most and least important. Again, consensus is the ideal in this exercise, but this is only a guide to the accurateness of the factor analysis scheme.

- ☑ Test some key, or benchmark, jobs with the new scheme, ascribing them the points that each level of each factor generates as a result of considering the different elements of each benchmark job. If you rank them by total points and they come out in (roughly) the same order as in the other ranking exercise, you have probably got the points to levels equation right.

- ☑ You may need to make some adjustments between factors and levels until not only is the ranking right, but the relative scores also seem to reflect your values.

- ☑ Once the trialling exercise has been completed, you then need to develop a points to salary grade formula, one that can avoid the accusation of providing arbitrary divisions but which draws together all jobs of approximately equal value. Again, a considerable amount of trial and error may be needed before you get this right.

- ☑ You will then need a set of operational guidelines, the rules of the scheme – who does the evaluation, how it is checked or appealed against, guidance on the interpretation of the scheme notes, when jobs can be reconsidered, what to do with new and revised posts, how to protect staff whose jobs are downgraded, and so on.

- ☑ Finally, apply the scheme to all jobs, including the benchmarked posts if late adjustments have been made. You will now have a job evaluation scheme that provides an assessed salary for every existing post, and which can equally be applied to future new ones. All you now need do is to work out whether you can afford to implement it!

As a manager, you should be aware that it is extremely difficult to introduce a new job evaluation scheme, particularly a factor analysis one, without some degree of 'grade drift', that is, salaries rising (or remaining protected) to fit in with the new scheme. You should always remember that you are measuring the post, not the postholder (the appraisal scheme is for that). And you should also be aware that for all its attractions, factor analysis is still not entirely scientific or objective, it merely reduces the subjectivity.

It will still reflect core values rather than hard facts, and there will always be some problems in interpretation. It's just that it is normally so much better than the alternative – at best, confusion and resentment over who gets paid what, and why; at worst, painful and expensive Employment Tribunal proceedings.

Salary levels and reviews

The burning question on salaries that remains, however, is: how much?

Unfortunately, this is not a question that can be answered in this book. We do know that, apart from a very few cash-rich charities, and for even fewer types of highly specialised jobs, voluntary sector salaries are, in the main, significantly below their counterparts in the private sector, and often also still lag behind parts of the public sector. Chief executives and other directors earned, in 1999, about fifteen per cent less than their commercial counterparts, and middle managers nearly thirteen and a half per cent less. Only really junior staff tend to be paid above the average, presumably reflecting the philanthropy of the sector. These trends are unlikely to be reversed quickly, but beyond that, it is not easy to go.

For a start, salary data get outdated very quickly. Actual figures here would not help you to decide how much to pay your staff in a few years', or maybe even a few months', time. More significantly, there is rarely, if ever, one straightforward answer. Even if you slavishly follow someone else's pay settlements, it is most unlikely that they will have a salary grade or job equivalent that exactly matches all your posts, particularly if you have already determined your internal relativities through a job evaluation process.

So I would advise instead that you turn to the salary review process. You don't need to do this every time that pay rise time comes around, but it is worth checking your position against the world beyond your own charity every now and again. There is a considerable amount of data to choose from – after all, there are thousands of charities employing getting on for half a million staff. The problem is knowing where to start.

Like job evaluation, the salary review process should never be seen as entirely objective – it all depends on which organisations you choose as your comparators and the size of your sample. But it can at least be subjected to statistical analysis, so that you can be sure to a particular degree of certainty how close to representative your data are. There are also many published salary surveys, which can form the basis for your salary-setting decisions. But again, which you choose to consult will determine the results.

> **MODEL 7.3** A (very) simplified factor analysis job evaluation scheme
>
> *The XYZ Charity* determines its salaries through a factor analysis job evaluation scheme. The key elements that are used to measure the value of each job are:
>
> **Factor 1: Responsibility**
>
> This factor measures the degree of resources – people, property and money – for which the postholder has direct or indirect responsibility.
>
> | | | |
> |---|---|---|
> | Level 1: | Responsible only for own personal work equipment, and no staff supervision | 10 points |
> | Level 2: | Responsible for supervising up to five other staff and their work equipment, and/or for local premises and limited financial assets | 40 points |
> | Level 3: | Responsible for up to twenty staff and equipment, and/or significant financial or physical assets | 100 points |
> | Level 4: | Responsibility levels above these | 125 points |
> | Additional factor: | Staff responsible for or handling valuable assets that may endanger their safety are entitled to an additional | 30 points |
>
> **Factor 2: Care**
>
> This factor measures how far the postholder is involved, and at what professional level, in the core purpose of the charity, that of delivering care services to our client group.
>
> | | | |
> |---|---|---|
> | Level 1: | Normally needs to use care skills only in relationships with day-to-day contacts with non-dependants | 25 points |
> | Level 2: | Significant contact with clients in need of non-specialist care | 60 points |
> | Level 3: | Significant specialist care skills needed, particularly with users with difficult problems | 90 points |
> | Level 4: | Occasional contact with full range of users through managerial responsibility for carers | 100 points |

Three approaches, broadly, are possible. First, you may decide to look at all comparable salaries for similar jobs – all finance directors, computer operators or drivers, for example. You will need to determine whether you want to consider information about the whole country or just your local area. Generally, the higher paid the job, the more likely staff are to relocate to it, so the broader your comparison can afford to be. Alternatively, you may feel it to be more appropriate to consider all jobs in a particular sector – comparing all charity welfare jobs, for example, or all housing officers employed by housing associations. Finally, you may combine these approaches.

Which route you follow is, in the end, determined by whom you consider to be your competitors (the charities and other organisations from whom you may expect to recruit staff, and to whom you may lose them if your service conditions aren't right),

Factor 3: Creativity

This factor measures how far the postholder contributes to the development of the charity.

Level 1:	Works generally within routines set by others	20 points
Level 2:	Organises own work programme within broad parameters	50 points
Level 3:	Organises the work of others, including developing new ideas and activities within broad parameters	100 points
Level 4:	Creativity and initiative levels above these	125 points

Factor 4: Education

This factor measures the level of skills and knowledge the postholder will need to do the job effectively. Possession of a qualification is not as important as the ability to work at the level indicated by it.

Level 1:	Basic education up to GCSE standard	30 points
Level 2:	Education to A-level or HND standard	50 points
Level 3:	First level professional qualification	100 points
Level 4:	Graduate or higher level professional qualification	150 points

Points to salary bands

0–120 points	Salary band 1 (*currently £12,000–£14,000*)
121–225 points	Salary band 2 (*currently £15,000–£19,500*)
226–350 points	Salary band 3 (*currently £21,000–£24,000*)
351–475 points	Salary band 4 (*currently £25,500–£28,000*)
476+ points	Salary band 5 (*currently £29,000–£32,000*)

Author's health warning: Do not attempt to use this model in your organisation. It is for illustrative purposes only. You must choose values, points and salary ranges that match your charity's values, both internal and external. And most schemes need to be far more complex than this one.

and how widespread that competition is. You can then tackle the problem either by asking them directly how much they are paying, or by analysing the often detailed statistics provided within the published surveys. The latter have the particular advantage of normally including large numbers of organisations in their results, so they are more likely to be statistically representative and capable of disaggregation. However, local comparisons with individual organisations can also be useful, particularly if you want to get an idea of a spot salary rather than a general trend.

Once you have determined your comparators, it doesn't stop there. Not only do you need to find out what others are paying, you need to know how much you want to pay in relation to them. Some charities, for example, seek to pay their staff in the top quartile (that is, better than seventy-five per cent of the comparator group); others might feel that the non-salary benefits are sufficiently attractive to pay below the median (midpoint). These matters will change over time and between different types of job, so you need to be aware of such changes, to monitor your recruitment and retention trends, and adjust your salary policies accordingly.

With sufficient understanding of statistical techniques, such as is often to be found in the better personnel departments, you should be able to make sense of the published survey data and apply it to your own charity. You may also wish to commit the not inconsiderable resources involved in conducting your own salary survey of comparator organisations, although many are becoming more and more reticent, especially if they feel that you are a competitor and are about to make use of commercially sensitive organisations. For this reason many charities, particularly smaller ones, are tending to ask specialist external consultants to conduct salary reviews for them, since they can often secure information, on an anonymous basis, that rival charities would otherwise be reluctant to supply. Whether you choose to implement your consultants' recommendations is, of course, entirely up to you!

... But there's more to life than money

The key to any successful remuneration strategy has, of course, to be acceptable salary arrangements. But any strategy that totally ignores other aspects of working life is doomed, sooner or later, to failure. Unless you consider non-salary elements as part of the overall package that you offer staff, then discontent is likely to grow, staff will start to drift away and you will find it increasingly difficult to recruit. Indeed, one of the great ironies of British industrial relations is that the more you get salaries right, the more staff's attention and interest focuses elsewhere.

This final section, therefore, briefly considers some of the most common employee benefits and approaches that you might adopt in determining what is appropriate for your charity. As with job evaluation, there are whole books devoted to this subject, and I cannot therefore do more than highlight some of the main issues here; doubtless there will be other examples you can draw on from your own experience that will enable you to establish a comprehensive benefits package for your organisation.

Leave

Next to salary, in my experience the benefit that most candidates seem most interested in is how much time they will have off from the job. You might question their commitment if that is at the front of their minds, but it's a fact of life and you need to be ready to respond to it.

All employees in post for thirteen consecutive weeks are entitled to four weeks' paid leave, and a more typical level is twenty-five days. Some organisations still operate different levels for long service and grade, although the logic of why someone who is more senior and therefore presumably more indispensable should have more time off, at greater cost per absence, has always escaped me. In the last few years, there has been a slight retrenchment, with the number of days' entitlement reducing slightly. In the voluntary sector, at least, this reflects the fact that many staff, particularly senior executives, have struggled to take their full allocation, and some of them have been paid compensation instead. The realisation of this factor has encouraged charity employers to reappraise the entitlements, particularly for new starters.

You may also consider it beneficial to link annual leave entitlement to other, special, leave which you can (and in some cases must) grant for a variety of reasons – although there is generally no obligation on you to do so with pay. You must allow reasonable time off (the law is silent on a definition of reasonable) for employees to undertake public duties – serving as a magistrate or a local councillor, school governor, on a jury, and so on. If you recognise a union, you must allow some time for its members to conduct union business – and this must be paid if they are union officials carrying out union duties in connection with their role related to you, their employer. The only other paid time off obligations are for pregnant employees to attend ante-natal care, and for potentially redundant employees to look for alternative employment.

As well as these rights, you are statutorily obliged to consider leave for caring responsibilities, and parental leave (neither of which currently need to be paid, and which are discussed in more length in chapter 6). Further, you might want to grant time off for service in the armed forces, and perhaps for reasons that reflect the specific culture and objectives of your charity.

There is a wide range of experiences throughout the sector, ranging from the amazingly generous to the downright mean. How much you choose to grant, and how much of it is paid, has to be a decision that only you can make; but in making that decision, you need to satisfy yourself that it is a sensible use of charitable resources (time, and time off, is money), and whether the circumstances of working in your charity, and of the kind of staff you attract, do call for such provision.

Hours of work

Closely linked to the question of how much time off staff should get is how long they should work, and when. Traditionally, charity staff have been employed on so many hours per week (the typical range is thirty-five to forty), and equally traditionally, on something like a nine to five basis. I would suggest that this is no longer a sufficient approach, and suggest that you consider the following aspects when determining your policy on working hours, always ensuring, of course, that you keep within the complex Working Time Regulations:

- If staff are regularly working more than their contracted hours, you either have a dedicated workforce who may sooner or later take a different view and feel they are being exploited; or you are paying a hefty overtime bill. Either way, you do need to review whether your staffing levels are right, or whether staff are working at the right times – work at other times might be more efficient.
- If staff need to work outside 'normal' office hours on a regular basis – and many, particularly in care and fundraising areas, do – then you would do better to avoid systems of premium payments (such as double time on Sundays) that have dogged public sector bureaucracies in particular, and instead pay staff to work so many hours a week, whenever those may be.
- If the demands of the job are erratic, and the staff's own needs are variable, then a system of flexible working hours (flexitime) may be to everyone's advantage. You need to have clear sets of ground rules, and you will always get someone who tries to abuse the system, but in general this can be an advantageous development at very little cost.
- If your work patterns are cyclical (perhaps your care staff are busier in the winter months), you may consider an annual hours approach. With this, you base the workload for the year on a standard number of hours per week, but then deploy staff flexibly so that they work more at some times of the year than at others. For example, if you have a thirty-five hour week and, excluding leave and bank holidays, staff are expected to work forty-six weeks in a year, you will have 1,610 hours to deploy, perhaps with twenty weeks of forty-five hours, twenty-four weeks of twenty-seven hours and two weeks of thirty-one hours.

Dealing with sickness

There are two aspects to managing sickness: the degree of sickness absence your charity considers reasonable and how much staff who are away sick should be paid during their absence. There is no statutory obligation to provide either, but if an employee is off sick, then she is normally entitled to receive Statutory Sick Pay (SSP). The rules about managing this are laid down by government, but basically mean that provided employees self-certificate the reason for their absence for the first week, and produce doctor's statements thereafter, they are paid by you; you may then be able to recover these payments against the employer's national insurance contributions and, if necessary, deducted income tax.

Be warned. Although you are not obliged to pay anything more than SSP, if your contracts of employment are silent on the matter, the courts are likely to rule that staff can be off sick as often as they like, and will get full pay while doing so. If you don't want to grant any sick time off, or you want to say that anyone off sick will get only SSP, then you must say so in the statement of particulars (see chapter 6).

Probably, however, yours will not be a charity that takes such a hard line. Most voluntary sector organisations recognise that good employer practice means giving their staff a degree of peace of mind, so that if they are genuinely ill, they can take time off to recover and to get back to making a full contribution without worrying that they can't afford the mortgage. Unfortunately, those that don't recognise the need to manage sickness absence tend to get the balance wrong between the employee's needs and the impact their absence has on the charity's work. All too often, I have come across sick pay schemes that permit six months' full-pay absence, followed by another six at half-pay, and that in a staff team of less than a dozen. It does not take great imagination to work out the effect that has on operations and finance.

Many organisations also tie in the level of sickness absence to the length of service – almost as if they were offering a long service award of the right to be off sick. But unless you are particularly benevolent, and your contracts are loosely worded, there should not in general be any right to be off sick, only a right to be treated reasonably by your employer if you are. So it is worthwhile making it clear that, if management accepts the reasons for an employee's absence, then she may be allowed up to a certain period of absence at a certain rate of pay, but beyond that, it is entirely up to the charity as to whether the job is held open. Even before that point, if the prolonged absence is causing impossibilities for the charity, it may be fair to dismiss the employee on the basis that she is no longer able to fulfil her contract, and that this failure is having a significantly deleterious effect on the charity's work. Employment Tribunals may consider that fair, provided that you have handled the process reasonably and that you have not treated other comparable workers in similar circumstances differently.

As a general rule, however, it is probably not a good idea to dismiss people who are off sick until they have exhausted their sick pay entitlement (you may need to think differently about key workers); and you may well wish to be compassionate, particularly if the employee is suffering from a life-threatening illness, or if the dismissal could affect her pension entitlements. As with many aspects of voluntary sector employment, it is a matter of getting the balance right, and the nature of your charity should determine where that balance will lie.

Pensions and retirement

With the reducing emphasis on state pension provision, and a movement into the voluntary sector of staff who previously enjoyed generous company or local government pension schemes, pressure is growing on charities to provide some form of retirement benefit. Indeed, such provision is very often a key part of the overall package that candidates will consider before deciding to work for you.

I am not an expert in pension provision, neither am I registered to offer pensions advice. Quite properly, that should be left to the professionals, and if you don't yet have a pensions adviser, you should think seriously about getting one. All I can point to in this section are some of the key issues that you need to be aware of and ask your adviser to address – if she can't help you, get another adviser.

- All employers with five or more employees must provide access to stakeholder pensions, and whilst neither employee nor employer is obliged to contribute, best practice is increasingly likely to demand that there is some element of employer top-up.
- Final salary schemes generally depend on a large sinking fund being set up, and tend to be expensive, particularly for smaller organisations who may need to underwrite the pension obligations in the early years. Typically, an employer contribution may run at 5 to 10 per cent of gross salary or more. They are, however, more generous in most cases to the employee, and can offer a wider range of benefits, variable contribution rates and other attractions.
- Final salary schemes are owned by the charity and the staff jointly – you will need to set up control mechanisms through a separate board of pension trustees, or join someone else's scheme. For this reason, changes can sometimes take a long time to effect, and it may not be possible to make them at all.
- Staff increasingly want their pensions to be portable; whilst many final salary schemes are in the Public Sector Pensions Club, where benefits can be transferred between schemes, some aspects can be lost, and some values reduced, on transfer, and many private sector schemes will not support transferability, or only at a high penalty cost.
- Support to personal pensions may be an alternative, particularly for smaller charities and where staff join who already have their own arrangements. You can agree how much to contribute to the employee's own arrangements, or you can set up

a group scheme, again with the decision on subsidy under your control. This makes it easier for staff to move in and out without having to leave little packages of different pensions scattered behind them with a range of previous employers.

Whichever way you choose to go, you will need to be absolutely sure of one thing. Recent court rulings, and now impending legislation, mean that it is no longer be permissible to discriminate on the grounds of sex in the provision of pensions benefits – and hence, by extension, on retirement age. There is only one sensible route – agree the same retirement age for men and women (which is in any case a legal requirement). If at all possible, make your arrangements flexible, so that either sex can retire within a range of ages without loss of pension benefit. Many employers now allow their staff to retire any time between sixty and sixty-five – something which, until recently, was generally easier when supported by a well-constructed personal pension than with a final salary scheme. And think very carefully before you allow any employee to work on, except on a very temporary and clearly defined basis, beyond the normal retirement age. Not only might you be putting a block on other staff's development, you might be undermining some defences in Employment Tribunal claims from other staff not treated in the same way, particularly if the retirement age is relatively low.

Transport

Many staff are concerned about issues such as mileage rates, expenses claims for journeys, car loans, bicycle loans and so on. It may well make sense for you to develop a transport policy that covers all these, underpinned by a review of what you are doing at the moment. There are specialist consultants who might save you a fortune in your transport bill: one housing association reduced its mileage claims by over forty per cent when a standard rate was introduced, whilst local government negotiators realised that they could save nearly five per cent of the country's salaries bill by restructuring the claims system. It took them three years to get there, but now the costs are coming down and the many charities who follow local government settlements are also benefiting.

Checklist 7.2   Developing a transport policy

☑ Is it really a good way of tying your charitable reserves up by giving staff loans to buy cars, when finance is so readily available elsewhere?

☑ Should you use charitable funds to subsidise such loans through preferential interest rates, unless it is vital that staff have a car to do their work, and you cannot be sure that they will otherwise provide one?

- [✓] Should you have a mileage allowance scheme that reflects the cost of running different sizes of cars, or one that encourages staff to use more economical vehicles by using a standard rate for everyone?
- [✓] Do you want to offer a benefit to staff who don't have or need a car, such as a bicycle loan or a loan to buy a season ticket to enable

---

MODEL 7.4 A transport policy

1 Transport loans

Subject to the agreement of the director, and the availability of the necessary funds, the *XYZ Charity* will make the following available to staff:

- *For staff whose duties require them to drive extensively*: a low interest loan for the purchase of an appropriate car.
- *For all other staff, and for eligible staff not in receipt of a car loan:* an interest-free loan for the purchase of an annual season ticket or travel card.
- *For staff either cycling to work or using their bicycles in the course of their duties:* a low interest cycle loan, repayable over one year, based on the model for car loans.

2 Car loans

A capital sum up to the value of two-thirds of the employee's salary is available to purchase a vehicle the director deems suitable for the employee to carry out her/his duties. The loan may be used to cover all on-the-road costs apart from road fund tax and insurance.

- The vehicle to be purchased may be new or up to four years old. If the vehicle is not new, a satisfactory report from a qualified engineer (such as the AA or RAC) must be provided at the employee's expense before the loan is agreed.
- Repayment of the loan will be by monthly instalments over a period such that the vehicle will not be more than five years old when repayment is completed.
- The employee must provide at her/his own expense comprehensive insurance for the vehicle throughout the period of the loan.
- No further loan will normally be provided until the anticipated expiry period has passed. Exceptions to this must be agreed by the director.
- In the event of an employee leaving the service of the *XYZ Charity* for whatever reason, the remaining capital outstanding on the loan will be immediately repayable. No interest is payable on this sum if it is so repaid, and the *XYZ Charity* reserves the right to deduct monies owed from any final salary payment.

Interest and monthly repayments will be calculated as follows:

$$\frac{(\text{Original capital loaned} \times \text{number of years of loan} \times 5\%) + \text{Capital}}{\text{number of years of loan} \times 12}$$

them to get to work? If the latter, can you turn it to the charity's advantage as well by making it a travel pass that allows them use it when travelling on the charity's business?

Model 7.4 encapsulates some of these issues.

Some examples of car loans

A Salary   £22,000
    Loan   £12,000
    Age of car   2 years
    Period of loan 3 years

Therefore

$$\frac{(£12{,}000 \times 3 \times 5\%) = £1{,}800 \text{ interest} + £12{,}000 = £13{,}800}{3 \times 12 = 36}$$

i.e. £13,800 to be repaid in 36 instalments (3 years × 12) of £383.33

B Salary   £18,000
    Loan   £12,000
    Age of car   new
    Period of loan 5 years

Therefore

$$\frac{(£12{,}000 \times 5 \times 5\%) = £3{,}000 \text{ interest} + £12{,}000 = £15{,}000}{5 \times 12 = 60}$$

i.e. £15,000 to be repaid in 60 instalments (5 years × 12) of £250

3 Car/bicycle allowances

- In recognition of the current disadvantageous tax position and of the availability of car loans, and in order to reflect actual costs incurred, essential car user lump sums will no longer be available.
- Rather, all staff who with authority incur mileage in their own vehicle or their own bicycle in the course of their duties, including staff eligible for a car loan who drive extensively, and those who only occasionally drive, will be paid the same lump sum mileage rates. These rates will be set at the prevailing tax-exempt standard levels set by the Inland Revenue, which in the tax year 2001/02 are 12p/mile for bicycles and the following for cars:
  Up to 4,000 miles   42.5p per mile
  Over 4,000 miles   25.0p per mile
- Employees must submit claims for payment of mileage allowances on a monthly basis, and must keep an accurate log of journeys undertaken. The *XYZ Charity* reserves the right to check claims and logs, and to make adjustments as appropriate.

4 Public transport

Wherever possible and appropriate, staff should use public transport for work journeys. Fares will be reimbursed at cost, where travel cards or season tickets cannot be used, and staff must use second class fares wherever these are available.

And that's not all ...

Staff groups in every charity will press for different benefits, and many voluntary sector organisations will seek to provide additions to the salary package that reflect their values. For some, paid paternity leave will be important; for others, enhanced carer's leave or childcare benefits such as an on-site nursery or childcare subsidies. Every charity will be different, but you should be aware of the tax position on many of the benefits in kind that are now available – if you don't deduct tax on some of them, you could finish up with a hefty tax bill to meet on behalf of your employees. Take specialist advice on this and other areas of benefits where you are not quite sure what you want to do, but do want to reflect your charity's core values.

Giving staff the choice

Increasingly, staff's needs vary, as the world becomes a more diverse place. It may therefore make sense for you to offer benefits at different rates to different employees. But, of course, you don't want to be accused of discrimination, so why not give them a choice of the benefits they want to enjoy, so that, for example, younger staff may find childcare subsidies attractive, while others would welcome more carer's leave; staff with families might prefer to have longer holidays, and others could opt for extra sick pay. This is known as the cafeteria or menu approach, where staff choose from a 'menu' of benefits up to a certain value.

You must, of course, avoid denying staff any statutory rights, so what gets included in the menu should generally be those items that are subject to negotiation under the employment contract rather than those externally imposed. Whilst this idea is relatively new in Britain, and in its infancy in the voluntary sector, it is proving attractive to many staff, well beyond choices around pension and associated provision, which is where it started.

Again, it would be inappropriate for me to be at all prescriptive as to how your charity might put such a menu together, but I hope that the following model will at least provide food for thought. You will need to decide which items to include, their relative values, and how many benefit points employees should receive (and whether they should all get the same amount).

Finally, it is worth being aware that the world is not static. Hence what may be an appropriate package of benefits for you now may no longer be so useful in a few years' time. Not only do you need to get the mix right now, you need to be ready to review and change it on a regular basis. Some models for doing just that are set out in the case study on page 124.

MODEL 7.5 A benefits menu

The *XYZ Charity* non-salary benefits policy: employee choice

1. The *XYZ Charity* recognises that the needs of its staff will differ both between individuals and over time, and that some of the benefits it offers to staff will not always be appropriate or wanted. It has therefore adopted a flexible approach to such benefits, offering each employee the opportunity of choosing between a certain range of benefits. Benefits that derive from a legal right, such as maternity leave, or from standards of best practice, are not included in this scheme, since the *XYZ Charity* does not wish to encourage its staff to deny themselves such basic entitlements.

2. Each benefit in this scheme is ascribed a certain value, expressed in terms of points, and each employee is given a certain number of points with which to 'purchase' benefits of choice. The choice of benefits will in most cases be reviewed annually, and the *XYZ Charity* reserves the right to refuse a particular combination if this proves economically or operationally inappropriate.

3. *Either***

    Points available are determined by the employee's grade, as follows:

Band 1	XX
Band 2	XX + 10%
Band 3	XX + 20%
Band 4	XX + 30%
Band 5	XX + 40%
Director	XX + 50%

    Employees changing jobs and moving from one band to another will have their points' entitlement changed at the next review of benefits.

    Or**

    All staff will have the same number of points available, currently XX + 20%.

    ***for the XYZ Charity's choice*

4. The benefits that may be 'purchased' are included in the schedule to this policy.

5. The range of benefits available under this scheme, and the number of points granted and 'charged', is subject to approval by the management committee, and may be adjusted from time to time. Benefits included in the scheme are in addition to those in the basic service conditions package available to all staff.

Schedule of available benefits in the Employee Choice scheme

Additional annual leave days above 20, subject to a maximum of *5:*
YY points per day

Paid special leave for public duties:
YY points per day

Access to flexible working hours scheme:
YY points

Additional sick pay entitlement above one month, subject to a maximum of three:
YY points per month

Childcare vouchers @ £zz per week
YY points

Permanent health insurance   *YY points*

Additional Voluntary Contribution (AVCs) to pension provision – not open to annual adjustment once chosen
YY points per cent

> **CASE STUDY 7.1** Changing employment conditions
>
> Two rather contrasting charitable organisations were faced with the same problem: the service conditions their staff enjoyed no longer met the needs of the organisations. In particular, there was no provision for working from home, and the incremental scales were very long and did little more than reward the ability to stay in the same job for ever.
>
> In one of the charities, the staff were quite contented to leave their managers and the trustees to deal with personnel issues (provided, that is, the situation was not exploited); in the other, there was a well-developed system of employee consultation and a recognised trade union; staff expected to be involved in their employment environment.
>
> Both sets of management recognised that they needed advice on what conditions would be appropriate to meet the very different employment and service delivery conditions that now prevailed. After extensive research and the assistance of, in one case, the personnel officer, and an adviser to the board's personnel panel in the other, they both identified a new package and hence the changes that would be needed to implement that package. It was at this point that their ways forward diversified.
>
> The more traditional charity sent a note to every employee explaining what the changes would be, and that they would be implemented from the following month. The charity with union involvement put a set of proposals to the staff representatives and publicised the consultation process (although not all the details) widely throughout the organisation, inviting comments through the normal channels.
>
> In the first charity, nobody said anything, and the next month, the changes were implemented and, in accordance with the law, amendments were issued to everyone's statement of particulars. In the other, the union, whilst recognising that in general the changes were for the better, also saw an opportunity of gaining concessions and of raising the concerns of individual employees whose circumstances would not be benefited by the changes. The union therefore refused to agree the changes, a prerequisite under both the union recognition agreement and within each statement of particulars prior to the implementation of any new arrangements.

In summary …

- Employee benefits can be a complex matter, particularly for longer established charities where practices have grown up over time, the historical significance of which may now not be clear and which may now be internally contradictory.
- If you're starting from scratch, then it is worthwhile taking a strategic approach to determine what is appropriate for your charity, now and in the future, and put together a package of benefits that is both attractive and affordable.
- If, as is far more likely, you are struggling with the arrangements you have inherited from your predecessor managers, then you may consider adopting a softly, softly approach,

In the first charity, everything went along fine until three months later when it was faced with a claim of unfair constructive dismissal from someone who had resigned shortly after the new arrangements had come into effect. She claimed that the new working from home arrangements had made her life intolerable because she went to work to get away from a bullying husband whom she could no longer avoid as the charity had withdrawn her right to work in an office away from home. She had not really realised that this was the effect of the changes, but as soon as they were in place, her manager had insisted on her setting up an office at home. The charity lost the subsequent Employment Tribunal case.

In the second charity, because of the union's power to delay agreement, substantial and unnecessary costs were incurred, which eventually led to a major funding crisis. Good staff drifted away and by the time the dispute was resolved, the impetus for change was lost.

Both organisations had key lessons to learn. The one without a union (a situation that did not last long once the staff had realised that in certain circumstances they could be very vulnerable to change) realised that, whether or not there was an obligation to consult, it was always better at least to be sensitive to individuals' needs and to try to accommodate them sensitively. Had they done so, both the employee and her manager would probably have understood the potential problems and sought to overcome them.

In the other charity, management eventually (but too late) realised that, however intransigent employees or their union may be, there comes a point when it is not reasonable to hold back any longer. Once all the reasonable concerns had been raised and considered, even once some unrelated concessions had been made, then was the time to act. In those circumstances, most staff would accept changes, provided they understood them; for the really intransigent ones, the charity discovered that they could give notice under the existing contract, and then offer a new statement of particulars on the revised basis. Whilst technically that would be a dismissal, very few Employment Tribunals would not in those circumstances support employers who had done their best to meet legitimate concerns and to explain the need for what they wanted to do.

changing the odd benefit here or there to suit your current circumstances. Or you may undertake a more radical review of all such benefits (this is usually done through a complete rewrite of the Staff Handbook, where most such benefits are to be found).

I hope that the various models and options that have been outlined in this chapter will at least give you food for thought on what will be appropriate for your particular charity.

CHAPTER 8

Effective recruitment

INTRODUCTION

In the following two chapters, which, many would argue, are the most important ones in the book, I offer guidance to managers on making what are probably the most critical decisions most of them have to face – whom to appoint to jobs, what is involved in the process and how to identify which candidates are up to it. In my view, it is in the area of recruitment and selection that a structured and 'scientific' approach to people management is of the greatest value to any organisation. In the voluntary sector, where there is often the added agenda item of not only getting the right person for the job, but also of being seen to be doing so transparently fairly, it is even more important for you to be able to demonstrate a clear link between your work as a manager and the outcomes desired by your organisation.

The traditional approach to recruitment has been to rely on the interviewing skills of the appointing manager, and on very little else. The trouble with that approach is that every serious study over the past fifty years has shown that interviews alone are poor predictors of future job performance – which is what the whole recruitment process is about. Interviews, whilst important and what people tend to expect, are but one possible method for selection. Therefore this, and particularly the next chapter, whilst not discarding interviewing entirely, put it in context and suggest that consideration might well be given to enhancing its effectiveness by using a wider range of techniques within a general framework of a recruitment programme culminating in an assessment centre. Hence this part of the book might better be entitled 'Beyond the interview'.

Why make such an effort?

For most voluntary sector organisations, the choice of whom to appoint, and how to go about it, are the most critical decisions managers will make. The wrong decision can result in:

- Poor job performance by inadequate candidates who quite innocently applied to do a job they thought they could do, exuding confidence at the interview and convincing the interviewer of their merits.
- Disruption and resentment in the workplace, as those same underachievers have to be carried by their colleagues, until the inevitable point arrives when, usually too late, management action is finally taken to remove the problem employee, by which time you have a demoralised workforce.
- Loss of income, efficiency and credibility, as the poor performers get it wrong.
- Expensive remedies through retraining (if they're capable of it); redeployment (if the organisation can make such generous provision to remedy its earlier mistakes); or removal from the staff and possible Employment Tribunal judgements – all leading in the end to the need to recruit all over again.

It is the received wisdom within the professional recruitment industry that the real costs of recruitment (advertising, management time, selection process, initial low productivity, etc.) can be as much as the equivalent of up to twelve months of the appointee's salary. Whilst there is undoubtedly some degree of hype from people who want to sell you their consultancy services and thus may be prone to a little exaggeration as to how much money they will save you, there is nevertheless a considerable element of truth in the view that recruitment is expensive. It makes sense to minimise the risk of getting the decision wrong, and to plan the recruitment process in some degree of detail from the outset – it always takes more effort than you think, and early planning will identify the actual level of resources of time, skills and money that you will need to deploy.

Job analysis

Until you know what the job is about, the demands on it and the level of skill required to do it successfully, you won't have the faintest idea of who could do it successfully – or indeed, whether you need it done at all. So I suggest that the first stage in any recruitment process is to ask yourself: can this job be done in another way, by somebody else, or can we make better use of the money we would have spent on the employee by meeting our objectives in another way?

The wise manager will not normally leap into filling a vacancy as soon as it is announced. The considered approach to justifying a job's existence will pay immense dividends, both through identifying the real worth of the job and hence securing commitment to and support for it; and in clarifying what it is about and what it needs – in terms of people skills and other resources – to improve the chances of the successful candidate becoming a successful performer. Note that I do not say *guarantee* success – recruitment and selection is an inexact science, and the best we can hope for is to raise significantly the probability of a positive outcome. Leaving it at interviewing alone will keep that probability abysmally low. I explain why in more detail in the section on interviewing in the next chapter.

The wise manager will also consult widely in undertaking a job analysis of the vacancy. Colleagues of the previous incumbent (if there was one) will have views on how the job worked (or didn't). So will other managers, customers and the trade union or staff group, if you have one. And then there's the thorny questions of affordability and appropriateness.

If you decide not to fill the post, either temporarily or permanently, then you are of course faced with a different series of issues to confront: how you can persuade remaining staff to cover the reallocated duties (if there are any), how the customers feel about what they will perceive as a loss of a service, and what it may do to the aspirations of staff who saw the vacancy as an opportunity for promotion. These are issues of general management and industrial relations beyond the scope of this chapter, but it is important that they are not ignored.

In a general guide like this one, no detailed models of job analysis techniques would be appropriate – I suggest that all that is needed is to put in your mind the thought that you should not automatically replace like for like without considering whether that is what you actually need and can afford. But there are two tools that are vital in the process of ensuring that you know what the post does and what qualities the postholder needs to do it: the job description and the person specification.

Job descriptions

Every organisation has its own views on what constitutes a job description. There is a wide spectrum. At one end there is the 'your job as an administrative assistant is to do what you're told in assisting with administration' approach (hardly helpful in indicating to poor job applicants what they are likely to be facing, to the manager in setting targets for acceptable performance, or to job evaluators in setting a price on the job). At the other end there is the detailed book of rules, long ago made famous by the railway industry and its rule books, which can be so prescriptive that the poor administrative assistant is told what a paper clip is and how to use it (equally unhelpful in encouraging initiative and enabling change and personal growth in a job). Good practice would therefore seem to lie somewhere in between, with a statement of the principal purpose of the job, followed by a short list of the main tasks normally facing the postholder, and what is known in the trade as a slave clause: 'such other duties as may from time to time be reasonably expected of you'. Good practice would equally argue that for the sake of flexible deployment of staff from the manager's point of view, and greater job satisfaction and the space to grow for the employee, both parties should agree that the job description is indicative of the nature of the employment relationship, but is not in itself part of the contract of employment.

I know of very few job descriptions that cannot be confined to one page, with not more than a dozen key elements listed altogether, and it is a good discipline to try to write them in this way. Anything more than that and you are drifting back to the railway industry syndrome, and inviting a 'more than my job's worth', work-to-rule attitude on the part of the small minority of employees who could seek to exploit such a situation.

All sorts of things get included in a job description which, strictly, are not descriptions of elements of the job, but rather rules or policy statements which the employer wants to draw to the attention of the postholder. This is particularly so where the organisation is keenly conscious of equal opportunity issues or aware of its employer responsibilities; often, the job description includes a requirement to abide by the charity's equal opportunity policies, to maintain confidentiality and to work in a safe manner. Whilst I would argue that they are better placed in the statement of disciplinary rules that every employer (more or less) now has to issue to employees, the culture of some charities is such that the wish to highlight their importance means that these matters are brought to the fore in the job description itself. And if that's what you really want, who am I to argue? To help you, I've drafted an appropriate clause to cover these issues in the model job description to be found in model 8.1.

Job descriptions often include details of reporting lines and staff for whom the postholder is responsible. This is generally helpful, as it offers some indication of where in the hierarchy (assuming that you have a hierarchy) the post sits; a proposed format is included in the model offered. But for recruitment purposes, especially in more complex structures, you would do potential candidates a great favour if you supply them with an

MODEL 8.1 Model job description

The Charity

Post: ....

Grade: ....

Reports to: ....

Responsible for following staff: ....

Date of last revision: ....

This job description is indicative only, and does not form part of the contract of employment of the postholder

Main purpose of job

Key elements in job

1 ....
2 ....
3 ....
4 ....
5 ....
6 ....
7 ....
8 ....
9 ....

10 At all times, work pro-actively to promote *The Charity's* equal opportunities policies, both in respect of service delivery and employment issues, to maintain the confidentiality of clients and others, and to ensure the health, safety and welfare of the postholder, colleagues, clients and visitors.

11 To undertake any appropriate duties as may be reasonably required, on either a short- or long-term basis.

Received on ....
                (date) (signature of postholder)

organisation chart as well as the job description when you embark on the recruitment process.

One of the difficulties that has been experienced with job descriptions in the past, particularly in the public sector and in those voluntary sector bodies that have tended to model their practices and structures on local government, has been that they have been used for two distinctly different purposes. Very often, they are the key tool – sometimes the only tool – in job evaluation, where it is necessary to write them in a standardised format that lends itself to analysis of the different parts and requirements of the job, and hence its relative value. This is rather different from a statement of the main duties, and has a tendency towards over-long job descriptions with standard phrases. I would argue that this is not generally helpful as part of the recruitment process. If job descriptions are to be used as part of the salary setting process, then they should be complemented by other documentation in the job evaluation process, and left in a usable and intelligible state for employment candidates and their managers. You might even consider two versions – one to tell postholders what the job is really about, and one to keep the job evaluation people happy. How (or whether) that can be done is discussed in more detail in chapter 7.

Person specifications

So now you've decided on what you want done. How will you make sure that the potential candidates will be capable of doing it?

In the same way that you analysed what the job is really about and identified the main elements that the person appointed will have to undertake, so also will you – and the candidates – find it easier if you can list all the qualities they will need to make a success of the job. Easier for you, because you will know what you are looking for; easier for them, because they should be able to recognise what they will have to demonstrate to make it worth their while applying (or what it is that will block their way if they apply regardless). This is the person specification.

There have been many different models for person specifications over the past forty-five years, since Rodger introduced his model in 1952 as the *Seven Point Plan*, describing what was then called a man specification (equal opportunities was in its infancy). In my view, it doesn't much matter what scheme you adopt, excepting that the more categories you use, the greater the risk of double counting. Rather than follow a mechanistic schema (when there's always something that doesn't fit into the categories, and something else that gets forgotten because there was no prompt to remind you), I find it easier to work with a new format for each job, working as it were from first principles, within a very wide framework. So long as you keep to the following points, you are unlikely to go far wrong.

Checklist 8.1: Developing person specifications

- ☑ Only include elements that can be measured. It might be nice to learn whether a candidate will stay in the job for five years, but how could you possibly find out for sure?

- ☑ Only include matters that are relevant, and exclude the irrelevant ones – you are measuring people's ability to do a job (however widely you define the concept of ability) and nothing else. Failure to do so is the single largest cause of unfair discrimination in selection. These criteria are sometimes referred to as 'competencies', a measure that is also used on occasion to assist with developing pay structures; but competencies are only about demonstrable skills, in their best application with specific standards attached to them, and you will probably be looking for a far wider range of attributes, including matters such as experience and attitude.

- ☑ Be as objective as possible when setting measures; for example, 'substantial experience at a senior level' is vague in the extreme. Far better would be: 'experience in a second-tier post with a budget of a minimum of £1m, not less than twenty staff directly supervised, and at least five successful new projects completed in the past three years'. But also be ready to accept that the equivalent of such criteria could be demonstrated in alternative ways, not necessarily in the work context – particularly so in the voluntary sector, where charity experience may have been gained as a trustee or volunteer.

- ☑ Make sure that the standards you set are legitimate, defensible and understandable. You might well need management trainees to be of graduate calibre, but do they need to be graduates, or can their level of skill be measured in other ways? A postroom worker clearly needs to be able to read and write, but an A-level in English is probably unnecessary.

- ☑ You may wish to distinguish between things that are absolutely vital – the *essential* elements of the person specification, without all of which you cannot consider appointing a particular candidate; and the *desirable* elements, which will make it easier for the candidate to pick up or do the job, and for you to distinguish between all the candidates who have equally met the essential criteria. But if you do use this distinction, make sure you keep to it, or your judgements will start to become less objective.

You are far more likely to get it right if you share your ideas with colleagues, so don't be afraid to produce a first draft, discuss it, defend and amend your proposals, until you have a clear list of attributes that will be the key to your decision-making.

At this stage you need to determine, not only that you can measure candidates against these requirements, but what measures you are going to use. And that is where we came in – going beyond the interview to obtain objective judgements on all aspects of candidates' performance and potential. This is all part of the planning for the recruitment exercise, and an absolutely key one, for from it flows the whole structure of the selection process. Basically, if you can't identify how you are going to measure a criterion, cut it out – but when you have decided on your evaluation method, you can then plan your assessment centre.

The construction of that assessment centre, and the balance of importance between the different elements within it, will come with experience and should reflect the essential/desirable measure of the selection factors. The various possibilities available to you are discussed in more detail in chapter 9, and you may well benefit from advice from personnel professionals or from other managers who have experienced the significant advantages of adopting this more comprehensive approach.

Again, in a book of this nature it would not be practicable to go into a great deal of detail that would meet your needs in every case when developing a set of criteria. My view is that, with good-will and an openness of approach, most managers who understand the basic tools – what this book seeks to give you – are not going to make many mistakes, and the ones you do make will be spotted early enough for corrective action to be taken. It is, however, worth making a particular note that the setting of selection criteria will, if done objectively and comprehensively, contribute significantly to improving equal opportunities performance. Irrelevant criteria are swept away, and the candidates' real worth will have the chance of shining through. Poor specification, of course, could have the opposite effect.

Whatever person specification model you choose to adopt, a final word of advice is: keep it simple to understand and all-embracing – no elements untouched, no secret selection agendas (not that you would, of course ...). One possible model is shown in model 8.2.

This model is, I trust, largely self-explanatory as, indeed, are the many others on offer, of which this is essentially an amalgam. Experience can be gained at work or, just as validly, in other contexts – a member of a trustee board will already have considerable insight into the issues of senior management. Qualifications can often be just as appropriately measured through individual study and practical application as those gained through a formal course of study. Skills can cover a wide range of job-related abilities and aptitudes (potential), including intellectual, manual and technical competencies. Personality characteristics should help you decide how well candidates will fit in (or not, as the case may be) to the organisation or their immediate team. Personal cir-

---

MODEL 8.2 Model person specification

The Charity

Grade: ....

Reports to: ....

Responsible for following staff: ....

Date of last revision: ....

This person specification is indicative only, and does not form part of the contract of employment of the postholder

Areas	Criteria	Essential/ desirable	Measurement method
Experience			
Qualifications			
Skills			
Personality characteristics			
Personal circumstances			
Contra-indicators			

cumstances are the limitations that each individual may bring to the job, such as a willingness to relocate or being physically mobile; and contra-indicators are qualities (if that is the right word) that would rule candidates out – no convicted paedophiles to work in a children's home, please!

Finding the candidates

However well thought through your job description and person specification may be, you will only have undertaken an academic exercise if you are not able to target them effectively – that is, at people who may be interested in applying for the vacancy. It may seem a trite point, but the fact remains that however good a job you have, however well constructed its elements and attractive its benefits package, more recruitment exercises have foundered on the failure to put together a good advertising strategy than for any other reason. Unless you operate in one of the relatively small minority of voluntary sector bodies who operate some form of succession planning (whether individual career development or internal-only recruitment), you are going to have to go public in one form or another – and to do so can cost a great deal.

There are, to simplify matters, basically three different approaches you can adopt. You can run the whole recruitment exercise yourself; you can engage consultants to do everything for you, right up to the final choice of successful candidate (you will want to make some decisions if you want to own the outcome!); or you can combine the two. If you decide to use specialist recruitment consultants, you will have the bonus of access to their database of candidates that they will have built up over several years, which may obviate the need to advertise at all – unless you have strong policy reasons for advertising. Whichever route you choose, you will also need to make choices about whether and where to advertise, what to provide to candidates, the structure of the decision-making process and who is involved.

Consultancy or do-it-yourself?

The costs of recruitment are high, but as I hope I have demonstrated above, the costs of getting recruitment wrong are even higher. Whichever route you choose, it is worthwhile investing considerable management time – and, if you have it, money. Figure 8.1 offers a typical timetable for the recruitment of a middle manager, say a financial controller. I have included in it some indication of the time this will take the organisation, its managers and anyone else it chooses to involve, indicating a typical split of responsibilities and anticipated volume of activities.

EFFECTIVE RECRUITMENT 135

FIGURE 8.1 Typical recruitment timetable (Financial Controller)

Week	Activity	Effort needed
	(numbers typical at time of publication)	(hours/days work)
1	Vacancy announced Need for job to continue confirmed	0.5 management days
2	Decision on use of consultants taken First draft of job description and person specification (JD, PS)	0.5 management days 0.5 management days
3–4	Consultation on job details Appointment of consultants JD, PS and other job details finalised Advertisement drafted and agreed	1.0 management days 1.0 management days 0.5 consultant days 0.5 consultant days 0.25 management days
5	Consultant register search Recruitment packs prepared (150) Advertisement placed Selection activities and timetable agreed	1.5 consultant days 1.5 consultant days 0.5 consultant days 1.5 consultant days 0.5 management days
6–7	Responses to advertisement: Job packs despatched (c100) Applications received and acknowledged (c50)	2.0 consultant days 1.0 consultant days
7–8	Applications (50) read, longlist drawn up (c10) Unsuccessful candidates advised	3.5 consultant days 0.5 consultant days
8–9	Longlisted candidates (10) interviewed Final assessment centre details confirmed Assessment centre (AC) material prepared	2.0 consultant days 2.0 consultant days 0.5 management days
10	Final shortlist (5) drawn up References/medicals requested Unsuccessful candidates advised Shortlisted candidates advised of AC details	1.5 consultant days
11	References/medicals confirmed AC details confirmed	0.5 consultant days 0.5 consultant days 0.25 management days
12	AC for final shortlisted candidates Offer of appointment made and accepted Unsuccessful candidates advised	1.5 consultant days 1.5 x no mangers days 0.25 management days 0.25 consultancy days
13–15	Candidate induction prepared	3.0 management days
16	Appointee takes up post	1.0 management days

You can do the sums for yourself on the value of the management time taken up; there is obviously a trade-off between consultancy fees and savings in management costs, which only you and your director of finance can resolve. A typical consultancy fee (although rarely stated in such terms) will be between 15 and 25 per cent of the full-year salary of the post being filled, depending to some extent on the anticipated level of involvement of the consultant; consultants coming from the private sector are likely to charge more. To these figures you should normally add VAT, candidates' expenses, advertising costs and some direct consultancy expenses that are not usually included in the base fee, e.g. charges for the provision of psychometrics.

If you do choose to use consultants, it would be advisable to ensure that they are able to comply with at least some if not most of the following quality standards that you would be entirely within your rights to expect:

- Abides by the prevailing codes of professional practice in the recruitment industry and of the Chartered Institute of Personnel and Development.
- Where applicable, accredited by an appropriate body, e.g. the National Council of Voluntary Organisations' consultancy registration scheme.
- Able to understand and work with the particular needs and practices of the voluntary sector, especially to demonstrate a sensitivity to the role of trustees and the issues of governance.
- Good record of working with similar organisations to yours (yes, every charity is unique, but there are some common threads) and of recruiting to similar positions.
- Strong database of potential candidates already known to them.
- Acceptable standards of presentation.

It would not be appropriate for me to recommend any particular recruitment consultants or consultancy organisations, but there are several recruitment and executive placement agencies operating specifically in the charity world (see Directory), and ACEVO (the Association of Chief Executives of Voluntary Organisations) has published a very useful guide on the selection of consultants; it will give you many pointers and will help you decide which is best for you, whether you are using them for recruitment or for a wider purpose. The golden rules on the use of consultants prepared by their institute are set out at the end of the last chapter of this book.

If you do decide to use consultants for recruitment, then I would strongly advise the following:

- Agree fees and payments beforehand, and clarify the VAT position.
- Agree a very clear programme of action (including the extent of the consultant's database search), a timetable and division of responsibilities, but don't be afraid to ask to review these in the light of experience.
- Pay promptly, but don't be afraid of raising concerns if you are not satisfied with progress. Once you have started down the

road with a recruitment consultant, you are locked into the process, so you'd best get your money's worth.
- Don't try to play the field once you have decided on consultant support – most reputable organisations work on an exclusive basis most of the time, and are likely to pay scant attention to your needs if you are asking them to compete against others for the remote possibility of a placement fee if their candidate is successful – not to mention the hassles you face between agencies if, as is often the case, they put up the same candidate and then both claim the fee.
- Keep in touch with your consultants regularly – they need to be loved too, and are always happy to let you know how they are getting on, but once you have appointed them, do let them get on with it.

If you choose to go it alone, remember that you will need to make time from your own staff resources for all the activities that consultants normally undertake for you, either by themselves or in consultation with your organisation:

- Planning the recruitment timetable and activities.
- Writing and placing the advert.
- Compiling recruitment information and sending it to interested applicants.
- Receiving and acknowledging applications.
- Reading applications and longlisting.
- Interviewing and evaluating longlisted candidates and preparing a final shortlist.
- Organising the final selection assessment centre for finalist candidates.
- Taking up references as required.
- Advising candidates at every stage of the progress of their applications.

What you will not get if you do everything in-house is access to the consultant's database, which could have saved considerable time and effort by avoiding any advertisement.

Of course, this will vary considerably, depending on whether there is a public advert, whether you have a dedicated personnel department or consultant able to spend a lot of time on the exercise, whether you have to do the lot yourself, with a bit of help from your secretary, the number of selection tools you choose to use, and the availability of the candidates. But it does give some idea of the extent of your commitment if you are to respond to the proposal that appointing could be the most important decision that you take, and that it is worth making the effort to get it right. The model timetable will, at the very least, help you plan your own recruitment exercise.

Why advertise?

At an early stage in the recruitment process, you will need to decide whether to advertise your vacancy and, if so, how and where. Whether you are using a recruitment consultant or running the exercise yourself, you will no doubt want to be involved in the key advertising decisions – after all, anything that appears will be presenting your organisation's public face, so it's as well to make it as impressive as possible – and that goes for any job information that is sent out to potential candidates as well.

The reasons you may want to advertise are:

- Your consultants are unable to provide a sufficiently strong shortlist from their database alone.
- You don't have sufficient suitable internal candidates, or no obvious candidate emerges, or you want to test the strength of your internal candidates against the external competition.
- It is your policy that on the grounds of equality of opportunity, posts should be externally advertised to offer the chance of employment on the widest possible basis.
- You want to get the message across that your organisation is going places, and is using the opportunity of a job advert to do so.

It could be suggested that if your reason is the last of these, or if you advertise in minority journals not only to attract candidates from disadvantaged groups but also to get the message across to them that you want to recognise them, the costs of such advertising should come from your PR rather than your staffing budget. Try having that argument with your director of finance!

However it's being paid for, once you've decided to place a public advert, there are two things that need to be done: choose the media and write the copy. Neither is particularly easy, and the advice of specialists is often worth considering – even if they are specialists only by dint of having done it themselves a few times.

If you are using recruitment consultants, listen to their advice – they write copy all the time, they know what is cost-effective and, if they're any good, they'll be sensitive to your needs. If you're into DIY and you place a reasonable number of adverts (anything upwards of ten a year), it's worth considering using an advertising agency – just as your consultants will be doing.

Advertising agencies make their money in two ways. They charge for setting (preparing camera-ready copy) your adverts – usually asking a notional fee; and they negotiate wholesale discounts with newspaper publishers, including a special charity discount in some parts of the media, which are not usually available to you directly (although I have heard uncorroborated stories from a few charities who claim to be able to secure better charity discounts than those offered by the specialist voluntary sector advertising agencies). They will also usually offer a copywriting (as opposed to copysetting) service, for which they may charge an additional fee, and for which they will certainly ask for additional time in your timetable.

But if you're in the position of having to write and place the advert yourself, you will need to consider the following points:

- National newspapers and professional journals tend to be very expensive; Sunday papers even more so – the local press, some trade journals and minority papers rather cheaper, but not necessarily capable of reaching a sufficiently wide audience.
- Don't just advertise in a particular medium because you've always done so or because everyone else does – ask yourself whether it will really reach your target audience, and whether it is the most cost-effective way of doing so.
- All reputable media will be able to supply audited circulation and readership details – ask them for the information before you buy space from them.
- Very small adverts won't be seen, so they won't be cost-effective, but very large adverts, especially placed by charities, can be criticised for an apparent waste of resources. The ideal is probably a quarter (tabloid) or eighth (broadsheet) of a page, with lots of white space, minimum text and something striking or unusual about it.
- Recruitment adverts are your shop window – ask yourself, would you really want to work for an organisation that presents itself like that?
- If you are hoping to make an impression as an organisation that is a little different, or if you are already well into new working methods, consider setting up your own web site (if you are big enough) or tapping into others' (such as that operated by NCVO and some of the charity recruitment agencies) and advertising there as well as or instead of the more traditional media. Most of the other aspects discussed in this section will still apply, wherever you place your advertisement.
- You don't need to put too much information in the advert, because you can send that out with the recruitment pack.
- Keep your advert to the basics – a catchy 'hook', the name of the organisation and the job, probably the salary, certainly where to get more details, a brief summary of the key elements of the job description and person specification (so that candidates can self-select) – and, if it is culturally important to your organisation, some form of equal opportunities statement (although I would advise against the long 'shopping list' type statements favoured by some local authorities that seem to take up as much space as the rest of the advert put together!).

> **MODEL 8.3** Model job advertisement
>
> ### CAN WE COUNT ON YOU?
>
> *The Charity* needs a
>
> # Financial Controller
>
> **£25,000 pa**
>
> Our last controller has recently been appointed as our Director of Finance. We need a replacement who has at least three years' experience at third-tier level in an equivalent organisation and who can bring a particular understanding of charity finances. The successful candidate is likely to be of FCIA standing and will have the ability to work at a range of levels in a small but pressured department.
>
> You will head a team of two management and three cost accountants with an administrative support team, and will have overall responsibility for the day-to-day running of *The Charity*'s finances, for preparing annual accounts and budgets, as well as deputising for the Director of Finance in her absence. Resilience and flexibility are the keys to a successful appointment.
>
> The post is located at our head office at: *123, Bottom End, Downtown, FA1 2ED, tel: 01789 123456,* from where further recruitment information may be obtained.
>
> The closing date for the receipt of applications is 24 December.
>
> *The Charity* seeks to apply good equal opportunity principles in all areas of its work, including in the recruitment and selection of staff.

A model job advertisement is offered in model 8.3. This advert has fewer than two hundred words, but gives a clear indication of what the job is about, what the main requirements of the person specification are, the salary (which for many casual job-seekers is the only thing they look for!), as well as how to apply. It would fit easily into a space about 10cm x 3 columns, which is an eighth of a broadsheet page.

The detailed planning

The final part of this chapter offers some thoughts on preparing for the key decisions you will have to take and for making the process run smoothly. The next chapter will concentrate on the selection methods you can deploy to make your decisions most effective.

CASE STUDY 8.1 Over-enthusiastic equal opportunities

A long-established charity campaigning for social justice in an international context needed to recruit several new employees. Its young and enthusiastic staff group, conscious of their inner-city location, wanted to ensure that the workforce reflected the local community, which up to then it did not.

With three posts to fill, they decided to make sure that a black candidate was appointed to the secretarial vacancy and to make the recruitment to the two campaigns officer posts open. Accordingly, they used their equal opportunities monitoring form to shortlist only non-Europeans, and a relatively inexperienced young woman was appointed after she and four others were interviewed. The other posts were both filled by white men.

It soon became apparent that the new secretary was unhappy in her post, and she was not able to relate well to overseas enquirers, of whom there were many. After only four months she resigned, and during her exit interview she explained that she had found out about the decision to appoint a black person and had felt that hers was seen as no more than a tokenist appointment — there was no incentive to do well, and in any case, nobody had offered her training; they had assumed as a black person that she would be able to relate to other (overseas) black people.

After taking advice from outside, the charity learnt some important lessons:

- It is illegal to recruit people because of the colour of their skin, even if you are trying to redress an imbalance.
- You need to be absolutely clear about what the job is about, and measure candidates for their potential to meet its requirements.
- People who are not appointed on their own merits rarely succeed, and always need support.
- A more structured approach to recruitment would have avoided these pitfalls, and would have enabled the charity to make a more effective choice from the outset.

Next time round, they developed a clear person specification, identified a series of tests to measure the key criteria and then targeted their recruitment drive at all local people. Their shortlist this time had black and white candidates on it, and the successful one was a black man with extensive secretarial experience in the Third World. He is now doing very well, especially in handling overseas contacts. Confident that he won the job on merit, he is not afraid to ask for help in performing it better and expects to stay there for several years. But they still had the expense of recruiting twice, when a clearer focus on the law and a better planned campaign would have saved money and effort in the long run.

Figure 8.1 has already demonstrated that recruitment can be a complex process. A lot of things can go wrong, most of them arising from people's unavailability. It is therefore well worth the effort, right from the outset, to plan a detailed timetable, taking account of the following points.

Checklist 8.2: Planning a successful recruitment campaign

- ☑ Identify who will be involved at what stages of the recruitment and selection process and seek to plan activities around their availability rather than expect them to drop everything to fit in with your proposals.
- ☑ Allow maximum flexibility for response times from candidates, including when they can be seen at preliminary interviews.
- ☑ Be ready to make adjustments to your timetable in the light of new evidence becoming available – for example, if you have more requests for information packs than you expected, you are likely to need to spend more time than anticipated on reading applications.
- ☑ Where dates are fixed (usually the final assessment centre), let all candidates know about them – they can then choose whether to apply, and whether to approach you with any problems they may have.
- ☑ Avoid arbitrary cut-off dates whenever possible – there's little point in rejecting potentially good candidates just because they've missed a deadline, especially if you can still easily fit them in.
- ☑ Build slack into the system, particularly around the time of the final assessment centre – you'll be almost certain to use it.

If you follow these principles you will find with experience that your recruitment exercises will run smoothly. You may even start to enjoy the process.

Who gets involved?

Every organisation will have different ways of making decisions, although under charity law ultimately, of course, the responsibility lies with trustees; however they may have delegated powers to the chief executive and other senior staff. Some voluntary bodies prefer a formalised panel process where every interest is represented; others will delegate some or all of the selection stages to one or two individuals.

There are many views, mainly based on differing approaches to equal opportunities but occasionally bordering on the absurd, on how formalised interview panels should be, ranging from the informal one-to-one meeting much favoured by recruitment consultants at the longlisting stage, to a panel of eight or nine people sitting in a row and offering no body language or facial feedback at all in case they treat one candidate marginally differently from another. My experience is that most charities will feel comfortable somewhere in between, perhaps using different levels of formality at different stages of the selection process. There is certainly no single prescription that I would recommend – you will have to do what is culturally appropriate for your organisation.

The following, however, is a summary of everybody who at some time different voluntary bodies have involved in their selection processes. (If you include them all, make sure that you hire the local sports hall for the day!) Usually, only a few of those listed might participate at any stage, but as far as it is possible without being tokenist, it is a good idea to have a panel that reflects the gender and ethnic make-up of your current workforce, the area in which you operate and the people you are seeking to serve. So, unless your charity is a very specialist one, avoiding all-male white selection panels is generally a good idea.

- Trustees
- Chief executive and directors
- Departmental heads
- Immediate line manager
- Fellow team members to vacant post
- Trade union representatives
- Representatives of special interests, e.g. from a black workers' or women employees' group
- Personnel department representative
- External recruitment consultant
- Independent external adviser, e.g. from ACEVO
- Internal 'customer' of post's services
- External service users
- External funders

Information for candidates

Whilst the public advert (or the approach by consultants to possible candidates on their database) is your shop window, inviting people to come inside and start bargaining about a job, the information you send them once they have taken up that initial invitation needs to be sufficiently detailed to enable them to make an informed decision on whether to proceed. At the same time, it will be the only set of information that many people (some of them very influential in the voluntary sector and amongst its funders when you are recruiting to senior positions) will get from you about your organisation, so it is an opportunity for publicity not to be missed. It is one which, if handled badly, will reflect badly on your charity (which is another criterion for the selection of consultants – how impressive is their presentation, and therefore their efforts on behalf of clients?).

Depending on the seniority of the post being filled, you may consider including in your pack of information sent to enquirers some or all of the following:

- Covering letter from the chief executive or another senior line manager, to include details of the selection process: timetable, who will be involved, what will be decided when and by whom
- Job description
- Person specification
- Structure chart
- Annual report
- Full annual accounts
- Background to your charity – its history and objectives
- Equal opportunities policy statement
- Equal opportunities monitoring form, if you do monitor
- Application form, if you use them

Some organisations include a guidance note on how to submit an application. Whilst this may be appropriate in some cases, you can run the risk of appearing patronising, particularly when recruiting to posts which require administrative or managerial skills, so use such documents sparingly.

If you have the resources, enclosing the whole pack in a corporate folder greatly enhances its appearance and is particularly appropriate for senior posts. If, on the other hand, you are running to a tight budget, you may wish to ask enquirers to send a stamped addressed envelope – but beware, there will always be some candidates who send the wrong sized envelope, and others who leave the stamp off! Tempting as it is to throw these candidates' requests in the bin, avoid the temptation – they will remember your failure to send them information long after you have forgotten their failure to play by your rules.

Application forms or CVs?

This is the final thorny problem that many organisations agonise over. Traditionally, job application forms tended to be used for more junior white collar jobs, and CVs expected for senior posts (manual workers didn't get a look in – a quick phone call from the Labour Exchange or factory gate recruitment was the norm). With the advent of more structured recruitment processes, the use of application forms spread both downwards to manual positions, and in some organisations upwards for even the most senior posts.

This latter phenomenon was particularly marked in organisations with a high equal opportunities perspective, which often still go so far as saying that candidates submitting CVs will not be considered, arguing that only by using a standardised application form can all candidates start on a level playing field.

Most recruitment consultants tend to invite the submission of CVs, because in the main the people they see are initially interviewed not for a specific job but for general inclusion on their database, and so application forms may not be sufficiently generalist. Candidates known and contacted by these consultants are often puzzled when asked then to complete an application form.

For about fifteen years, as more and more people got access to good quality typewriters, application forms gained in popularity and quality of presentation, whilst the CV producers found ever more ingenious ways of submitting their CVs in support of the standardised application form and not getting ruled out. Then word processors arrived and typewriters vanished almost overnight; people who had got used to typing on application forms had to go back to hand-written submissions where CVs were not allowed (have you ever tried using your word processor to type onto someone else's form?). The result is a mess, a mix of bad handwriting and a myriad of 'see attached sheets' that are difficult to follow.

Whilst the standardisation argument still has some merit, the availability of word processing, at least for candidates applying for positions that require even a modicum of administrative skills, is now extremely widespread, and there is little legitimate argument against the submission of applications prepared in this way. Coupled with a more structured approach to recruitment, where in effect you are asking candidates to respond to the requirements of a person specification, it is not unreasonable, and certainly not against the practice of equal opportunity principles, to expect them nowadays to tailor their CVs on each occasion to show how they do meet those requirements, either directly or in a covering letter.

Having said that, if you do still wish to use application forms (perhaps for more junior jobs or where the only selection criteria are those related to objectively measurable historical data such as details of previous history and academic success), then I would suggest that the forms should be neatly designed, professionally printed, systematically set out and separate from any equal opportunities monitoring questions.

Promotion or recruitment?

Somewhat cynically, at the start of this chapter I suggested that some organisations avoid the drive towards objectivity outlined above, because there are other agendas, including the appointment of favoured sons (yes, they do tend to be male!). Clearly, if you are in a charity that uses jobs for the boys as its selection process, you've got your work cut out.

But that doesn't preclude developing your own staff to fill vacancies. This is called (when it's done properly) 'succession planning', and has a lot to be said for it. If yours is a charity that values loyalty and continuity above the regular injection of fresh blood, you may wish to consider modifying the advice in the rest of this chapter to suit your purposes.

However, I would urge you not to throw out everything and appoint the chair's nephew anyway. He may or may not be competent, and how will you tell unless you set out the standards you expect, and then try to measure him against them?

The true succession planning organisation – and this is far more likely to apply in larger organisations that can offer a range of different roles and can adopt a generic approach to working – is one that will identify career routes over twenty years or more, and will recruit a pool of candidates to junior posts, develop training and career development programmes for them, and analyse its own workforce to establish which vacancies are likely to become available and when. There are likely to be extensive considerations to be had on different salary and benefit structures in such situations, and the industrial relations implications will need to be handled sensitively.

If you do choose to adopt this approach, then most of what is proposed in this chapter will still be relevant, but will only be applied at the point of entry to the organisation. Provided that you have open access to your charity at that point, then any subsequent criticisms about internal promotion being against equal opportunities should become muted.

But there will also be occasions for organisations that normally undertake open recruitment exercises when it is quite evident that there is an ideal internal candidate. Do you still go through the whole process described in this and the next chapter? I would suggest that to do so, particularly to advertise publicly, may not be the best use of charitable funds, but each decision will need to be taken on its merits, and if equal opportunities is of paramount importance to you, you will need to satisfy yourself that you are not unreasonably excluding other candidates who might be equally capable of doing the job. What I would urge is that, in order for you to be able to confront any criticism that you have not been open about the recruitment process, a modified version of the processes outlined here is applied to the internal candidate to be promoted. If you do this you can be absolutely sure that she really does meet the requirements of the job. And if there is more than one person who has the potential for promotion, the whole approach is adapted to enable you to select between them.

Where have we got to so far?

If you have gone through this chapter step by step, you should be aware by now of all the issues you are likely to confront in undertaking a comprehensive and effective recruitment exercise. Of course, not every appointment will need such detailed attention, but you will be in the best position to judge what level of effort is needed to secure a cost-effective and successful outcome.

Having put in place your recruitment process, you will now be embarking upon selecting your chosen candidate. What methods you have available to you, and how you can best deploy them, is the subject of the next chapter.

In summary ...

- A planned and structured approach will minimise the risks of, and high costs associated with, a poor appointment.
- The key to getting it right is job analysis – knowing what the job is really about, and developing accurate and comprehensive job descriptions and person specifications.
- Job descriptions should be indicative but succinct, enabling not contractual.
- Person specifications should be comprehensive but not narrowly restricting, appropriate and measurable.
- Always share ideas and consider expert help – you may well save money, and will certainly save effort, if recruitment consultants are used.
- Agree the terms and brief with consultants very carefully beforehand.
- Carefully evaluate where you are targeting your recruitment efforts to ensure cost-effectiveness.
- Spend the extra effort on getting your advertisements and job information right – they are a window onto your organisation.
- Involve key people at all stages – it's much better than having them complain afterwards that they've been excluded.
- Provide as much information as possible to candidates to help them decide whether they want to work for you – you're asking them to do the same thing to help you with your decision.
- Don't get too hung up on application forms – most people prefer CVs, and there's nothing intrinsically wrong with them.
- Plan as much of the detail as possible beforehand – who will be doing what and when, and what slippage you can allow – you'll nearly always need it; and make sure you tell everybody.
- If you do choose to follow a promotion rather than recruitment route, apply as many of the techniques and suggestions in this chapter as appropriate to satisfy yourself of the internal candidate's suitability.

CHAPTER 9

Selecting fairly and efficiently

INTRODUCTION

In the previous chapter I dropped some pretty heavy hints that interviewing alone was not necessarily the best way of ensuring that the right recruitment decisions are made. In this chapter I will explain why this is so and then explore what other selection methods are open to you to help determine that most important of questions – whom to appoint to key posts so that you are as sure as you can be that they are going to make a success of their appointment.

There is no simple formula to determining between different selection methods – the choice will be assisted, as we saw in chapter 8, by what is measurable within the person specification. So I am not (within limits) going to tell you in this chapter which tools to use and which to avoid – your choice will depend on your circumstances and you will quickly learn to identify what works best for you, and when. As before, it is always worth considering the advice of experts; this is particularly true when choosing between different psychometric instruments, where the distinctions are fine but critical.

What follows, then, is discussion about methods that are both alternative and complementary to interviewing. You don't need to read this chapter from start to finish, but rather may wish to check the details of any of the main selection methods available. At some stage, however, you may find yourself faced with the possibility of using any of them, and the descriptions I offer should be sufficient for you to make informed choices that stem from your person specification and will, when properly put together, create a pretty impressive assessment centre.

So what's wrong with interviewing?

Probably not a lot in itself – interviewing, like poverty, is likely always to be with us, at least until all the nation's charities have fulfilled their objectives and eliminated poverty and we can all go home. I suspect that, even then, we'll still have interviewing, if for no other reason than that both candidates and managers expect it at some point in the recruitment process and old habits die hard; we do therefore need to accept it as a fact of life. But poor interviewing will lead to poor recruitment decisions – just as any other poorly applied selection tool will distort information and results, and will lead to inevitable mistakes.

The real problem is that there is a great deal of sound statistical evidence that interviews alone are poor predictors of future job performance, particularly when they are carried out by untrained people in an unstructured, unsystematic or haphazard way. At this point, I am going to indulge myself in a little bit of statistics, but don't worry, I won't keep repeating the habit, and before your eyes glaze over, a little effort now will help you greatly in understanding the strength of the alternatives to interviewing later.

A measure of the closeness of agreement between two variables is called a 'correlation coefficient'. A value of 0 means there is no relation at all, a value of 1 that the prediction of one variable by the other is perfect. In the social sciences, where measures are affected by human variability and environmental factors, a 0.65 correlation is considered very good (you can get 1.0 only in pure science and mathematics). Using these rather clever statistical techniques and correlating interviewers' opinions on how well a candidate will perform against how well they actually perform, there is an average predictive coefficient of only 0.1, meaning that the prediction is almost useless.

Some studies of interview prediction have actually shown a negative correlation – i.e. a good interview assessment is linked to poor job performance, and vice versa. With rigorous equal opportunity procedures and a systematic approach to interviews, the correlation coefficient for interview prediction may, with luck, go up as far as 0.2, still a figure that is of almost no practical interest!

Try as they may, the traditionalist advocates of the 'I've got a nose for these things, I know when I interview someone whether they're any good' school of recruitment have never been able to better this – that is, when it's been possible to get hold of any objective data from their previous efforts.

Enough of statistics, except to remind you to ask the right questions of people who will seek to advise you on different selection methods – 'what's the predictive correlation coefficient of your test, then?' will soon sort out the sheep from the goats.

Interviewing by itself can be improved towards the high point of 0.2, but I am clear that further improvements in prediction can be achieved only through adding in other measures. So many books have been written about interviewing, from both sides of the table, that I am not going to offer my own tome here. Rather, I would suggest a few pointers that are often missed by the traditionalists which, if taken on board, could ensure that their interviews yield better results:

- Focus on the requirements of the post through thorough job analysis, expressed through the job description and person specification and any other reliable sources of information obtained from the analysis.
- Ensure that interviews are formalised and structured, avoid first impressions, irrelevant assumptions and subconscious personal agendas.
- Involve a panel of interviewers, who can then debate their impressions and retain the rigour of the results of job analysis, or require that managers interviewing alone prepare a comprehensive and objective written report on each candidate they see, a report that they are ready to defend (and if recruitment consultants aren't willing or able to do this, don't use them).
- Whichever approach you adopt, carefully plan the interview process so that all parties involved derive the maximum benefit (see checklist 9.1).

Checklist 9.1 Planning for successful interviews

- ☑ Ensure candidates are given clear travelling instructions, and take into account the distances they have to travel when planning the interview schedule.
- ☑ Tell the candidates beforehand what they should expect, e.g. the length and nature of the interview, who will be on the panel and when they can expect to learn the outcome.
- ☑ Allow plenty of time for each interview, including a period at the end of each candidate's appearance when notes can be made and initial impressions shared, taking into account that the timetable nearly always slips.
- ☑ Plan questions that are as far as possible open-ended, seek to explore the requirements of the job and are not over-complex.
- ☑ Recognise that you will be looking for a combination of factual and theoretical responses, and will need to be able to tell the difference and assess accordingly.
- ☑ Determine who will ask which questions and how flexible follow-up questions will be asked.

☑ Be prepared to answer the candidates' own questions, recognising that it is their choice as well as yours whether they take the job, and try to engage more in a conversation with them than conducting an interrogation.

☑ Be friendly and professional, using and noting body language and other non-verbal communication as part of the evaluation.

These improvements can be achieved only through effective training, backed up by keen equal opportunity awareness, and are likely to show at best a marginal improvement. But however poorly interviews predict job success, both managers and applicants do still expect them, and most successful candidates will not feel they have been properly appointed without a face-to-face meeting, where they will have a chance to assess the organisation as well as be assessed. So you are advised not to discard interviews altogether, but to make them part of a wider and more effective process.

But doesn't that mean a great deal more effort?

Nobody said management was going to be easy – but it can be effective and certainly enormously satisfying when a job is well done. And what could be more satisfying than knowing that you have appointed someone who shares your vision of where your charity is going and has the ability to help you get it there? There is no doubt that in the short term, yes, there will be more work to do – it means better planning of the whole of the recruitment process (not just a few interview questions thrown together at the last minute when the panel can squeeze in a late afternoon meeting). But that planning will pay off:

- It will offer a clearer operating framework for the appointing managers.
- It will build on the work already done on job analysis, thus lending greater credibility to the process.
- It will, with modification, provide a bank of information and exercises for future appointments.
- Most importantly, it will improve the chances of a successful appointment. A day planning now can save months of agonising later.

I am not suggesting that for every job, every recruitment tool is used – far from it. But in this chapter, I seek to identify those that you may consider, to help you with your decision-making. In the end, it is part of the manager's job to decide, not only whom to appoint, but how that decision will be made. That decision will depend on what is in the person specification, what it is you are actually trying to measure and what is the best way of measuring it.

The recruitment assessment centre

As with all other management activities, the terminology around recruitment varies, so don't be put off by different descriptions and attempts by gurus selling popular paperbacks to mystify you with intriguing titles and impenetrable jargon. What I mean by a recruitment assessment centre is a collection of different measures, the results of which, taken together, will lead to decisions on the appointment of staff. It is worth noting that assessment centres can also be used for training, development and teambuilding purposes (these are discussed elsewhere in this book). In this chapter, all references to assessment centres should be taken in the context of the recruitment and selection process.

The keys to an effective centre are:

- Identifying the elements and techniques that will properly measure the attributes in candidates that the person specification identifies as being required.
- Giving appropriate weight to each element, including avoiding falling into the trap of ignoring the results of the other elements in favour of traditional assessment in the interview stage, particularly as the people making the final decision tend to be the same ones who conduct the formal interview panel.
- Planning and managing the process effectively, both leading up to the final selection centre and for the day(s) of the centre itself, and afterwards. The recruitment assessment centre should be viewed as part of the wider employment cycle and not as an end in itself.
- Having all managers who have contributed to elements of the centre participating in the final decision-making.

What techniques are available?

Whole books have been written about each selection technique that I discuss in this chapter, and there is really not enough space here to do more than highlight the possibilities. As an experienced manager, you will recognise most of those outlined, at least by name. What I hope to offer is sufficient information about them to consider them in a structured way, to make informed choices on which techniques to use. I have spent rather longer on psychometrics, because a great deal of unnecessary mystification surrounds what is otherwise an excellent selection tool, and I think it only right to throw light on what is a technical subject about which many myths have grown up in recent years.

Interviews

- They can't be avoided, but they can be more focused and structured (see above).
- They can and should be used, not just to test out elements of the person specification, but also for candidates to ask *their* questions, and for personal details (such as 'do you need help with relocation?') to be sorted out away from the actual decision-making process.
- They can be used to promote a positive image of your charity; they offer you the opportunity of telling other people about what you do, and if the interview has been well conducted, candidates will go away with a positive impression of your organisation, whether or not they are appointed.
- They can be undertaken at the initial stage by recruitment consultants to draw up a shortlist for your approval, thus taking a great deal of the burden off your hard-pressed shoulders. But do make sure that, whoever is doing the initial screening to produce a final shortlist, they apply to the written applications only those criteria you have identified as appropriate for shortlisting purposes; other criteria can be applied later.

Presentations

Candidates are often given a subject on which they are asked to speak for a given time, usually at the start of an interview, with or without the assistance of visual aids. There are three possibilities:

- Give the candidates the subject well in advance – in which case, you will be measuring their ability to deliver the material, but won't be sure that they have prepared it (unless you quiz them closely on the content after the presentation).
- Give the candidates the subject on the day, with time to prepare – in which case, you will know that they have used their own skills, but they may not be able to offer such a considered or polished response.
- Give the candidates the subject and ask them to speak straight away – in which case you are testing their ability to think on their feet, but maybe not much else; some candidates could be unfairly intimidated by this approach.

It is important, as with all selection measures, to ensure that you are consciously measuring the right thing. You therefore need to determine beforehand (referring yet again to the person specification) exactly what it is that you are interested in, and try to exclude consideration of other matters. This can be particularly difficult with presentations, where a poor delivery exacerbated by nervousness may distract you from considering excellent content; and brilliant performers may hide the fact that they have nothing to say. So decide which of the following you are actually measuring:

- Oral presentation skills and 'presence'.
- Design/IT skills (PowerPoint, OHPs, flip charts, handouts, etc.).
- Analytical or debating skills.
- Ability to keep to a time limit.

Security and objectivity are important – don't let some candidates have a time advantage or overhear other candidates' presentations, and ensure that both the standards and the criteria for the evaluation of the presentation are established beforehand.

Report preparation

This is like a written version of asking the candidates to make a presentation, and some of the same issues may apply, but doubly so. Can you be sure it's their own work if they produce the report outside controlled conditions? If you are interested in measuring candidates' ability to prepare pieces of written work, some options for reducing the difficulties are available. You may, for example, consider giving them the subject in advance, asking them to specify the information they'll need, but explaining that they will be required to write the report on the day under controlled conditions; or you can ask to see a report they have prepared for other purposes and so know (or can be reasonably certain) that it's all their own work.

When considering reports submitted by candidates, it is very important to keep clearly in mind what is being measured – is it knowledge of the subject or the ability to produce reports (which are not the same thing)?

In-tray exercises

An in-tray exercise is typically a simulation of a manager's in-tray, which may include letters, e-mails, memos, messages, etc. The exercise is completed under more controlled conditions than is possible with the report-writing exercise and, if properly structured, can offer a good simulation of real work life and hence a good measure of how the candidate will actually perform. The purpose is twofold: to see how well candidates prioritise work, and to measure how well they do the work.

- Considerable planning needs to go into preparing the elements of the exercise as they need to be accurate to be a good predictor. This is a fairly skilful process, and unfortunately the same exercise cannot be used too frequently – it either loses topicality or becomes easier for candidates who have done it before. On the other hand, a skilled writer of in-tray exercises can quite easily modify them to suit new circumstances.
- It is important to ensure that there is strict timing for all candidates, that all tasks given are real reflections of the job, and that if tasks are other than written (e.g. telephoning someone to make an appointment), all participants are fully briefed and have objective measurement yardsticks.
- Clear written guides are vital for evaluation, and either all marking should be done by one person or, as with public examinations, there should be a separate overview offering independent invigilation.
- Exercises can be structured either to enable a good candidate to finish everything, or to give all candidates the choice of undertaking a specified number of tasks within the set time-frame. Either way, you need to mark the prioritisation skills and the quality of response on individual items separately.

Examinations/tests

These are rarely used in recruitment, particularly in the voluntary sector, so I mention them only in passing. They usually comprise a pen and paper set of questions to test factual knowledge, as an alternative to asking direct technical questions in an interview. If they are to be considered, the questions need to be checked for ambiguity and clarity, and the weighting between them needs to be carefully established.

Simulation exercises

Typically, a simulation exercise is where a candidate's performance is observed during an interpersonal exercise with a particular agenda and objectives, for example, giving them a brief to role play the part of a manager faced with an industrial relations issue, and then confronting them with a staff representative with whom they have to negotiate towards a satisfactory conclusion. In devising and using such exercises, you need to ensure:

- Observers are briefed to evaluate the processes and skills displayed at least as much as the outcome achieved.
- Observers do not judge on how they would have done it, but rather the effectiveness of the candidates' own performances.

- Role players seek to maintain an equal approach to all candidates, but keep within character and are drawn in as part of assessment. Their perspective from the inside is just as valid as yours as an observer, so it is well worth asking the role players, for example: 'How did it feel to you when the candidate responded like that?'.

Group exercises

These are similar to simulation exercises, except that typically the candidates are put together to deal with a particular problem, and are observed doing so. Whilst they are an interesting study in human dynamics, there are some drawbacks:

- They are very difficult to measure objectively: some candidates may dominate, others may make a small but crucial intervention, or play specific roles, such as volunteering to take the minutes. How do you measure their performances when there is no like-for-like comparison?
- They can only really be useful when clear criteria have been established and observers are fully trained in their task – which can be extremely time consuming.

'Spy' observations

These involve observing certain behaviours of candidates when, in theory at least, they are not aware that they are being observed. One crude but genuine example was experienced in one somewhat old-fashioned charity, where candidates were watched over lunch to see if they ate peas off their knives! They can be very subjective, and it is difficult to be sure that you are actually measuring work-related criteria. In any case, you may wish to consider whether it is morally defensible for candidates not to know that what they are doing may affect the outcome of their application.

Staff feedback

It's good practice to give candidates a chance to meet their potential future colleagues, as part of a general introduction to their future working environment – it will help them make up their minds as to whether to accept a job offer. But there is the issue to consider of whether the staff themselves should offer feedback that may influence the appointment decision.

This is largely a matter to be determined by the culture of the individual charity, but I would suggest that if a decision is made to involve the staff, such involvement should be properly structured, and the candidates are told that the meeting with staff is part of the assessment process. If they are not, it's like the 'spy' observation process.

Graphology

Whilst graphology is popular in France as a measurement of personality, there is no evidence in Britain that it can measure job-related personality traits and hence, here at least, it is a poor predictor of performance. It's fine if you want to identify criminal tendencies, but there are probably better ways of doing that too!

Astrology

Although still used by some people to help with business decisions, it might as well be used for predicting the National Lottery. It certainly won't tell you how someone will perform in a particular job, however well their star sign tells you what kind of person they may be! And no, there's little or no proven scientific correlation between characterisation as portrayed by astrology and the rather more scientifically-based approach of self-assessing personality profiling discussed below,

References

These are fine for telling you how well someone has performed in the past, but the past may not relate to the requirements of the future. However, like interviews, they are likely always to be with us, so it's best to make the most of them. They can serve as a useful check on other measures used by appointing managers, but are no substitute for them. Indeed, I would suggest that they are best kept out of the selection process *per se*, and are mainly useful for confirming (or otherwise) decisions later, particularly when you are dealing with sensitive positions, and information such as police checks and medical reports is needed. If so, any potential job offers should be made on condition of receiving satisfactory references.

There is a lot of concern about the liability of both those who give, and those who receive, references, and it is therefore worth considering the whole issue in rather more detail. Without some clear explanation of the position, both legal and managerial, the more faint-hearted employer may never give a reference again!

That's an easy temptation to fall into – but think how you'd feel if there was a constant stream of 'sorry we don't provide references' to your enquiries about potential employees. But if references are to be of any real assistance in decision-making, then they will need to be full and accurate. With the legal constraints now operating (many would say not before time), it's vital to get it right if you are to be protected, and it's critical to your organisation's image to be known to be acting fairly and professionally. The following points offer some suggestions on what you need to consider when drawing up a policy on references that is just that, one that is consistent between the two activities of giving and asking for references, although obviously the emphasis will be different. Probably the easier side to get right is how to ask for (and get) useful information.

Requesting and obtaining a reference

If you have a personnel department, they will have far more experience in reading (between the lines of) references than the average manager who may recruit only once or twice a year. So it's a good idea for personnel not only to request and receive references, but also to evaluate them. However, as with recruitment decisions, let personnel draw a draft conclusion on any reference, good, bad or indifferent, but involve the line manager and others taking part in the recruitment process in the final decision.

If you don't have a personnel specialist, then the recruiting managers (or their secretaries) will probably have to do the work themselves. In those circumstances, it would be advisable to share an evaluation of a reference with colleagues before a final decision is made.

So what do you ask? The factual stuff is obvious, and probably no more than confirmation of what's already been written by the candidate. As with application forms, don't ask for more than is really necessary to know for the job (e.g. you won't in most cases need to know marital status to decide on an appointment). What is really useful to the appointment panel is the assessment of ability and personal attributes.

It is tempting to ask the previous employer or other referee whether the candidate can do the job you are advertising. They won't know. All they can tell you is how well the candidate did their previous job and – if you're lucky – how closely it resembles your post. So do send the referee a copy of the job description and person specification, but remember that you have already decided that you think the candidate meets them – otherwise you would not have made the decision you did.

What can give a lot of useful information is to ask how well the candidate performed in the previous job, what were their strengths, weaknesses and constraints, and how flexible or adaptable their performance has been.

Most employers keep references on personal files. Many employers have an open file policy – and in any case are under the obligations of the open access provisions of the Data Protection Act. So you will need to decide what to do about references, and to tell the referee if what they have written may be readily available.

This normally doesn't cause a problem when the decision is to confirm an appointment. But if the reference is so bad that, after due consideration, you withdraw a conditional offer, you will need to have a clear and consistent policy of what you tell the failed candidate, and why. Again, letting the referee know what your policy is can make them more objective, help to explain the decision to the candidate and inform how you do that.

So what should you do if the reference is bad, or has unexplained gaps? *Don't panic.* Don't make any hasty decisions. You will need a series of policy processes ready to help your decision. First, you should satisfy yourself that the bad reference was not given maliciously, by getting in touch with the referee, to let them know what the effect of their reference may be. This can be done over the phone, although initial telephone approaches to referees are usually best avoided, as it is hard to act consistently that way, and the inexperienced giver or receiver of references may say something they later regret. But it would be wise to make a file note of the conversation, perhaps even write to the referee confirming what has been discussed. This checking out process may produce amendments: it should certainly produce clarification.

Then, if the situation remains roughly the same after this contact, you may choose to discuss the situation with the candidate. It may be that the poor aspects of the reference relate to areas of their ability on which they feel the referee was ill-equipped to judge, or that they feel the referee was biased. You will need a consistent policy on whether you then offer them an opportunity to provide another referee. One response may be to offer a six month probationary period in which you can monitor performance.

Finally, you make the decision to accept or reject – and it is *your* decision. There's no rule that you must reject candidates because of poor references. If they highlight weaknesses, this can be part of a development programme for an appointee who will need more careful managing. But if you do reject – especially after making a conditional offer – then you need to be honest with them, including giving feedback and remembering that such a rejection will be a real body blow. If it ends up in court, you'll have to disclose your reasons anyway, and the problem will then largely be the referee's, not yours.

There is one issue about asking for references that often causes problems – that is when the referee offered is internal to the organisation. This is often the case when an employee is going for promotion.

Your policy should cover whether in these circumstances you need a reference at all, or whether you prefer to depend on appraisal information – the less structured and effective an appraisal scheme, the more likely the need for internal references. Then there is the question of the proffered referee being part of the recruitment process. Very often they are in the best position to judge the candidate for both the old job and the new, but there are obvious conflicts and potential for accusations of bias. Alternative referees, especially in smaller organisations, don't grow on trees, and your policy will need to be clear on what is acceptable. If the manager can play both roles, you will need to give guidance on being detached in the writing of the reference and its subsequent consideration with the other information about the candidate.

Providing a reference

You are just as likely to be asked to give references as to request them. This is the area where real sensitivity is needed and where you need to be very conscious of your legal obligations. You can safeguard your organisation's position only if tough controls over reference giving are the norm, so that you meet the test of giving the information in good faith, having taken every reasonable care to ensure that it was accurate.

A good reference policy will make it clear who within an organisation has the right to act as a referee in an official capacity. Both managers and staff needing to quote names as referees should be made aware of who may act. Generally, I would advise that a senior manager, normally above the candidate's own line manager, should be the person whose name is used and who scrutinises any draft reference prepared by the managers themselves. And if you have a personnel department, let them review what's being said – they'll have an input on the factual information anyway.

You may wish to consider making it a recognised disciplinary offence to give a reference outside the authority of your policy. You will certainly need guidelines to all staff on what to do if they are asked to give a reference which they are not authorised to give – do they send it back to the prospective employer, pass it on to a colleague or tell the candidate they need to get an alternative referee? You cannot stop them giving references in a personal capacity, but your policy needs to include matters such as control on the use of stationery and how the referees describe themselves, to avoid any suggestion that they are speaking with authority they don't have.

In general when providing a reference, it is unwise to go beyond what is asked of you. If you volunteer information that was not requested, particularly if this has a deleterious effect, the courts may readily conclude that you acted maliciously or recklessly. Even if it is positive, you may be influencing the prospective employers in ways they do not want to be influenced, and may be contributing to breaches of their own policy.

However, the real issue comes with answering the 'give us your general assessment' type of question. It is at this point that referees need to avoid waxing lyrical, and stick to an evaluation of the employee's strengths and weaknesses as you know them, not as they might be in a new situation. And even if the prospective employer asks you whether you think the employee could do the job, your professional evaluation (and hence your liability) should be confined to those aspects of the new position that have a close parallel with the old.

Best practice suggests that you should be as full and honest as possible – it is in everyone's interests, including the candidate's. In the end, you need to remember that next time it will be you asking for a reference – think how you would feel if something vital was left out or distorted. Writing a reference is not a game, trying to be clever in not saying things (although there are many experts around who can do just that), it should be a genuine sharing of information to assist a decision-making process.

You will want to establish a policy on what you tell your own staff of what you're saying about them. You may decide to reveal nothing, you may let them see what you have placed on their file, or you may choose to discuss a draft with them before the final version is sent, which may clear up misunderstandings. Whichever policy is right for you, you need to apply it consistently.

In conclusion: whatever policy choices you make, everyone likely to be affected by references – and that means most managers and probably every employee – needs to know what the rules are. So good communication of what is required, and the consequences of not following it, is critical if the integrity and reputation of your organisation as a fair employer is to be maintained.

Psychometrics

Increasingly, employers are recognising that the most effective way of evaluating potential (for that is, in essence, what judgements in the recruitment process are about) is to use objective and independent measurement based on an understanding and study of human behaviour, translated into workplace applications. This is what psychometrics (*measurement of the mind*, from the Greek) is about. It identifies how people in general act, and then uses benchmarks against which to measure individuals. Good psychometrics is (as far as anything human can be) value free, unbiased in terms of race, gender and disability, capable of self correction, and founded on extensive research both in general and in relation to specific instruments. Bad psychometrics, partly tarnished by the dubious practices of racist applications of fifty years ago by people such as Hans Eysenk, and partly just through sloppiness, is at best a set of party tricks, and at worst downright dangerous, discriminatory and illegal.

Needless to say, what follows is about good practice, about what is happening almost universally outside the voluntary sector. Over seventy per cent of blue chip companies and half the public sector regularly use some form of psychometrics in recruitment. The old suspicions about the biases in the processes are slowly being laid to rest, and it is likely that in a few years' time we will look back and wonder how we made legitimate recruitment judgements without the help of such instruments.

Aptitude/ability tests

These examples of the use of psychometrics are measures of particular skills and abilities, conducted under controlled conditions which, properly used, are powerful predictors of certain aspects of job performance. The terms 'aptitude tests' and 'ability tests' are for all practicable purposes interchangeable. They are usually timed multiple-choice tests where there are right and wrong answers; the best ones are designed so that a wide range of ability can be measured with the same test, which means that, in many instances, most candidates will not complete all the questions.

They do not measure current performance, but how well candidates will be able to perform a range of functions in the future, that is, how suited they are to particular job requirements. There are many tests available, which can be broadly categorised into four groups:

- Tests of general office skills ability, e.g. classification, accuracy, understanding, numeracy.
- Trade-specific tests, e.g. typing or a practical measure of brick-laying ability.
- Tests measuring how well suited candidates are for technical jobs, e.g. spatial awareness, diagnostic or computing logic.
- Advanced managerial tests, measuring depth of understanding and ability to deal with critical information, e.g. in the use of language or numerical data.

Good tests will have the following characteristics:

- Published validation data.
- Norm tables against which to measure candidates' performance.
- Strict information on their application and interpretation of the results.

Accurate job analysis, and hence your person specification, will enable you to identify the technical (in the broadest sense of that word) skills that successful postholders will need. It is my experience that, when you peel away the layers of mystique that surround most jobs, particularly professional ones, with which the previous incumbents have surrounded themselves, you will usually find the jobs actually require, apart from specialist knowledge, a relatively small number of key abilities (the 'right' personality characteristics are usually at least as important). A selection of appropriate tests, pitched at the right level, will nearly always be of great assistance in measuring those abilities.

In addition, testing can be used cost-effectively when you are faced with a large number of applicants for relatively junior posts, where the evaluation criteria are limited but the quality of candidates' potentially extremely variable. For example, you might be faced with hundreds of applications for a care assistant, office junior or assistant fundraiser post. Tests of clerical skill, verbal comprehension and numerical competence would identify candidates with the greatest potential strength in these areas, which are likely to be important, although not sole selection criteria with such posts. You can easily test literally scores of candidates in a single day to bring your candidate list to manageable proportions, and from that can select interviewees to be tested on the other, people-oriented aspects of the job, safe in the knowledge that they have an appropriately high degree of the technical skills required.

You do need, however, to beware of rogue tests. Any that can't show the characteristics listed above for good tests cannot guarantee to be good predictors. Anyone offering to conduct tests for you who is not bound by the British Psychological Society's (BPS) code of conduct, will only be able to offer rogue tests. So it's well worth asking to have explained to you the validation data on the test that you are proposing to use – if a blank look is the response, or panic seems to be setting in, use a different adviser.

Tests have to be conducted under strict conditions if their results are to be valid. Vigorous training is offered to specialists in psychometrics, which includes the administration of tests in such a way that the results obtained can be legitimately compared with the previously established norms – or even to your own organisational norms, if you make sufficient use of such instruments to start to build up your own database. The training is equally thorough in the interpretation of the results and their application to your circumstances. If, therefore, you want to make legitimate and defensible use of aptitude tests, you will need expert advice in both test selection and test use, but the investment in time and money will pay off, both in terms of the savings in managers' efforts in coping with huge responses to your advertisements, and from the quality of the final selection decision.

Personality profiling

This is a more advanced and sometimes controversial part of psychometrics – the attempt to measure personality characteristics or traits. Where it is important for the success of a job that the employee performs in a particular way, has an approach to colleagues, funders or clients that complements your charity's style, then a personality profile will be able to play a key part of the assessment, and one that is far more accurate than the subjective judgement of personality so often favoured by interviewers.

The main reason why personality profiles are so accurate is that they are based on candidates' assessment of themselves. Whilst in the interview situation interviewees can talk themselves up, and the better actors are quite capable of fooling the interviewer, when doing a personality profile the only gallery they are playing to is a series of questions that are not obviously related to the position for which they are applying. They may try to exaggerate some traits (for example, overstating how empathetic they are to clients in need), but the internal checks of the better tests – the lie detectors, if you like – will invariably throw up the fact that the candidate has sought to distort the responses. And since part of the best practice approach to the use of such instruments is for the evaluator to feed back to the candidates the results before they are shared with the interviewer, any anomalies can be resolved before a final report is submitted to the employer.

It is worth stressing that, unlike aptitude tests, there are no right or wrong answers, so these are 'measures' rather than 'tests'. The range of personality variations amongst humanity as a whole is virtually infinite, and it would be a strong-willed moralist indeed who suggested that one was better than another. Rather, what we are seeking to measure is appropriateness for a particular job or membership of a particular team, by measuring candidates on how strongly they possess a particular personality trait or combination of traits.

Personality profiling has a wide range of uses, not only in selection, but also in personal development, counselling, team-building and organisational analysis. These are all important parts of the work of managers in their responsibilities for the people and organisations they manage, and are touched upon elsewhere in this book. However, the principles of the operation and use of personality measures remain the same whatever the application.

The real key to profiling is not just the measurement of separate traits, but the interpretation of how they interrelate. This is an extremely skilful process and, with respectable instruments, can only legitimately be undertaken by people registered with the BPS. The results of good personality profiling instruments have been agreed, time and time again, to be startlingly accurate when discussed with the person undertaking the measure. They can reveal intimate information about people, so must be used sensitively and only by trained evaluators, in accordance with strictly controlled rules.

Good preparation for their use is therefore vital. You will need to agree in advance:

- What information you will need from the evaluator's feedback.
- What combination of traits you are looking for, what you are seeking to avoid, and why.
- What team types you need to complement or develop existing working arrangements, and whether individuals have a range of such types and can therefore be supported in modifying their behaviour appropriately.
- Whether you need the evaluator to highlight areas of potential concern, which can then be pursued at the interview stage.

Selecting the appropriate instruments, applying the measures and interpreting the results is a highly skilled business – there are subtle differences between tests which, if not acknowledged, will largely invalidate any results. I would therefore stress the importance of getting expert assistance if you are to use such instruments with any degree of confidence or validity. You may wish to discuss some or all the following issues with your advisers, and should rely on their specialist knowledge.

Checklist 9.2 Selecting psychometric tests

- [x] Always ensure that the person advising you accepts the BPS code, and preferably is registered with them or with the test publishers. Reputable test publishers will not supply material to unqualified people, so it is worth asking to see your adviser's certificate of competence.

- [x] Ask about the statistical data held on each instrument. In particular, ask your adviser to explain to you the following:
  - its validity – how relevant the test is in contributing to prediction
  - its reliability – the accuracy of the test
  - its construction – particularly the size of the samples upon which its norm data has been based, and the history of its development. The larger the sample and the longer the research, generally the better the instrument.

- [x] Be sure that your adviser distinguishes between the different types of test and their applications. For example, the Myers-Briggs Type Indicator produces scores on wide-sweeping scales that, some would argue, are well suited to counselling on personal development but may lack the detail of discernment of the thirty separate personality factors identified and measured in Saville & Holdsworth's (SHL) Occupational Personality Questionnaire (OPQ). Equally, there is little point in giving senior management candidates easy clerical aptitude tests, or vice versa.

- ☑ Check that the instrument is culturally appropriate and properly normed for your use. It may, for example, be an American test (Myers-Briggs), or a British version of an American test (Cattell's 16PF), or a British instrument that has been translated into other languages (all SHL products, and the Test Agency's Rapid Personality Questionnaire – RPQ).

- ☑ Ask about the age of the test. Of the leading personality profiles, the 16PF was originally developed in the early 1950s (and has subsequently been updated on several occasions); Myers-Briggs has been around since the 1960s; OPQ is based primarily on research undertaken in the 1980s, with the new version, OPQ32, developed in the late 1990s. Aptitude tests can get stale as they become used by more candidates; alternative versions of the same test can minimise this effect, and reputable publishers will produce replacement versions every ten years or so.

- ☑ How accurately do you want the test to measure performance or potential? You will tend to pay a great deal more for marginally greater accuracy, e.g. SHL products cost roughly twice the price of Test Agency ones, but properly used offer the chance of ninety-nine per cent predictability as opposed to perhaps ninety-five per cent.

So how do you make up your mind?

By this point, however well you may have been convinced of the merits of an individual measurement method, and however closely these relate back to individual parts of the person specification, you may be wondering how to make your final decision, particularly if the results of different parts of the assessment centre are fairly similar. You may feel that you have too much data, and could start to wish you were back in the bad old/good old days when you made up your mind on the spur of the moment straight after a short interview. Resist the temptation.

If your assessment centre has been properly planned, there will be plenty of time at the end for a genuine evaluation of all the information available. If it has been a comprehensive process, it is likely that several colleagues will have made a contribution, and in most voluntary sector organisations the culture is such that their contribution to the final decision-making will be equally valued.

You can either adopt a relatively mechanical approach to scoring candidates' performance and adopting various weightings for each element, depending on whether they are measuring essential or desirable criteria, and within those bandings their relative importance; or you can conduct a more general assessment of all the information through an open discussion. Whichever route you choose, you will find that after the first assessment centre you are involved in, you will be sufficiently familiar with the process that all the pieces will drop into place and the decision will normally become self-evident.

However you go about it, always make sure that at the end all candidates, whether successful or not, are advised of the outcome and treated with respect and, if you are confident with your decision, have the time and are asked, provide feedback to candidates on their performance and why you made your decision. You are likely to gain that confidence if you remember the following points when structuring your decision-making process:

- Never overlook the equal opportunity implications of your decision (see below) because genuine equality of opportunity leads to the best appointments; but also remember that equal opportunities is about outcome, not processes, so do whatever you feel it is right to do to secure the right outcome.
- If you use a points system for each element of the centre, do not necessarily give the job to the person who gains the most points, particularly if you are looking for an all-rounder rather than someone who shines in a few areas; and ensure that you set a minimum threshold for each element – you don't want to find yourself appointing someone who fails to meet an essential criterion just because they are brilliant at everything else.
- Try to avoid making a decision on the evidence of any single element – it's the package that's more important. This is particularly the case with psychometrics (which has been given a bad name on occasion by some rogue practitioners who have used aptitude tests and even personality measures as the sole screening mechanism), but it can equally apply to panel interviews. If the people making the final decisions are those who conduct a formal interview, make sure that they take everything into account when making that final decision.
- If, at the end of the process, you are still not convinced that you can make a safe appointment, don't make one at all, however much effort you have been through. It will be even more effort unscrambling the mess of a wrong appointment later, and the whole purpose of the process is to get it right, not to minimise the degree of wrongness. Start again, learn the lessons of the process, if necessary modify your expectations, and only then make an appointment you are comfortable with.

> **CASE STUDY 9.1** Selection techniques: no time please – we're a charity

In general, charities tend to handle recruitment and selection through their internal personnel department, if they are lucky enough to have one, leave it to line managers to get on with it, or in a few cases use either a recruitment agency or perhaps the services of trained internal psychologists as a source of additional expert advice. Working for the one of the UK's larger charities, Saville & Holdsworth Ltd (SHL) provided opportunities to influence and change assessment procedures. One of the most pressing factors facing both them and the charity's management was the issue of time or, to be more precise, the lack of time.

The children's services department was the core business of the charity – providing drop-in or residential projects and influencing government policy to help socially and emotionally disadvantaged children. Within this department many assessment practices were commonplace; within head office and across the regions practices varied widely, in fact, inconsistency was the one consistent thing that you could be assured of. The common theme running through assessment procedures was the need to cut down the amount of managerial time needed to make effective selection decisions.

Recruiting for Principal Policy and Practice Officers (PPPOs) during the peak periods could be a tediously regular affair – at times as frequently as three in one week. PPPOs were selected using anything ranging from one interview to an interview and some psychometric tools backed up with an in-house written exercise, usually designed by an expert in the children's services field but not trained in objective assessment. Such exercises tended to consist of asking for a commentary on a government White Paper or other forthcoming current issue that was likely to have a major impact on the quality of childcare and protection offered to children and young people. Questions would be asked of the candidate to inform the panel how they would go about tackling the problem within the confines of their role.

SHL introduced a selection system making it easier to measure key competencies after a thorough job analysis had been undertaken to establish the exact requirements of each role. The challenge was often finding the time to meet with job incumbents, heads of departments, directors and managers to carry out the job analysis as they were frequently committed to other pressing engagements, but eventually sufficient information was gathered by SHL. They used a range of techniques, including visionary interviews, repertory grids, explored critical incidents and the job description to ascertain the key skills and attributes required for success. As a result of this very rigorous job analysis – admittedly it is not always necessary to be quite so comprehensive – SHL introduced a two tiered system: for less experienced, and for more senior PPPOs. The type of exercise used for both levels of PPPO was similar but the level of difficulty differed.

SHL went on to advise that competency based interviews should be undertaken only by trained managers to streamline those coming through to the assessment centre. The aim of this was to increase the calibre of applicants who were selected.

This of course meant that in the short term more managerial time was required, which met with some resistance as time was a scare commodity in this charity. However, by demonstrating the long-term benefits of taking more time initially to ensure that only the 'cream of the cream' were invited to the assessment centre, resistance to this change in assessment practices was reduced. Whilst senior managers now spent more time conducting interviews, observing exercises during the assessment centre and participating during the integration session, they were less concerned with earlier design stages. The benefit to the charity was that these managers bought in to the process far more, because they were able to observe the entire process, increasing their knowledge of candidates and commitment to the objective evidence cited by the trained assessors. This increased involvement consequently raised their confidence in their ability to make the final selection decision.

This more thorough approach also reduced the number of applicants invited to the assessment process, as only those who had proven they had the basic skills required to do the job through a competency based interview were invited to the assessment stage. Recruiting managers soon acknowledged the benefits of using this two stage process. The first stage consisted of a twenty to thirty minute competency based interview, which focused on the technical skills. Depending on the success of the applicants at this stage only a few were invited for assessment to the second stage.

The second stage focused on the assessment of the key competencies through the use of psychometric tools and assessment centre exercises (designed and validated by SHL), written exercises (designed jointly by the consultant and the client) and the final competency interview, which concentrated on the softer interpersonal skills required for the PPPO role. The tools used during the assessment centre were a presentation, an in-tray or written exercise, a personality questionnaire, ability tests related to the real skills of the job, including numeracy, oral and written skills, some administrative attributes and, of course, the competency based interview. In circumstances where the numbers invited to the assessment centre were limited, a group exercise was also included.

The outcome was that, over time, not only did the charity and all its senior managers focus more closely on the real nature of some key posts within it and what was required for their effective operation, but that more qualified, suitable and motivated staff were recruited to these key posts. The previously high and alarming turnover rate was drastically reduced, greater stability in service delivery was achieved, and in the longer term the investment in planning for more effective recruitment was more than repaid through reduced recruitment and advertising costs.

Adapted with grateful acknowledgement to Saville & Holdsworth Ltd.

The great equal opportunities in recruitment debate

Back in the bad old days, people used to interview informally, if at all, blissfully unaware that their own subconscious prejudices and cultural starting points were affecting differentially and adversely how they perceived the people they were interviewing. Put crudely, they were much more likely to favour people who were just like them. No wonder that black applicants, women, people with disabilities and those of a different generation usually fared so badly.

It was largely to redress these unconscious biases (there really are very few overtly racist interviewers around) that organisations, first mainly in local government and then more recently in the voluntary sector, started to systematise the recruitment process, in order that recruiters would follow standard approaches to their work that raised the level of awareness about prejudice and sought to eliminate it. Whilst in some cases, it could be argued, it went too far and completely removed any discerning skills or human touch from the appointment process, in the main the more structured approach worked, and we do now have the evidence available that more people from disadvantaged groups are getting to the top. There is, nevertheless, a long way to go before generations of unconscious bias, institutionalised racism and sexism will be fully eliminated.

Because the main cause of biased recruitment decisions was seen to be poor interviewing, equal opportunity specialists concentrated their efforts on improving interview skills, and a whole industry grew up in the early 1980s offering training in equal opportunities recruitment, although in reality this should better have been called equal opportunities interviewing. As a result, the belief emerged that all you had to do to secure fair representation was to advertise your vacancies widely and follow to the letter the detailed advice from the latest training guru on how to interview fairly. The training gurus then reinforced the belief that any deviation from this path was a serious breach of equal opportunities – and 'deviation' often meant any selection method other than the very same (but now allegedly improved) interviews whose shortcomings they themselves had criticised (and which, as I demonstrated earlier in the chapter, are of limited predictive value even when perfectly conducted).

The point that was missed in all this is that equal opportunities is about *outcomes*, not process. The key issue for any organisation undertaking recruitment is to ensure that the best people for the job are appointed, free of bias, which in the end will result in a more representative workforce. The issue for any selection method used is for it to be shown to produce a representative range of decisions. It is not sufficient for any organisation – and particularly for any charity, with its responsibilities to its trustees, funders and users – simply to pride itself on its equal opportunity procedures, when those procedures often take precedence over the outcome.

Panel interviews, representative membership, focused questioning, avoiding discriminatory attitudes and the like in interviews are all necessary. But they are not sufficient. Despite all these improvements in technique, interviewing is still a poor predictor of job success, which, ultimately, is what managers should be concerned with. What is more, despite these improvements, there is still significant evidence of women, black people and people with disabilities doing less well at interviews than their colleagues – and in some cases, evidence of (unconscious) positive discrimination that has led to bad appointments where people from disadvantaged groups have been set up to fail. In other words, interviews standing on their own still tend to be discriminatory, despite every effort to improve them. They're just not quite as discriminatory as they used to be.

The assessment centre approach will work towards a significant reduction in this bias, both by putting the results of the interview in a broader context and by introducing less subjective measures of performance.

As with every other recruitment decision, the key is the selection of the appropriate instruments of measurement – ones that can be justified in terms of the job's requirements. To use as wide a range of different measures as is appropriate, offering all candidates the opportunity of showing off their potential for the post, is the true modern equal opportunities approach. This is the approach that has been endorsed by both the Equal Opportunities Commission (EOC) and the Commission for Racial Equality (CRE), through their support of best practice guides prepared by the leading psychometric test publishers. Both the EOC and the CRE favour a broad-brush approach, and methods such as in-tray exercises have generally escaped equal opportunity criticism. But regrettably, a great number of myths have grown up about psychometrics and equal opportunity, very often put about by people who fear they may 'fail' a test and hence not get a job. It is worth considering the following points:

- All reputable aptitude tests are measured for gender or race bias, and the few differences in performance are openly published and explained; the publishers constantly refine their tests to reduce those differences.
- Such few differences as exist in gender performance tend to demonstrate cultural norms – for example, women perform

marginally less well on technical tests because girls' education generally does not encourage their interest at a formative age. People whose first language is not English may not do quite as well in tests that rely on written instructions. Some personality traits vary marginally between the sexes.
- In most cases, these differences are not statistically significant, and most recruitment decisions are unlikely to be determined solely by such a marginal distinction.
- In any case, it is not illegal to compensate for such differences when considering the results of all candidates – and test publishers produce data to allow for such adjustments.
- Any small biases shown in psychometrics are insignificant compared with those in even the best interviews – and, unlike interviewing, there is always room for improvement in the development of tests.
- The very conduct of psychometric measures encourages the best performance from all candidates, by offering practice sessions and pre-test briefings, thereby eliminating any differences external to the traits or skills being measured. Interviewers have not generally been prepared to offer candidates such advance notice of what to expect – yet tests still produce a much better prediction of job performance.

In summary ...

- Interviews are just one way of effective selection, and should really be used judiciously in conjunction with other selection techniques.
- It might not be cost-effective to run the relatively high risk of a poor appointment based on interviewing alone; the extra cost of running a more comprehensive assessment centre will be amply rewarded. It has been estimated that the real costs of recruitment (advertising, management time, selection process, initial low productivity, etc.) can be as much as the equivalent of up to twelve months of the appointee's salary. It makes sense to minimise the risk of getting the decision wrong.
- As an integral part of the planning process for a recruitment exercise, managers should ensure that job analysis leads to a clear person specification, and that that specification includes within it clear indicators of how each element will be measured.
- Those measures will best be achieved through combining elements of an assessment centre, each properly planned and chosen. Each job will be different, and it is unlikely that the same combination of elements will apply to different jobs. Proper planning at every stage will ensure the most effective

evaluation and application of results, including planning for the decision-making process itself.
- As a general rule-of-thumb, the more complex a job, the more senior or the more it relates to other people, the more detailed an assessment centre is likely to be.
- Managers trained in the past in good equal opportunity recruitment practices will recognise the principles underlying the assessment centre approach, and will be able to apply them to the choice of different elements within it. There will be advantages in discussing the details and planning with colleagues who will participate in the recruitment decision the nature of the process.
- Guidance should always be sought, from those qualified to offer it, on the choice of psychometric aptitude tests and the application and interpretation of personality profiling. Bad tests should be avoided, but credible tests used by credible advisers, and the sensitive interpretation of validated personality measures, offer an extremely powerful predictor of future job performance.

CHAPTER 10

Developing staff – motivation and training

INTRODUCTION

For every personnel manager who points to the recruitment and selection process as being critical to the future success of an organisation, you will find a trainer who will argue equally convincingly that unless you develop your staff properly, you are equally doomed to failure. The truth is, both statements are true. You do, of course, need to get the right staff in the first place, but then you have to work hard to keep them as the right staff. That doesn't happen by itself, however well motivated they may be. As we saw when the question of capability was discussed in chapter 4, the charity world is rapidly changing, and staff skills need to change with it, just to keep up, not to mention gaining or maintaining a competitive advantage.

This chapter will look at how you can motivate your staff to keep them keen to contribute effectively to your charitable objects; how they can be developed to make an even more effective contribution; and how this can all be structured into an effective review and feedback process.

Theories of motivation

A managing director from an underperforming company went to a conference where the theme was motivating staff to achieve success. He learnt that morale was a key component to improving staff performance. On returning from the conference he decided that questions of morale had to come from within, that his staff had to believe in themselves. So he came up with a simple solution. 'Unless,' he said, '*morale in this factory improves, the sackings will continue.*' They were out of business within six months.

There are many academic theories that seek to explain what encourages and discourages people to act in particular ways. As this is a book primarily about the practicalities of managing people in charities, I shall not dwell too long on these. But it is clear that managers do need to look beyond the legal and practical basics of the employment contract to encourage staff to greater and better things, to secure their ownership and commitment and to make their aspirations compatible with your charitable objectives. This is especially true when, as is nearly always the case in the voluntary sector, the one thing that you are unlikely to be able to do is throw money at a problem. Neither can you just dump the problem onto the staff themselves or threaten their very existence – it rarely works, as our newly inspired manager found to his cost.

It is when you start to consider rewards other than those associated with 'the basics' (reasonable working conditions, acceptable wage levels, for example) that you begin to motivate staff to get off their bottoms, and your balance sheets and services to get off their bottom lines.

There are two levels of reward relevant to any organisation, but which in the voluntary sector are absolutely vital, and will probably be found in a different combination than in other sectors. They are the rewards that cost money and the rewards that cost effort. And since the former can often be in conflict with charitable objectives or with the ethos of the organisation, or both, voluntary sector managers have to concentrate far more on the latter than do some of their commercial sector counterparts. I discuss monetary rewards in later chapters; the softer-edged people approaches are just as critical, and in fact probably go further in meeting employees' needs for recognition and hence motivation. They are the rewards that make staff feel good about coming to work once all the grubby little things like salary, performance-related pay and leave entitlement have been sorted out.

The Industrial Society has done a great deal of work on how you can secure that feel-good factor. They suggest there are three things that any employee needs to know, and when they have that information, they are far more likely to be amenable to positive leadership and to making a significant contribution themselves:

- *What is my job?* – clarity of roles and tasks, with clear targets and how these fit in with those of others, and in particular how the employee's work fits in with the basic cause.
- *Who is my boss?* – where do I go for guidance, whom do I answer to – and, just as importantly, whom not? Letting me know whether I've got it right or wrong, being my mentor or my coach, and showing an interest in my progress and that of my team, is a great way of letting me know that someone really does care.

- *How am I doing?* – I need clear ways of measuring progress, so I know that what I'm doing is acceptable and that I have realistic targets to grow towards. There is no better way of ensuring pride in and commitment to the job.

By involving staff in developing, monitoring and reviewing both their team's operational plan and the organisation's strategic plan, however indirectly, you enable them to see and measure their contribution to the cause. Some of the techniques for doing this are discussed below.

Motivational management

Good management is not just about good organisation, however important that may be. Voluntary sector managers need more than anyone else to harbour and deploy scarce resources effectively and efficiently. But because those resources are so scarce, and because everyone, at least in theory, is expected to share the same objective, charity managers need to be able to lead as well, to keep everyone on course and enthusiastic. That's why, time and time again, people looking at or coming into the sector from private industry are perplexed by its complexity and impressed by the skills of its managers in coping.

Of course, charity managers need all the organisational skills to make decisions over pay levels, recruitment, discipline and other personnel issues. They also need the strategic skills to develop and operate incentive schemes, appraisal systems and staff training and development programmes. But they also have to have highly tuned people skills, to inspire and lead their staff to ever greater things.

I do not profess to be an inspirational manager myself – maybe that is why I now work as a consultant! But I can recognise it in others. I do not intend to repeat in this book what scores of writers on leadership have offered over the decades – how you go about it is as much about personal style as anything else, and it's therefore a matter of personal choice which particular route you follow. But just a few pointers, some real basics that people sometimes forget to mention – they're so basic – and then sometimes also forget to do:

- Always thank, always praise, criticise only when you have to, and then only in the context of how you're both going to improve. In transactional analysis terms, keep to the positive strokes. Be nice to people – they'll usually want to be nice in return by making a commitment. The few who try to exploit that will soon be frozen out by their colleagues, and there's always the disciplinary procedure to fall back on.

- Always try to say YES, rather than no.
- Acknowledge your own shortcomings and show that you can deal with them, so that your staff are inspired to deal with theirs.
- Recognise that you are more capable than most of your staff – but to them be a partner with a different role, someone who is there to help them do their best, not to eclipse them.
- Show just as much enthusiasm as your staff, work equally hard, demonstrate your unswerving commitment to the cause and don't stand on ceremony (unless there's a royal patron visiting your charity!).
- Acknowledge that status is very important for many people. Whilst it is dangerous to rely on it yourself, it can often be a good way of rewarding and encouraging effort and achievement.
- Include staff in planning and decision-making: this will increase their sense of self-worth. Whilst you will probably still need to distinguish between staff views and trustee responsibilities, the more staff can control their own environment and destiny, the better contribution they will make. There's a lot to be said for the good old-fashioned suggestion box, provided management does empty it occasionally.

What applies to individuals also applies to teams – but here, the sensible manager will apply a degree of caution, because every employee is different and wants to be treated as an individual. Yet it is often the collective team effort that achieves the best results, through setting team targets related to organisational goals. So motivating teams has to be a combination of group enthusiasm and activities (bonding, if you must) and bringing together the separate parts to create a greater whole. The good manager will identify the strengths in the team and ensure that they complement each other, will make allowances for the weaknesses and seek to build them up, and will ensure that the gaps are plugged by developing existing staff and introducing new team members. She will praise publicly and criticise privately; she will be part of the team, but will always be seen as a leader, not a follower; and she will ensure that the team neither smothers individual members' efforts, nor develops a culture of its own that is at odds with the objectives and culture of the charity as a whole.

Some key issues for charities

It would, of course, be foolish for me to suggest that managers in the private sector do not also have to face these motivational issues – of course they do. The difference for them is that they are in general able to focus on one measure, usually the level of profits, and can use cash and similar incentives more readily if they think it appropriate to secure a net gain. In the voluntary sector, with its emphasis on quality and quantity of output, it is more complex. I would suggest that the following issues are prevalent to a greater or lesser degree in charity management, and that this is what makes managing in the sector a unique challenge.

Ownership versus commitment

Voluntary sector staff are often drawn to a particular charity because they believe in the cause. They often stay because of a continuing belief, despite all the odds, even when they are poorly treated as employees. But question their commitment or find yourself in conflict with them over your charitable objectives and you can expect big trouble. In terms of meeting their needs, it's almost as if they have tacitly agreed to surrender some of their rights to having lower-level needs met, in return for high-level job satisfaction. Take that away, and it's little surprise that they start to get agitated about more mundane things such as a decent salary.

Commitment versus charitable objectives

A not dissimilar issue arises when staff's own enthusiasm for the charity's services conflicts with how you go about delivering those services. Their ideas may run ahead of the imagination of the trustees, or your finance director has to tell them that they would be breaking the law if they conducted an unlicensed house-to-house collection. The motivational issue for charity managers then is to channel that (perhaps naïve) enthusiasm into equally productive activities, without appearing patronising of the staff's good intentions. And what is true of professional staff may be even more true with some volunteers, whose unbounded enthusiasm is unfettered by constraints of employment, who will have a sharply focused view on the charity's objectives, but who may not yet have developed a broader managerial perspective.

Rights of trustees and users

Staff aren't the only stakeholders in the charity. A bit like shareholders in a limited company, others also want the charity to succeed. But unlike shareholders, who are normally content to let the management and staff get on with it provided they can reap dividends and profits (the average turnout at shareholders' annual meetings is less than one per cent), voluntary sector stakeholders are far more active. Trustees may well have founded the charity; service users may have strong views about how services should be delivered, with the inevitable impact on their interface with staff; service users may also be trustees. It is a complicated melting pot, and one where charity managers have to juggle many balls at once. Staff may be the single most important asset of a charity, but they are not the only interest group with a legitimate voice, indeed, there are many occasions when their voice has to come last. That can be a motivational nightmare for you as a charity manager, and there are no easy answers. Pragmatic solutions are, I suspect, the only ones that work, and the level of your success is likely to be correlated closely with the type of bad experiences you have had in the past.

Motivating volunteers

Staff can be motivated, or at least satisfied, by basic conditions and a continuing recognition of their contribution. You can never forget as a charity manager that they are in the main not like staff in other sectors – they are prepared to work harder for less, because they believe in the organisation. They can nevertheless be managed, at least in the shorter term, through a combination of standard management techniques, on top of which you can add a cupful of motivation theory and lots of warm strokes.

Volunteers are both very similar to and very different from paid staff: very similar, in that to keep them at it, they need the chance to share in the objective, to be part of the process and to be nurtured for a job ever better done; very different, in that unlike paid staff, you do not normally have to worry about the basic terms and conditions. Most, but not all volunteers who are given unnecessarily unpleasant working conditions are unlikely to come back, and they don't have the incentive of a salary to brave it out. Both staff and volunteers need to be treated with respect, to be given decent operating conditions, so that they can concentrate on the job in hand – the delivery of quality services to your charity's client group.

There is one particular issue that frequently comes up in the management of volunteers when there are also paid staff, and particularly when either the volunteers are service users themselves or the charity is a member organisation – 'Why should they get paid when we don't?'. This is particularly prevalent, and understandable, in those areas where there has been a tradition of voluntarism, or where it appears, on the face of it, that the staff and volunteers are doing the same thing. Some of the ways of tackling this concern – and they will vary considerably depending on the nature of your volunteers, your client group and the type of services you offer – are:

- Volunteers' and paid staff's roles can be structured in subtly – or not so subtly – different ways, so that the paid staff are seen to support the volunteers' activities.
- You can explain to volunteers that the paid staff are there because of a particular specialist skill which cannot easily be found.
- The separate roles can be seen to complement rather than mirror each other.
- Volunteers can be rewarded in ways that staff do not enjoy, such as free tickets to events, special supporters' clubs, etc.

What you need to avoid is giving the impression that you would rather use volunteers than paid staff – not because this flatters the volunteers, but because it has such a demotivating effect on those people who have chosen to make their career with you. Your charity has made a conscious (and, one would hope, strategic) decision to employ people to ensure its maximum effectiveness. Neither the charity nor its staff will achieve that if they are told they are not really wanted. A more detailed discussion of volunteer management, including issues of motivation and volunteer-staff relations, is provided in chapter 13.

Equal opportunities, motivation and development

The real success of any organisation depends on getting the best out of everyone and then applying that effort in the best possible way – which is a measure of a manager's own success. But unless your charity is aware of the causes of disadvantage and tackles the blockages that discrimination causes, it is highly probable that women, black staff, people with disabilities and perhaps even lesbian and gay workers will be so alienated from the processes that they will underachieve and, with them, so will your charity.

Equal opportunities is a common theme throughout this book. This is not because of any personal or political agenda, but because it is evident that our society has underachieved largely because it has failed to recognise the wealth of available talent, through the stereotyping processes that still favour white middle-class heterosexual males, and assume that people who don't fit neatly into this category are somehow inadequate, and that anyway everyone should seek to shoehorn themselves into its values.

The charity sector, above all others, is rich in its diversity, both of the groups it seeks to serve and, to a lesser extent, the people who staff it, either as employees or as volunteers. It is about addressing disadvantage, and it does that in a wide variety of ways. It is still, in places, a long way from being a genuine equal opportunities sector, as inevitably it will tend to reflect the values, prejudices and practices of our broader society.

To ensure that our staff and volunteers, both present and future, are fully motivated and the blockages to their success removed, we do need to place a particular emphasis on the issues facing those from disadvantaged groups. It is not a level playing field, but charity managers in particular have an opportunity of straightening it out a bit. So I offer the following pointers to equal opportunity motivation:

Checklist 10.1 Equality of treatment

- ☑ When evaluating performance, always focus on what the job and its targets are about, rather than the person doing the job.
- ☑ Try to understand the different background, the different perspective and the different expectations of staff who do not share your own experiences.
- ☑ Identify where, if at all, shortcomings lie, and seek to redress the balance by enskilling disadvantaged staff to play their full part in the team. For example, the education system in this country has failed many black people; just because someone doesn't have a specific qualification doesn't mean they don't have the ability, and you can offer training and support that will enable them to realise their full potential.
- ☑ Acknowledge that there are differences and build upon these as strengths rather than see them as divisions. Staff who can bring new approaches to the situation are an asset, and they can be well motivated if you recognise this.
- ☑ Acknowledge equally that the differences are outweighed by what unites us. A common commitment to the cause and a recognition of the contribution that every member of the team can make will not only motivate individuals, it will also lead to greater understanding and tolerance amongst all team members.

With such an approach to genuine equality of treatment, leading to genuine equality of opportunity, all your staff, black and white, men and women, disabled and fully able, gay and straight, are far more likely to make, and to want to make, their full contribution. And if they still do not do so, you will have removed the artificial barriers to their success and will be in a better position to deal with subsequent shortcomings managerially rather than politically.

It's a tough line to follow, but it will be that much easier in the end. And if you apply the principles of treatment that I've set out above to all your staff, and the same techniques of motivation to every situation, the chances are that your staff will develop and contribute significantly to the success of your charity. The mechanics of ensuring their development, through the whole range of training techniques and the appraisal and target-setting techniques, are the subject of the next chapter.

Investing in your staff

It is the done thing to claim that you invest in your staff. The argument goes that the greater the skills of the workforce, the more competitive the organisation. Hence the myriad of government initiatives, the latest of which is *Investors in People* (IiP). This is, essentially, a training management and evaluation system run by local learning and skills councils (LSCs), which accredits individual employers once they have demonstrated their ability to provide effective and appropriate job-related training; but its critics (and there are many) say that the emphasis is on measuring the process rather than the quality of training, and that the amount of paperwork necessary to gain IiP accreditation is a serious deterrent to all but the most determined smaller employers.

Whichever approach has been proposed, the private sector in Britain has been a bit slow to catch on, either relying on the state or other companies to do the training for it, or taking greater short-term profits and hence reducing investment levels – and make no mistake, training your staff is just as much an investment as buying a new piece of fundraising software or managing your pension fund portfolio wisely.

This argument is fine as far as it goes – but investment is not enough in itself. Giving staff the necessary training, even as part of an overall strategic development plan, is not going to make that much difference unless they can also be motivated to make best use of their new skills. And giving them training as a substitute for motivation or decent working conditions is even worse – you are just enskilling them to leave that much earlier!

That is why all training should be done within the context of your organisational development plan. Not only is it pointless – and a dreadful waste of charitable funds – to give staff training and skills that they cannot possibly need in your charity; but they won't see the point, except as a piece of personal development, and it will not help towards cementing their commitment to your future. Put their own developmental needs within the context of the organisation's growth, and they are more likely to see that by growing themselves, they are contributing towards the charity's objects – they will become that much more part of the organisation. Of course there may be some training needs that either conflict with each other or compete for scarce resources. In these circumstances, the overall organisational needs will normally come first, and your training strategy should identify where economies of training scale can be secured, especially if you have an effective appraisal feedback loop that identifies common threads and common needs.

Staff may of course not want to be trained, in which case the appraisal process (see chapter 11) should help to sort them out, or the training that is available may be only tangentially relevant to what is needed. But the point is to put training in the right setting, to make people want to do it and then to give them the space to learn, to make mistakes, and to improve.

There will, of course, be times when staff are given training that does not relate to the charity's objectives, directly or indirectly. But these occasions should be few and far between. If it's genuinely a way to motivate someone or to keep a key employee, then you can view it as another kind of investment. Conversely, you may want someone to leave and you can ease the pain of departure by equipping them with new skills to make them more marketable. This kind of expenditure may be justifiable within the broader context of securing your overall charitable objectives, although the Charity Commissioners are taking a tougher stance nowadays on many such payments, whether or not related to training, and the Housing Corporation is applying its Section 15 powers to limit the scope of extra-contractual payments far more narrowly than it used to. In one recent case, the Corporation even refused to allow a housing association to pay for career management counselling for an administrator who had worked for over twenty years – all his adult life – and who was terrified about his impending redundancy. Fortunately, the association was such a responsible employer that it found another way of providing the support. The employee left a happier man, and found himself a new job quickly and confidently.

So the key points in any training strategy are:

- Get yourself an organisational development plan first.
- Have a personnel strategy that supports that plan, and relate individual employees' training needs to the training strategy, within the overall training plan of offering courses that meet the needs of a maximum number of staff.
- Ensure that staff are trained because they want to be, to enable them to play a fuller part in the organisation.
- Offer personal training unrelated to organisational needs only in very special circumstances.

Why train at all?

Employers are not educationalists – unless they're in the education business. Even then, whilst they are educationalists to their students (or clients, or end-users, or whatever phrase best suits your organisational philosophy), they are still employers to their staff. If you are going to develop your staff, you need to do so in pursuit of your organisational objectives: to offer them new skills and learning for their own sakes, to meet *their* agenda is education; to develop them to meet *your* needs is training.

I am sure that there will be fierce debate around these, what I freely admit to be, very rule-of-thumb definitions. Most self-respecting trainers will argue that skills enhancement helps the individual as well as the organisation, whilst educationalists will rightly say that the kind of personal development a good college course can offer will often make an employee more effective either in the round or in the performance of specific tasks. Of course those perspectives have great validity. The point I am making, however, is simple: any expenditure you incur on training needs, ultimately, will be justified in terms of the end product. That is the stance adopted by the commercial and public sectors, and it needs to be adopted even more vigorously by the voluntary sector, with its scarce resources and its public scrutiny. It is often hard enough justifying to trustees and donors why you are spending money on, say, media training for your key staff who will be appearing in public – you understand the reasons why, but it's often an uphill struggle convincing them. Try running the same argument in support of an application to a childcare charity for an employee to do a history degree. However better a person she may be at the end of her course, it is difficult to see what added value that degree would bring to your organisation and, even more importantly, to the children it seeks to serve. The rule is therefore simple: if you can't convincingly justify the expenditure in terms of its effect on the end product, however indirectly or over whatever timescale, then it shouldn't be charged to the training budget.

Please do not for a moment assume that this is parsimony on my part. I have consistently argued, wherever I have worked, for an increase in the training budget. British industry has been notoriously poor at investing in its people. Our history of short-termism, whether in taking profits or in constructing budgets, is appalling. All major political parties in this country now agree that lack of investment in training is one of the main reasons that we have fallen behind our competitors – they only disagree on how to go about improving our performance. So I am not being mean when I argue that training has to be relevant to outcomes, just being more focused than either industry or the education world.

A few years ago, the CBI suggested that a target of three per cent of the gross salary bill should be spent on training. The average private sector company is at less than half that, and the public and voluntary sectors are not much better. And at times of cutback, it is often the training budget that is the first to go, especially when an organisation buys in most of its training and so doesn't have the problem of making the trainers redundant. But to get to these catastrophically low levels means that you are storing up greater problems for the future. Your best staff will go somewhere else where they can get their skills developed to enable them to make a full contribution; your weaker colleagues will stay on, not improving, and will continue to drag the organisation down.

The figure of three per cent does perhaps need clarification. Every organisation counts both its staffing costs and its training budgets differently, so comparisons are very difficult. But as a working definition, I would suggest that it includes all the costs of running an in-house training department, if you have one (staff, premises and materials) plus the cost of training purchased from outside (mainly places on courses and tutors brought in). I do not include the opportunity cost of trainees' time, but many organisations do have a ready reckoner figure for this, by indicating the average number of training days' absence each year they consider to be acceptable. The norm seems to range between five and ten days which, as a proportion of, say, 240 working days a year, is again about three per cent.

Often the development of new skills has an obvious link to improving performance. Training staff in the use of new computer software, for example, should enable them to keep more accurate accounts, structure their timetables better and provide better information services to users. Improving staff's lifting skills will lead to fewer back injuries, less time off sick and therefore reduced overheads. These are all direct skills where you can easily draw the link between training and effect. But other kinds of training are just as important. Enhancing managers' interpersonal skills will enable them to increase their understanding of their staff, motivate them better and hence get more out of them. Being enskilled to handle the media could make all the difference between a major public relations gaffe, leading to loss of confidence from funders and donors, cuts in income and retrenchment of services, and gaining their confidence that you have handled a difficult situation well, and are therefore worthy of support. Less tangible, less direct, but just as important.

All this can be summed up by the proposition that you need to know your organisation well before you can start an effective training programme – you need to know what its objectives are, you need to have a plan on how to get there, you need to identify the strengths and weaknesses in delivering that plan, and you need a training strategy to address the weaknesses. Hence my proposition that all training strategies are inextricably determined by your charity's development strategy. If you don't have a development strategy, you should have, but this is not the book to tell you how to get one. But assuming that you have something like it, then the rest of this chapter flows on from that critical starting point.

A SWOT analysis approach

Your development plan will have a series of target objectives and a range of indicators of how well you are achieving those targets. You are also, depending on the size and nature of your charity, likely to have a series of sub-plans, covering both different parts of your operation and different resources that will support its implementation. Since we all operate in the real world and not in splendid isolation, any plan worth its salt will take into account all the external and internal factors mitigating for and against its success – the traditional SWOT analysis that takes into account all the:

Strengths
Weaknesses
Opportunities
Threats

There are other models and other acronyms, but for non-specialists in the finer points of management theory, they all amount to roughly the same thing.

Thus each department will have a series of performance development objectives that will complement and together constitute the whole charity's development plan, and underpinning all this there will be development plans for support services such as information technology, finance and personnel. These latter plans are often included as departmental plans, but in my view, strictly they relate to the whole organisation, and should be seen as such.

In developing your strategic plan, your senior managers and trustees are likely to have gone through the process of identifying your current and future (usually five years) core objectives. Unfortunately, the world is changing so rapidly that it is very difficult for most organisations to have anything more than a vague idea of their environment five years hence, so there is a danger that you will set out to implement your five-year plan with the greatest of hope and the highest of skills, only to discover in five years' time that most of what you've been doing for the past two years or more has at best been irrelevant and, far more likely, counterproductive. That is why development plans nowadays tend to be written as rolling documents, and are reviewed every year, even if they stay with the five-year format.

Because corporate budgets in this country, particularly in the public and voluntary sectors, tend to be based on an annual cycle and because, like it or not, finance is central to organisational success, the development plan review process tends to get integrated with (or confused with, depending on your viewpoint) the budget-making process. There is, of course, always a danger here that money will drive outputs, rather than the other way round; but at the very least, the financial SWOT analysis will enable you to evaluate how realistic your chances of implementing your desired outcomes are, and then trim your plans accordingly. And in the same way as you are realistic about corporate objectives and outcomes, so also can you identify the ideal in terms of training objectives, and then move back to the realistically achievable.

Thus as part of your development plan, you will want to have an overall personnel plan, and part of that will be your training strategy, identifying at a corporate level the key staff development targets you will need to meet in order to deliver on your core strategic objectives. These are likely to be couched in terms such as: *All office-based staff will have a working understanding of the word processing system. All care staff will hold a current First Aid Practitioner's Certificate. All managers will be conversant with equal opportunities selection procedures. All housing officers will be competent to NVQ level four standard* and so on. There is likely to be a long and informed debate as to what are appropriate training and development standards, and it is healthy for an organisation that this should be so, as it indicates an interest in the effective deployment of its human resources. At the end of the process, my experience is that most organisations readily accept such a set of standards, set them within the context of their overall training policy, and then go on to work out how quickly the training can be delivered, at what cost, and how big (or small) the training budget can be to secure success.

You then have to go on to identify how you are going to deliver the training – what methods are most cost-effective, economical or culturally appropriate – and to whom – which staff already have the skills, and who needs additional support to enable them to develop.

A training policy

At one level, of course, your training policy is very straightforward – give staff all the necessary skills to enable them to meet our corporate objectives. But even though this gets away from the educational approach, it is still unfocused, as it fails to prioritise between competing demands for scarce resources (however convincingly you have won an increase in the training budget) and does not recognise that the timing and style of the training can be crucial to its later effectiveness. Thus you should consider adopting a training strategy or policy, which will help to determine such matters and, provided it has been sold well to the staff and their managers, should defuse much of the rancour of the type so regularly heard when organisations don't really know where they are going on the training front: *Why can't I go on that course? – she did. OK, so I don't need computer skills at the moment, but I might some day, and it's not fair that you are holding me back now. I know I failed the exams last year, but if you pay for my re-sits, I'll work much harder this time*, etc. A model that seeks to address most of these points is offered below.

MODEL 10.1 Training and staff development policy

1 *The Charity* recognises that for staff – both paid and volunteer – to be effective in their roles, they must be fully equipped in terms of information, knowledge and skills. Accordingly, it will place heavy emphasis on the provision of appropriate training and accessibility to source materials.

2 It is the responsibility of the leading professional, in consultation with the training manager, to ensure that all necessary professional reference material is available to the professional staff providing services to clients and that this and other sources of information are maintained, up-to-date and complete and are kept in an easily usable format. It is the responsibility of the training manager to ensure that the training needs of all staff, excluding those specifically provided for through the professional training arrangements outlined above, are met in accordance with this policy and *The Charity*'s development plan.

3 Every employee, at the annual appraisal, will identify jointly with their line manager what training needs they have to ensure that all personal performance targets are met for the next year. These performance targets will be set to accord with corporate and departmental development objectives. The training needs information from all appraisals will then be consolidated by the training manager into an organisational training plan, which will form the basis of budget planning for the next financial year.

4 Whilst every attempt will be made to meet all training needs, *The Charity* recognises that resources may not always be available. In developing individual training needs, therefore, the employee and line manager should prioritise separate elements, and this prioritisation will inform choices where they have to be made.

5 In developing an overall training plan, the corporate needs of *The Charity* will take precedence over individual needs, and in the event of competing demands on training resources between individuals, the following priorities will operate:

   ■ Employee/line manager prioritisation.

Adopting a policy along these lines will enable you to focus more clearly on individual training activities and should assist with the resolution of disputes. However, as with a development plan, the policy should be a dynamic document, capable of being reviewed and reprioritised as circumstances change, so should perhaps better be seen as a guideline rather than as a prescriptive policy. How such a development plan can be used by your charity to set its corporate and departmental objectives, and thence its training plans, is demonstrated in the model extracts on pages 190–192. You may not agree with their content, you may well think that they are rubbish and either don't reflect reality or wouldn't work for you. That's fine – it means that you are already beginning to think critically, and will be able to prepare far more realistic plans for your own charity.

- Training needs shared by more than one employee where economies of scale may be available.
- Updates on professional matters relevant to the work of *The Charity*.
- Other professional skill/knowledge enhancement.
- Continuing professional learning requirements of the appropriate professional lead body.
- Repeated courses after one failure, provided *The Charity* is satisfied that the employee worked hard on the first occasion and has a reasonable chance of success.
- Other individual directly work-related training needs.
- Non-directly work-related or personal development.

6 Wherever possible and appropriate, training will be provided in-house, either from *The Charity*'s own expert resources, or through a visiting trainer, in order to ensure cultural sensitivity and to minimise cost. Where this is not possible, *The Charity* will arrange for employees to attend external courses.

7 Where *The Charity* is unable to afford to provide training, employees may undertake it at their own expense; *The Charity* will give active consideration to granting time off with pay for this purpose.

8 *The Charity* recognises that as well as specific work-related training, individual employees may have personal needs that will, if met, assist them in career development or life enhancement. Whilst financial support will not normally be available to staff for such training, *The Charity* will consider granting time off, with or without pay, to individuals to pursue such training, using the following scheme of priority:
  - Career skills in a field complementary to the work of *The Charity*.
  - Skills in other, unconnected areas.
  - Personal development.

9 An employee who feels unreasonably denied access to training or development opportunities has the right to use the grievance procedure to pursue these concerns.

MODEL 10.2 Extract from a corporate plan

The Charity Development Plan 2001–2006

Operation area	Objective	Completion target date	Review date	Performance indicator
Homeless hostels	20% more bedspaces	December '03	March '03	Extent of growth
	Top quality service	April '02	December '01	Housing Corporation quality measures
	5% operating surplus	December '02	March '02	Accounts outturn
	Reduction in user complaints	September '01	Continuing	Complaints level falling
	More user involvement	September '02	April '02	Tenants' committees established and working

You will, I hope, note a few points from the models.

The further down the structure you go, the more detailed the targets and standards. This is partly to avoid the 'wood-for-the-trees' syndrome, and also to give individual employees the chance of a greater input at a level that really affects them, close to their own work areas, thus offering a greater chance of higher levels of motivation.

The different stages of the development plan are not just expanded or contracted versions of each other, but documents in their own right which are complementary.

I have avoided shoehorning every activity and every target into exactly the same format. Some managers insist on this, but the point about a document like this is to make it work – if you can achieve the same objective in a different way, I would suggest that it is unnecessarily bureaucratic to insist on every box being filled in the same way. Consistency is, of course, useful when you need to compare progress between very different areas, but you can go too far – it was once said that consistency is the hobgoblin of small minds, and even I, accused as I have been in the past of pedantry, can agree with that!

Whilst a training strategy inevitably should look at overall needs, it can also at the very least hint at how individuals relate to it: hence the identification of different levels of application of training targets for different staff and at different times. This can also serve to deter individual employees who see a training course

MODEL 10.3 Extract from a department plan

The Charity Homeless Support Division

Work area	Objective	Completion target date	Review date	Performance indicator
Development	Provide extra 20% bedspaces by:			
	– securing LS HAG	March '02, '03	January '02, '03	Level of HAG bids/ grants secured
	– commissioning/ building	(i) December '02 (ii) July '03	July '02 February '03	Work on site progress
	– improving client flow	Immediate	Continuing	Reduction in empties
Quality management	Secure all Grade 1s at next Housing Corporation inspection	April '02	Continuing	Performance score
Finance	Obtain 5% operating surplus through:			
	– improved efficiency	Immediate and continuing	Continuing	Local targets
	– tighter accounting	December '02	December '01	New accounts package installed
	– control of fraud	December '02	December '01	New procedures devised and tested
	– better liaison on HB	January '03	September '01	Liaison group with la established
Customer care	10% annual cut in complaints by:			
	– prompt response	Immediate	Continuing	New rotas introduced and working
	– new quality review process	September '01	July '01	Process adopted
	– performance management of estate staff	Immediate and continuing	Continuing	Effective training in customer care
	– tighter control of contractors	Immediate and continuing	Continuing	New review system operating
Tenant involvement	Tenant group set up in each hostel	First by September '01, then one every month	Continuing	Groups established
	– regular meetings			At least bi-monthly
	– good attendance			Minimum 15% of tenants
	– good communication channel			Regular liaison meetings with estate managers

> **MODEL 10.4** Departmental training plan
>
> ### *The Charity* Homeless Support Division
>
> The management and staff of the Homeless Support Division are totally committed to implementing the key objectives determined for the Division in *The Charity's* development plan. To this end, staff training needs will be assessed and the following training priorities met in 2001-02:
>
> | Key objective | Skill/training activity | Comments | Priority |
> |---|---|---|---|
> | Securing HAG and using it | Promotional and presentational skills | Needed for key staff | High |
> | | Housing needs analysis | In place | Nil this year |
> | | Project management skills | New staff next year | Low now, high next |
> | | More effective allocations | Insufficient current skill | Medium |
> | Quality management | Raise awareness of quality issues | Not a current priority | High |
> | | Implement quality review systems | Theoretical knowledge only | Medium |
> | Financial management | Efficiency target setting and operation | Already good, awareness raising needed | Medium, then review |
> | | Introduce and enskill on new accounts package | Must be right from start | High for finance staff, medium for rest |
> | | Develop and train in new fraud procedures | Good level of awareness – little training needed | Low, but keep under review |
> | | Train in advanced HB procedures | Management of LA process poorly understood | High for lead staff, medium for rest |
> | Customer care and tenant involvement | Better interpersonal skills, time management and report and letter writing | Some very poor examples | High for selected staff |

being offered and immediately want to jump on it. We've all known them – an appropriate response might be: *Yes, thank you for your interest. It is true that we think this training is needed for the charity, but not everyone needs it, and it's not so relevant to your area of work.*

How you determine the nature and extent of individual employees' training needs is the subject of the next section of this chapter.

Training needs identification

In the previous section I discussed how an organisation can go about determining its overall training needs, compared with the current level of skills and resources available within its present and future workforce. This is fine and necessary as a strategic approach, but that overall view needs to be converted into practical reality. How do you actually determine how much training individual employees need, in what areas, and how is it to be delivered?

In the same way as the collective process considered corporate needs and objectives, so also does every manager need to go through an individual process of assessing the skills currently possessed by each employee under her care, and identifying where the gaps are, compared with what that employee needs to do the job properly. And since we have recognised that job requirements change over time, nowhere more rapidly than in the voluntary sector at present, so also will the skills deficit vary; plugging the gaps one year does not mean that the issue is resolved for all time, and the state of training-readiness for every employee needs to be reviewed regularly if a skills deficit is not to re-emerge.

Every charity, however small, has to produce an annual set of accounts, which sets out its trading position and, provided a balance sheet is included, a statement of its financial worth. What tends not to happen is a similar exercise in terms of its human assets, although most of us pay lip service to the idea that its staff are the charity's greatest resource. We know how much they cost us – that is, in the income and expenditure account. But we rarely know how much they are worth. More enlightened organisations are now approaching this question by undertaking a skills audit, seeking to identify all the abilities possessed by its staff (both obvious and not so obvious) already deployed in support of the charity's objectives, and those just waiting to be used – either immediately relevant to the end product or even those that seem entirely tangential.

Such a bank of information could prove to be an invaluable asset, particularly if your charity is prepared to deploy its staff and their skills flexibly. If, for example, you are the housing organisation whose development and training plans appear in the above models, you are going to be able to provide a better service to all your clients if you know that a member of your office staff can speak a little known dialect, and a user comes in otherwise unable to make himself understood. Drawing on your skills bank, you can ask your finance clerk to stop processing invoices for a moment, and come to translate for the housing officer trying to help the homeless person. Result: a more satisfied client, and an employee who has, through a skill not usually deployed at work, made a significant contribution to the progress of the organisation.

Of course, unless you know about such skills, you are not going to be able to make use of them, which is why you need a systematic approach to information gathering. And you cannot necessarily expect that every employee will be willing to have you make use of all their skills all the time, especially if you have had a history of close job definition and strict pay differentials, where people have become used to being paid for the job they do, and nothing else. Whilst this 'more than my job's worth' attitude is, thankfully, fairly rare in the voluntary sector, it does still exist, particularly in larger charities that mirror local authority bureaucracies. So securing a maximum of such contributions may demand a culture change as much as anything else; this is the subject of further discussion in chapter 5. In the meantime, let us assume that at the very least, you are keen to gather the data, ready for use as and when it may become possible or is appropriate.

If you do not have all the information at your fingertips, or if you have it only in a piecemeal way, then I suggest that you will find it a very useful exercise to conduct a formal skills audit amongst your staff. It is probably not a good idea to make this compulsory, but if you set it in the context of identifying what skills your employees would like to gain, and what skills they can offer to make a greater contribution towards the charity's success, you should get quite a high response, which can be built upon as the non-respondents see the value of the exercise. New staff, of course, can be audited both as part of their recruitment and as a formal stage of their induction, so that over time, you will build up a pretty comprehensive databank of available skills and training needs. The latter, of course, should in the main be met in accordance with the training strategy of the charity as a whole, rather than in response to individual expectations, but experience has shown that, over time, these two strands will converge.

As well as undertaking the initial audit, there is a need constantly to keep the information up to date, as new skills are acquired and organisational needs change. If formal training has been provided by or through the charity, it is a routine matter to revise the records, but often employees will learn new skills without the assistance of their employer. There needs to be an opportunity to tease out this information, and the annual appraisal process provides the ideal opportunity. This is discussed in chapter 11.

You still need a starting point. Depending on the size of your charity, you may choose to handle the mechanics of the process in different ways, but I would suggest that you do need a standardised way of collecting the data, whether this is done directly from the centre or through line managers. However you do it, undertaking a full training needs analysis interview is a quite skilful affair, requiring acute listening skills and a clear perspective on organisational objectives. This should allow the person gathering the data to relate personal skills to the charity's needs and to tease out the whole range of other skills that the employee may possess but hasn't thought to tell the employer about. I would suggest that before you embark on such a process, you arrange specific training in needs identification for those about to undertake it.

Probably the best way to handle the process is to prepare staff in advance for the needs identification meeting by issuing them with a prompt sheet, explaining what you are doing and why, and helping them to identify all their skills. This can then form the basis of the full discussion, the results of which can be fed into the skills databank – which, if it is computerised, will become a powerful managerial tool in the enhancement of your charity's performance, both in deploying the skills the staff have, and in planning to give them the skills they do not yet possess. A model prompt sheet is suggested in model 10.5, on the next page.

Using a prompt sheet like this – and, of course, you will want to vary it to some extent to reflect the different operational emphasis within your own charity – can be an invaluable way of teasing out a wealth of information which can then be analysed against your real operational needs. You can then identify the skills gaps and set about in a strategic way to bridge those gaps, through a variety of training activities that are best suited to each training need. An overview of the different training approaches available is given on pages 198–203; all these approaches are equally applicable to responding to an organisational training audit as they are to dealing with individual needs, which will change over time and which will largely be identified through the appraisal process. The point is this: once you have conducted your skills audit, you have moved a long way forward, but you can't then sit back on your laurels. The world is still changing, there will always be a turnover of staff, so you will need to keep your skills register and training plan constantly up to date.

One aspect of training sometimes overlooked by trainers – though not so frequently by the managers who have to fund their activities! – is to ensure that it is relevant to the objectives of the organisation. Whilst there is always a place for personal development as well as the deployment of skills you never knew your staff had, it necessarily remains the case in a hard-pressed charity that you will need to focus your training towards ensuring that staff are actually equipped to do the job, however you go about it. An

MODEL 10.5 Training needs identification

The Charity Training and skills inventory

As a good employer, we are committed to ensuring that all staff are fully trained to enable them to do their jobs to the highest standards. We are also keen that staff are encouraged to make their maximum contribution to our objective of providing the highest quality of service to our users, by deploying all their skills on all appropriate occasions.

In order that we can support you in your work, and in order that we can ensure that your skills are used to the maximum advantage, we need to know all about what you can do, and what additional training you feel you need to do your job well. Your manager will shortly be arranging to discuss these issues with you; this will give us a snapshot picture of the skills available to and the training needs of *The Charity*. We recognise, however, that in the rapidly changing climate in which we operate, we will need to update this information regularly. This will normally be done as part of the annual appraisal process, but do please bring to *The Charity's* attention any new skills or needs you have before then if you want to do so.

The following questions should assist you to identify the skills and needs that will be helpful to our work.

Name:
Department:
Current job:
How long have you been:
   in this post?
   with *The Charity*?

Education:

Please list all the formal qualifications you possess, including:

Examinations and courses taken at school

Further education studies (degree courses, professional qualifications, apprenticeships, etc.)

Other studies (e.g. night school, correspondence courses, intensive training courses leading to specific qualifications, etc.)

What other subjects have you studied, without achieving a qualification at the end, and what is your level of skill in these subjects?

Work skills

Please list all work-related courses and on-the-job training you have undertaken, both in your current job and in all previous appointments. Also include skills that you have developed in your own time pursuing your personal interests. Please indicate what you consider to be the level of your proficiency in the subjects covered.

There are many different kinds of skills that you may have developed, and we cannot hope to list all of them. Here are some of the more common, to help you, but do try to include *everything* about yourself.

Office skills

Switchboard operation
Using/maintaining office equipment
Reception skills
Cash reconciliation

Computer skills

Word processing (which systems, what is your speed?)
Spreadsheets (which systems?)
Databases (which systems?)
Programming (what level?)
Hardware maintenance

General organisation and management

Time management
Project management
General administration and organisation
Supervision skills
Coaching skills
Leadership
Staff appraisal and target-setting
Public relations
Public speaking
Meetings management

Health and safety

Risk assessment
VDU evaluation
First aid
Proper handling techniques
Fire regulations and use of equipment

Care skills

Hygiene
Food handling
Care of older people
Paediatric care
Other nursing skills

Craft and technical skills

Building trades (indicate which ones, and to what proficiency)
Design skills
Cookery
Driving (what kind of vehicles can you drive?)

Languages

Which languages do you speak (including English) and to what proficiency, spoken, writing and reading?

Hobbies and pastimes

Please list any bodies of knowledge you may have gained through activities out of work; for example:

- Involvement in politics gives you an understanding of how local authorities work.
- An interest in railways gives you insight into logistics and transport and travel planning.
- Horseriding gives you an understanding of animal welfare issues.
- Helping in a children's home gives you a new perspective on working with volunteers.

The skills that you gain in this way can often be just as valuable as those you develop in the work context, so do provide as much information as you can.

What skills do you still need?

However well you feel that you are doing your present job, you may feel there are extra skills that would help you do it even better. Please set these out below.

What skills would you also like to develop?

Although not relevant to your current job, there may be other skills that you would like to have – perhaps to help you gain promotion to another position, or just to support your personal development. Please indicate these below, explaining why you want to develop them, and how you plan to go about doing so.

In order to maximise the effective use of this information, it will be stored on The Charity's *main computer. We may from time to time ask you to deploy some of your skills in areas not normally associated with your work. There is no obligation on you to do so, but we hope that you will find it a satisfying contribution to our work if you do.*

increasingly common way of doing this nowadays is to seek to express what is required for jobs in terms of standards that are universally understood – a competency-based approach. This can be in terms of the NVQ model, which defines different levels of performance for individuals in a range of distinct jobs; or it can be offered in the form of an inventory (for example, 'the competent recruitment officer will be able to advise an appointing manger clearly and effectively on the choice of appropriate aptitude tests for the vacancy in question').

Training techniques

This is not a book about how to be a trainer – that is a specialist subject aimed at personnel practitioners, and this book is specifically about personnel for the non-personnel manager. You may or may not have done your time before the flipchart, but what you need from this book is support in managing the process of training, rather than hints on how to do it yourself. Hence what follows is an overview of the techniques available, and a brief discussion on their differing values; this should enable you to plan the implementation of your training strategy in practical terms, offering you the skills to determine your unique combination of training activities that will meet your charity's particular needs.

Professional qualification training

This is the most traditional training method, often adopted by organisations that have established clear professional standards and expectations over a long time, and have depended on academic institutions to bring their staff up to an appropriate standard. Typically, it is provided through day release and evening classes, although increasingly distance learning, through the Open University, the Open Business School, and so on, is coming into vogue, and some courses are offered on a block release basis. Within the voluntary sector it is often staff pursuing fairly mainstream careers – housing officers, social workers, general managers – who are most likely to undertake this kind of training.

- You can usually be assured of high standards that are externally validated.
- Consistency of training is available, especially if you regularly use the same academic institution.
- Fees can be quite high, and are getting higher.
- You do not usually have much influence on what is taught, and much of what your employees may learn may not be relevant to your needs.

- Securing a professional qualification will make an employee more marketable, so you will wish either to have a retainer (or repay the fees) clause in the employment contract, or make your own internal job prospects more attractive.

Buying into short external courses

If yours is a small charity, and you don't have the resources to employ an in-house trainer, or your staff have a specific and focused training need, you may be able to identify a particular course for them to attend – there are after all literally thousands of training organisations trying to sell you their products. Your problem is picking the right ones, and that comes from experience – if the price is very low, trainees are unlikely to get much personal attention; if it is marketed very widely, the content may be bland. Don't be afraid to ask around amongst charities for recommendations (and the opposite!).

- These courses can, if properly chosen, provide new and updated skills quickly and intensively.
- They often offer an opportunity for your staff to meet and network with people from very different backgrounds.
- You have no influence on course content apart from selection of trainer.
- Evaluation of individual courses is difficult and subjective.
- Courses can be expensive, especially if you want to send more than one delegate (as the more trendy trainers insist on calling students).

Bespoke internal courses

You may decide that you want tighter control over course content or that you have sufficient numbers of staff with the same training need to justify dealing with them together. In such cases, it may well be prudent to set up a course tailored to your needs. If you don't have enough trainees from within your own charity, you can always consider selling places to other voluntary sector bodies – or even organisations in the wider economy – operating in a similar field. You may well be surprised by how many others have similar training needs to your own, and how many common threads, and subsequently transferable skills, your staff face and possess.

- There can be considerable economies of scale in running courses in-house, especially if they are repeated with the commensurate reduction in development and preparation time.
- If you are large enough to employ a training manager, then let her use her professional skills to design the course – and that

will include working closely alongside you in determining course objectives and outcomes.
- If you need to recruit a tutor to run the course for you, *do* rely on others' recommendations, *do* ensure that you are comfortable that he is sensitive to the needs and culture of your organisation, *do* prepare a detailed specification for what you want from the course (but be prepared to be flexible in how it should be delivered), and *don't* be overimpressed by glossy brochures – they sometimes mean that you will get an off-the-shelf product, not a bespoke course.
- If you go to external tutors who normally run their own courses for you to buy into, make sure you insist that they fully customise their course for you – after all, you are saving them all the effort of marketing their services to a range of delegates, so you can expect the extra effort in return.
- Occasionally, even if you have a fully competent in-house trainer, the subject matter may be so politically sensitive that you will want to have outside support anyway. This is particularly true when dealing with matters such as the effects of restructuring or when staff may be critical of management, and need a safer environment in which to do this. Staff are often suspicious that internal training staff are part of management and will report attitudes back to the director – and sometimes they are right!

Team development

So far, consideration of meeting training needs has been in terms of individual employees, even when several have the same need and it is all put in the context of organisational needs. But there is a further form of training and development which is more collectivist in its approach – when a whole team of staff needs to work together in order to improve their performance. This can either be because they are facing new challenges and do not yet have the skills to meet those challenges or, more commonly, a team of staff may have all the necessary technical skills between them, but they are still not succeeding in meeting their targets, still not gelling as a work group.

If it is just a matter of a lack of a skill, this can be easily remedied by bringing the team together with a trainer in that skill. This can often be a good team bonding experience as the staff learn together and can see their own ability grow towards new objectives. Unfortunately, the failure of teams is rarely ascribable to lack of skill, and far more often it is because personalities, leadership and attitudes are not quite right. This is a far more sensitive matter to tackle, but tackle it you must, if you are to get the most out of your employees in securing your charitable objectives. And it is a particularly prevalent issue in the voluntary sector, where not only are there the standard problems of individual motivation and questions around who fits in where and how, but also the added complication (which is usually a plus point) that staff are committed to the cause and can get very upset if they are told that their approach to work is hindering rather than helping it.

So approaches to team-building, whilst vital, do need to be handled very carefully, with a trained facilitator who understands a lot about motivation, can quickly become aware of your organisational objectives and, most of all, can evaluate team and personal dynamics to identify strengths and weaknesses, conflicts and complementarities, and gaps and potential solutions. Some training managers can do it; more commonly, an external facilitator with no suggestion of a personal agenda is more likely to achieve some success. There are several working models of team dynamics, but the one that most charity managers will be familiar with – and one which I generally use myself when assisting staff, both individually and in groups, to develop their contribution to their own charity, is based on the work of Meredith Belbin. Belbin argued – and there is a great deal of empirical research to support his proposal – that within groups, people can be categorised into eight different work styles, and that the most effective teams are those that ensure they have the appropriate mix of these styles to deal with the matter in hand. This is not to say that individuals have only one team type, or role, that they can play, but rather that we all have our strengths and weaknesses, and the skill of the team builder is to encourage development of some skills whilst suppressing some others.

The Belbin model and, more importantly, its use in practice is a complex matter, and has been subjected to various reinterpretations since it was first developed in the early eighties. I do not intend to discuss it in detail here – there are whole textbooks that do just that, and that alone. I shall simply outline the eight key roles and invite you to try to recognise which ones most closely reflect how you perform at work. If you work in a small team, you will quickly realise that you may need to play more than one role. And whilst you may find it relatively easy to identify your own team types, getting it right for everyone else is a far more complex process, which is why you will probably need support in getting your team balance right.

These various approaches to training are what most managers think of when deciding how to work on the development of their staff's skills as, one way or the other, they fit into the traditional classroom model of teaching skills to and developing the attitudes of groups of people. But there are also training methods

> **FIGURE 10.1** The Belbin team type model
>
> - *Co-ordinator* – likely to chair meetings and often be the titular head, this person will set goals, define roles and co-ordinate efforts through securing respect of other team members.
> - *Shaper* – will be the dynamo that makes the team succeed, the person with high energy levels who gives the team a competitive edge.
> - *Plant* – the team's ideas person.
> - *Monitor-evaluator* – will be the realist, bringing the team back down to earth and ensuring that all options are carefully weighed up.
> - *Resource investigator* – the person to secure the necessary resources to achieve the task, who will then sell the product to its users.
> - *Completer-finisher* – detail conscious, this team member will make sure that things happen to time and that accuracy is guaranteed.
> - *Team worker* – every team needs one, the member who will pick up and run with others' ideas, enjoys being in the team for its own sake, so always works towards a successful outcome.
> - *Implementer* – the realist who turns ideas into outcomes, making the process manageable by bringing logic and method to others' inspirations.

that concentrate on the individual, which in the right circumstances are no less valuable.

On-the-job skills training

This is probably the most widespread and least managed approach to training, in the voluntary sector as elsewhere. It is where a new employee works alongside an experienced one, learning how to do the job as she goes along. Even if your charity has a highly structured induction training process, I would be very surprised if this traditional training method does not still abound. It used to be called *Sitting Next to Nellie,* when Nellie was the hard-bitten worker who knew all the tricks, and you sat next to her to learn them. In more enlightened non-sexist days there is probably a better phrase, but the idea lingers on.

- It is always worth drawing upon the skills of your existing workforce, in which you have invested a great deal of effort, and it's usually cheaper than getting a specialist trainer.
- However, Nellie may have fallen into bad habits, which you don't want your new employees to inherit. Unless you watch her carefully, Nellie can pass on the bad bits as well as the good.
- If you do use your existing staff skills to develop newcomers, you need to do so in a structured way – identify training needs

and learning targets, develop a partnership with Nellie on what she will be teaching, and review progress externally on a regular basis.
- This approach only really works when you are in a steady-state situation, where the skills and approaches of one generation can be handed on to the next. The arrival of new staff may well be the occasion for Nellie herself to be retrained, rather than for relying on her to impart knowledge that is no longer needed.

Coaching

This can be a more managed version of on-the-job training, where a trainer with particular knowledge works through a programme with the employee to assist in the development of new skills. The coaching can either be in the real work situation, or the trainee can be taken out of the workplace to develop those skills, and then helped back at work to practise them. Nellie can be the coach, but only if she has been trained as the trainer – or you can bring in a professional trainer, or the responsibility can fall to the manager. However the coaching is approached, it does demand a clear programme towards a set of goals.

Mentoring

Mentoring is a little more abstracted from the immediate skills training situation and is more about developing personal confidence and the less tangible qualities of management. It is particularly useful in situations where a manager is new to the job, or where an employee is working in relative isolation, and therefore does not have either colleagues or a peer group to turn to for advice. It is thus particularly appropriate in the voluntary sector, where frequently staff teams are widely dispersed, or senior officers and chief executives are faced with trustees who, with the best will in the world, do not necessarily have the management skills themselves to provide the necessary support.

The key to mentoring is to be non-directive. The mentor, who is nearly always a person external to the organisation, acts as a foil to ideas from the mentee, can offer a more dispassionate analysis of issues as they arise, and above all is not critical. Rather, the mentor will listen sympathetically to concerns, suggesting alternative ways of addressing them, in a confidential and non-threatening environment in which the employee can admit to mistakes and weaknesses. It is the mentor's job to build up the employee's confidence to go back in there and tackle issues, and to help her develop the necessary skills to do so, whether directly or by identifying other sources of support.

It will quickly be realised that mentoring is a highly skilled profession. Be very careful before you decide whom to appoint as your mentor – and however technically good they may be, however laudable the reports of their work with other charities, the chemistry with the employee has to be right. So any good mentor will suggest a trial period before entering into a longer-term commitment.

Measuring training effectiveness

However brilliant the training package that you have finally decided on may be, it will all be worthless unless it actually serves the purpose for which it has been developed – the enhancement of skills towards organisational objectives. Anything less than that and you are wasting valuable charitable assets – and as I have been at pains to point out throughout this chapter, you should normally view employee development as justifiable only in terms of measurable outcomes related to your charitable aims. Not only should the training be designed to that end, it also needs to be acceptable to the trainees concerned; there's little point in devising the most focused courses, only to discover that the way you intend to deliver it – the style or personality of the trainer, the location or timing, the balance of activities in the course – are anathema to the trainees. In those circumstances, they just won't learn. And finally, however acceptable the training may be, however much it relates to organisational objectives, it's still useless unless it actually delivers on those objectives. You have to show that it works.

To summarise – there are three key components to measuring training:

- Does it relate to your charity's objectives and culture?
- Is it acceptable to the trainees?
- Does it actually improve their performance in their work towards those same objectives?

Unless you can say a resounding YES to each of these questions, you need to go back to the drawing board.

Whilst each charity will wish to adopt a different approach to setting its training objectives and measuring its training performance against them, all training needs to be evaluated as you go along, both by the trainees themselves, and by their managers who have, sometimes reluctantly, agreed to release them from precious work time to go off to be trained. When an employee comes back from the training course (or other activity), therefore, the first thing his manager should do is to discuss with him how the training went and what general lessons and skills can be learnt for the rest of the team. Both the trainees and, I would

MODEL 10.6 Training assessment

The *Charity* Training evaluation form

Training course: ....
Date(s) of training: ....
Name(s) of trainers/training
organisation: ....

Please score your evaluation of the training using the following scale and ringing the appropriate number where indicated. Please add comments as you feel relevant.

1 = Excellent
2 = Good
3 = Satisfactory
4 = Poor
5 = Bad

1 What were the objectives of the course, and how did these relate to your role with *The Charity*?

2 Overall, how well did the course meet its objectives?   1 2 3 4 5

3 Was the structure of the course:
   The right length?   1 2 3 4 5
   Well balanced between different activities?   1 2 3 4 5
   Logically put together?   1 2 3 4 5

4 Please comment on the quality of:
   Delivery by the trainers   1 2 3 4 5
   Visual and other aids   1 2 3 4 5
   Handouts and other materials   1 2 3 4 5
   Training accommodation   1 2 3 4 5
   Residential facilities   1 2 3 4 5

5 Your performance as a trainee
   Overall, how demanding did you find the course?   1 2 3 4 5
   How appropriate was the level and difficulty of the course?   1 2 3 4 5
   How much did you learn?   1 2 3 4 5
   How good was the feedback on your own performance?   1 2 3 4 5

6 What key points would you summarise as being central to what you learnt?

7 *(To be completed by the trainee's manager)*
   How well did the course meet your expectations for this trainee?   1 2 3 4 5

---

argue, their managers should evaluate the training, and that evaluation should then be fed back through the charity to the trainer. This way, the charity will begin to learn whether it is getting value for money, and the trainer will know what has worked well and where improvements are needed. Trainers who do not encourage and welcome feedback are bad trainers.

Some trainers provide their own evaluation form, some encourage organisations to develop ones that are appropriate to their needs. In model 8.6 I suggest a hybrid version that you can modify to suit your circumstances, bearing in mind that it relates primarily to formal courses; feedback on other forms of training is just as valuable, but the form will need to be adjusted significantly if you are to avoid being accused of being bureaucratic. And if you are either a trainer reading this, or a manager seeking to evaluate training, do be aware that, since trainees are all different, and you can't please all the people all of the time, it is not a sign of failure if you don't get a full house of 1s. Provided you get a good average, you are generally doing all right, and you then just need to pay attention to any extreme marks or unsolicited comments.

In summary …

- Staff skills and perspectives need continual development to reflect the changing needs of the charities that employ them.
- Unless staff are effectively motivated they will not, in the end, perform well; and motivation covers two separate though interdependent areas: the basics of giving staff acceptable conditions in which to work, and the less tangible aspects of helping people to feel good.
- This latter point depends on good motivational management, which is best provided by inspirational leadership that includes and thanks staff for their contributions, forever pushes out the boundaries of achievement and is applied equally to individuals and teams of staff.
- There are complex issues in the voluntary sector that are not reflected elsewhere in the economy – around ownership, control and use of services – which can be potential sources of conflict between staff, volunteers, trustees and users. This offers a particular challenge for charity managers.
- There should be considerable investment in staff training, but this should be within the context of the personnel strategy, which itself should be determined by the corporate development plan. Most training activity should be capable of being directly justified by specific organisational objectives.
- A sensitive equal opportunities approach to staff training and development is essential if the full potential of current and future staff is to be released.
- Training is about outcomes, a means to an end rather than an end in itself. The best training relates to organisational objectives and has to be measured against how well it contributes to them.
- Good training is training that is accessible to the trainees, ensures the maximum of learning and development from the minimum input, and can take a variety of forms.
- The wise manager, in determining what training will be done – there is no real choice as to *whether* to train at all – will be aware of the range of options, both short and long term, and producing either immediate results or deeper structural change.
- Training is a challenge to which every manager will rise, and one which, when properly addressed, will provide enormous benefits both to the charity and to all its staff.

Developing staff – supervision, appraisal and personal development

CHAPTER 11

INTRODUCTION

In the previous chapter I came back, time and time again, to the point that training should be related to organisational outcomes, an approach which tends to encourage a short- or at best medium-term perspective; if you can't see an immediate result in improving staff skills, you are unlikely to make the investment. But it is possible to take a longer-term view, one that argues that if you develop your staff in general terms, you will also enhance the performance of the charity.

This chapter looks at a range of techniques for monitoring and enhancing staff performance through target-setting, performance evaluation, positive supervision and formal appraisal.

Staff development in context

The problem for many smaller charities is that much as they would wish to see an overall enhancement of staff skills levels, with professional training, day release, management development and other background development initiatives, these are all expensive in terms of time and fees. It is only the larger organisations that can consider affording them, and staff, particularly managers, in smaller charities generally do not get many developmental opportunities. As a result, they tend to move on. The very nature of their staffing structures militates against long-term commitment, apart from those staff who really do work for the particular charity for love rather than money.

In the larger charities, the opportunity does exist, not only for such personal development in the confident expectation that it will, in the longer term, pay dividends; but also for succession planning, knowing where there are likely to be vacancies and preparing staff to step into them. There will be many who would argue that this militates against equal opportunities recruitment where, they say, all vacancies should be open to anyone to apply. There is some strength in that argument, particularly if the people being groomed for stardom were not themselves originally recruited in an open way.

But if you have genuinely open access to your charity for people starting their careers, there is at least an argument for considering adopting the practice that is widespread throughout the private sector, and concentrate your training resources where they will do the most good, with staff who will be with you for a long time and who will be the leaders of tomorrow. And, because you share the values of the voluntary sector, you will be able to be open about your succession planning, basing it upon sound principles and relating it to the charitable objectives to which you and everyone in the sector is committed.

The corollary of succession planning is personal career planning, supporting staff in determining where their careers can best take them, rather than where the charity would like them to go. Career management is becoming increasingly relevant as the job-for-life syndrome rapidly collapses, and we certainly need to enskill all our employees to make them more marketable. Even charities have to declare redundancies, and with the world of work changing so rapidly, career moves are bound to become the norm. Although I discuss career management in more detail in chapter 12 within the context of the kind of difficult decisions you may have to face, and how to secure win-win outcomes from them, it is equally valid to consider providing it to key people now, either to help them stay with you by enhancing their performance and presentation, or by equipping them now for what may happen in the future, thereby removing some of the sting if and when it does happen.

The need to be involved

If the previous section seems a little negative – or ambitious, depending on how many nettles you are prepared to grasp – then perhaps it's time to consider some more of the practicalities of ensuring that your staff are effectively managed towards excellent performance. I start from the premise that motivation is the main element in good performance. People don't live, or work, in isolation. They like to know what's going on around them, and they usually want to know what effect they are having. Although people come to work to be paid, the process of employment can be far less alienating if they feel they have some control over their environment, and that in the main is dependent upon how well they are motivated to be involved. If they know the effect of what they are doing and, at a deeper level, why they are doing it, they are far more likely to want to do it well.

Staff sitting on production lines, whether they are making cars, processing invoices, sweeping the street or delivering meals, get bored very easily. Introduce variation in the process and the boredom lifts – for a while. Explain to people the effect of what they are doing and they will be even more enthusiastic. Let them make suggestions about how they should go about it and tell them how well they are doing, and they will be better still. In the end it all comes down to a need to be nurtured – as study after study has shown, provided you pay people attention, they will be happier. And that even applies when you have to tell them bad things rather than good, and experiments have shown that workers are more productive when you smile or shout at them than when you ignore them.

So a key component in motivating staff is to let them know how they are doing, and for that to happen you need to set benchmarks to measure that performance. Those benchmarks may relate just to personal performance, but following the arguments of the previous chapter, it only really makes sense in organisational terms if they are set within the parameters of organisational objectives. In the same way that individuals need to be involved to be motivated, so also does your charity need to relate their involvement to your organisational objectives, otherwise yet again there is a danger of going off at a tangent and wasting valuable resources. And whilst a manager might, at least in the short term, get away with that in the public or commercial sectors ('it's all part of a long-term plan'), it is far more difficult justifying irrelevant targets and activities to trustees and volunteers who are there solely for the maximisation of the immediate end product.

The other key component is staff involvement, however you choose to do it, in the setting of those targets. Every charitable organisation will strike a different balance between top-down leadership and bottom-up involvement, but I suspect there will be very few where an edict simply comes down from on high as to what is going to happen, and even fewer where the staff accept this unquestioningly. Remember that they probably joined your charity in the first place because they were, at the very least, attracted to its objectives, so they are likely to want to have their say. That say is likely to relate to outcomes, and your job as a manager is to help your staff keep their eye on the end-product ball – working within the trustees' overall constraints – and encourage the appropriate level of contribution on how that end product can be improved, both collectively and through individual performance.

This chapter is therefore all about individual target-setting, and how this can be set in the context of your charity's overall development plans. It is about putting into practical reality, for every employee, the theory and broad statements of policy direction and training objectives discussed in chapter 10, supported by the development of employee involvement systems that enable your staff to be fully informed, fully signed up to the provision of a quality service and fully involved to the extent of their abilities and within the cultural limits of the charity.

Target-setting and performance evaluation

Measuring the performance of employees is similar to measuring the potential of candidates before they even become employees. Your objective is to ensure that, in all the circumstances, you get the best out of the people involved and you know when you've got it. However, when you are considering this aspect of measurement, the cards are not entirely stacked in favour of the employer, as they tend to be in the recruitment scenario. Then, the recruiter decides the standards, determines the measures and assesses the candidates against them. It is a brave applicant indeed who may seek to challenge the process, and an even rarer one who gets appointed as a result. Once they are members of staff, however, those candidates inevitably become far more part of the process, with rights as employees to be listened to and to be treated fairly. So the process of target-setting has to be acceptable, or at least accepted, by all concerned, or it just will not work.

In the voluntary sector (indeed, elsewhere as well), it makes good sense to involve the people who do the work in setting its standards, because not only are they likely to have more detailed knowledge of how things actually happen than the person responsible for their management, they are also likely to share the objectives and so will want the system to work. That is not to say that managers are in any way redundant in this process. Their role is to question, to push out the boundaries, to inspire and lead staff to ever greater performance. But if they try to do that without taking account of staff's professional skills and knowledge, and of their legitimate aspirations, they could appear very foolish. And if there are disagreements on occasions about standards, the manager's duty to make the final decision is more likely to be acceptable if she can show that she has taken full account of others' views and normally responds to them.

In chapter 10 we saw how an overall training strategy can be developed from the top down, giving shape to organisational aspirations and development plans. Whilst that is essentially a corporate process that trickles down and becomes more detailed as it goes, there is nothing at all to prevent those voluntary organisations who emphasise employee involvement to include staff in the development planning process. That involvement is however in the form of playing a corporate role, and it would of course be inappropriate for the organisation's training strategy to be influenced by the personal needs and limitations of individuals, needs and limitations which are addressed by their being consumers of the training process, not shapers of it.

We need to move on from the giddy heights of corporate strategies and training plans to their application in practice to individuals – the obvious extension of the detailed departmental training plans exemplified in model 10.4 in the previous chapter. That model hinted at this, in that it demonstrated a general awareness by its author, the manager, of the state of skills within the department as they were applied to the corporate and thence more local objectives. The next stage is to apply the overall aims to individual capabilities, and this can only really be done on a one-to-one basis.

I shall argue later that this is best done through a formal appraisal process. Before we get to the point of considering how appraisals can be structured, it is worth considering some of the principles and processes that underlie them. I would suggest that the keys to any successful performance measurement, just as when measuring potential in the recruitment situation, are:

- Targets must be capable of being achieved.
- Targets must be capable of being measured.
- Targets must be relevant to the objective.

There is absolutely no point in setting staff goals that do not meet either their own objectives or, even more importantly, those of your charity. Staff will quickly become totally disillusioned with that.

There is also absolutely no point in setting targets that nobody can reasonably reach. Constant failure is a deadly demotivator. If you want people to be able to do five impossible things before breakfast, you have to build up to it. By giving them only three difficult things before lunch, you will improve on the previous performance of coasting towards teatime and, once they've taken the first step, you can make the next one that bit steeper.

Finally, however fine-sounding objectives may seem, there is no purpose whatsoever to be served if you can't measure performance towards them – you won't know whether you've got there, and may miss the point when you have, with the waste of effort and loss of subsequent impetus that this implies. As a charity manager, you need to keep constantly in touch with progress, and to know what that progress means.

So how do you actually do it? Whether as a manager you do this alone, or you share the task with the staff involved, the basis is job analysis:

- Break down the objectives and the job into separate elements.
- Identify what is needed to achieve success in performing those elements and the job as a whole.

- Evaluate the resources available for that performance, and shortfalls.
- Determine how you will meet the shortfalls, and over what period.
- Undertake the necessary actions to reach the appropriate levels.
- Measure how far those actions have actually secured the improvements.
- Re-evaluate the objectives and the job to determine whether the ground has changed, and keep performance under constant review.
- ... start around the circle again.

An example of this in practice is offered in model 11.1, in which you will see a combination of supportive and corrective activities, all designed to ensure maximum corporate outcomes, including building upon the employee's strengths, developing her skills, supervising her weak areas and recognising that challenges are sometimes beyond her control and ability, and therefore providing additional resources – because, on balance, she is good enough for you to want her to stay as part of your team, warts and all.

You will have noticed in this model that some of the performance measures are more objectively measurable than others. There is a school of management thought that suggests that unless you can define a target precisely in numerical terms, then you should not use it. Such targets cannot be argued about once they are set, because the quality of the performance is all in the figures. This certainly has the superficial attraction of ease of measurement – even a computer could supervise an employee if all she has to do is tap in the data about what's she's been up to. But is that management? In any work area where quality is measured as much by how people feel about things as it is by hard statistics – and where is that more true than in the voluntary sector? – the idea that such measures are invalid is in itself utterly invalid. Management is about making judgements, some of them subjective. They are no less valuable for that, and the good manager is one who is able to combine in her decision-making processes all relevant information and measures. It is in the end, in my view, a measure of a truly effective manager to be respected for the judgements that depend on people skills, rather than on mathematical ability.

All you need is love?

Every manager needs to set targets – for herself, for her department and for individual members of her staff team. Just as important as setting those targets is giving people support in achieving

MODEL 11.1   Job analysis and training needs

Job: Regional fundraiser
Employee: Freda Bloggs
Job task: Organising regionwide raffle

Job elements	Performance measure	Evaluation of employee	Remedial action
Prepare budget	Budget reflects reality of previous similar activities	Never run a raffle before	One-to-one coaching by manager
Secure sponsors for prizes	At least four prizes worth £1,000 each	Has only previously secured small deals	Advice and review by corporate FR department
Prepare pre-publicity to members	Keeps within corporate style; likely to be read	Previously charity PR manager, fully capable	None
Order printing	Realistic timescales, adequate numbers, conforms to law	Not aware of legal requirements for tickets	Read up on lotteries law
Distribute tickets and admin details to branches	Prompt and accurate mailing, clear support materials, fall-back arrangements	Poor time manager, good at systems and logistics	Regular checks by manager
Chase up branches regularly	Diplomatic but firm skills, detailed application	Very convincing but needs to be pushed to make calls	Formal training on admin systems
Collect in money and counterfoils	Knowledge of security, visit all outlets in 48 hours	Left petty cash tin open, got mugged last year	Formal training in personal security
Organise unbiased draw	Appropriate accommodation secured, understands basic statistics	Has always promptly booked meeting rooms, has A-level maths	None
Despatch prizes, produce and distribute results sheets	Proper transportation organised, effective publicity with winners, attractive sheets	Good at logistics and photography, needs help with tight deadlines	Extra staff for final stage

them. Employees need to know you care about their performance as workers, because that way they can work on the assumption that you also care about them as people (whatever your real feelings may be!). Lots of positive feedback, encouragement and helpful advice is what best motivates the vast majority of people –

loads of carrot and as little stick as possible (although even that is better than being ignored).

However, if there is something wrong, if improvements *can* be made, then you will be undermining yourself and your staff if you don't act. They don't want to be in a position of not knowing whether to believe your fulsome praise because you never criticise – everyone knows when they've made mistakes and are confused if you thank them for them. The trick is to offer criticism in a positive way, so that staff will want to change and improve, and will look to you to help them do so. (There follows the only joke in this book: *How many trainers does it take to change a light bulb? Only one, but the light bulb has to want to change.*)

If someone has got it really wrong, find out why. Perhaps they weren't briefed properly, or the task was different from that expected. Maybe other things came along and they made the wrong choice of priorities. Perhaps they were not up to the task and it was your mistake to ask them in the first place. They could just be unlucky. (Some of the most successful managers are the lucky ones, and work hard to build teams of lucky people around them. Whether or not you believe in luck, the point is to capitalise effectively on what resources are available, including the operation of fate and statistics.) Whatever the cause of the mistake, most of the time you will be able to get a better performance next time by combining all the factors in a different way. And if you can't secure acceptable change, you are probably facing a capability, or at the extreme, a disciplinary case.

When you do confront the failure, be pleasant but firm. Don't show your anger or disappointment – it only generates anger or defensiveness back. You want to improve, not punish, and confrontations are not the best nurturing grounds for positive thinking. Use phrases like: *You seem not to have hit the target here, which is disappointing because The Charity was relying on that income. Do you know what went wrong?* and *I'm sorry that you weren't able to make it to that important meeting last week – would it be more helpful if we scheduled our sessions for a different day in future?* Try to avoid the Big Brother (or Sister) approach of: *I can't understand why you didn't finish that, it's so easy, I've done it myself a dozen times. You're going to have to pull your socks up if you want to stay around here;* and *How could you possibly have forgotten the meeting – it's been in the diary for months? Any more of that and I'll cancel your support sessions, and then see where you'll be.*

Supporting staff is about helping them to grow, to make a greater contribution towards your charity's corporate objectives. Most of the time, most staff will accept most support, even positive criticism. Most people want to succeed; your job as a manager is to help them to do so. If you don't, and instead see them merely as a pawn to move around the board, as units of production rather than as people with feelings and expectations, with strengths and weaknesses, they will very quickly get very isolated: isolated from their colleagues, isolated from any chance of a positive relationship with you as their manager and, worst of all, isolated from the objectives of your charity. An employee who started with a flush of idealism can rapidly deteriorate into a bitter and twisted thorn in the charity's side, and it's normally management's fault when they do. So, always think positive, approach problems positively and firmly, look for the positive sides of your staff's work and praise them. And even if it's not love you can give them, your respect will be an invaluable motivator.

It's not just when things go wrong ...

Life in the voluntary sector can often be a pretty lonely business. Despite a sharing of ideals and objectives that is hard to match, our staff have to face and deal with a series of conflicting demands on an almost daily basis, and often find themselves desperately short of support and advice. The majority of charities employing staff are likely to have only one or two employees, often working out of their home and reporting to a management committee comprised of well-meaning amateurs who rarely have management skills. Many other organisations may have a handful of staff scattered around the country, rarely seeing colleagues but expected to be the public face, its eyes and ears, of the charity employing them. Too often titles such as 'Regional Fundraising Manager' disguise a job with long hours on the road, evening meetings miles away from base and a boss who's on the end of a phone an hour a week if you're lucky. Even in larger charities, everyone is so busy thinking about the key objectives that they can forget the support needs of others – and there's nowhere lonelier than a busy office when you don't feel that you fit in.

This all points to a need to manage contact and support between staff and their employing organisations carefully and regularly, to let them know that you are there, to make space in busy diaries to discuss problems, ideas and successes. If you only arrange to see your staff when things have gone wrong – and of course, they will occasionally go wrong, and you will need to discuss those matters – there is unlikely to be any great trust or confidence built up between you. If you have regular support meetings, praising the positive, planning realistically and pushing standards ever higher, the occasional correction session has a greater chance of being seen in a less threatening light.

The position can be particularly difficult for chief executives, who not only have to contend with the legitimate (and sometimes illegitimate!) demands of their staff to be nurtured, they often do

CASE STUDY 11.1 Staff supervision

A care-providing charity received, somewhat to its surprise, a large lottery grant that would enable it to expand significantly its support to its client group and establish links with various other agencies that should enable it to continue that work once the tapered funding had dried up. In the hope of ensuring operational effectiveness, it introduced a new layer of managers, establishing two regional manager posts that would each lead the work of a team of home-based specialist social workers. Arising from the recruitment process, one of the existing social workers was promoted, and the other vacancy was filled by a person new to social work and the voluntary sector who had previously worked as a nursing officer in the army.

Both new managers were largely left to their own devices, as their own senior manager was involved in developing the public image of the charity, consolidating good governance practice with the expanded trustee board, and strategic management of a much wider range of services. The senior manager felt that they had the right mix of experience not to demand constant supervision.

The former field social worker knew the charity inside out, having been one of the first to have been appointed fifteen years before. He was personal friends with most of the team he would now be supervising, and fully sympathised with the pressures they had all been under. Now that there was more money around, he felt that his former colleagues would be able to perform better and, having resented his previous manager breathing down his neck, gave them the space and authority to get on with it, with an open invitation to get in touch if things went wrong. The former nursing officer, on the other hand, not being fully conversant with the ways of the charity or the work of individual social workers, set up systems whereby she spoke to each of her staff once a week, receiving from them regular progress sheets (something they'd never been asked to produce before) and ensuring that she met them face to face on a monthly basis.

The staff supervised by their former colleague basically carried on as before, providing the kind of service they'd always offered. Most clients seemed happy with this, but some of them heard about the new image of the charity and started to complain either that they weren't getting the kind of services being promised, or that 'head office was wasting money that could be better spent on people like us'. The social workers tended to agree, and their newly appointed manager – when he heard about these things at all – didn't disabuse them of this perspective. Rather, very aware of the pressures they were under, he agreed every leave request and was sympathetic to any sickness absence, particularly those that were stress-induced arising from client

not enjoy professional managerial support themselves. This suggests a strong case for management training for those chairing trustee boards or charged with the responsibility of liaising with the paid staff, and there is an increasing move towards joint training of both parties. It is also a matter that has increasingly been

contact. After all, he'd been there himself and had never felt supported by his own manager.

The former nursing officer, on the other hand, sought to impose a much harder and more corporate line. She explained with monotonous regularity what the charity's new approach was about, producing information about it to be given to clients, she checked regularly on sickness absences, only agreed holidays when cover was available, and proactively discussed both straightforward and complex cases with her staff.

After a year, an internal audit on progress in developing a wider range of clients and services showed:

- Social workers in the team managed by their former colleague were, on average, doing no more than twelve months previously, and in some cases were doing much less.
- Their sickness levels were rising, despite their manager being sympathetic to the stress they faced.
- The number of complaints from clients had risen significantly.
- Staff turnover had increased.
- The team managed by the newcomer had shown an initial increase in turnover amongst previously disaffected staff who didn't like her more interventionist style.
- Staff were offering a wider range of services in line with the new corporate image.
- The number of complaints not properly dealt with was falling.
- Staff casual sickness levels were reducing.
- Two grievances against the new manager had been investigated but not upheld.

Two contrasting styles of supervision – the former initially producing an easier time for staff but in the longer term little by way of challenge and an unfocused workforce; the latter a shock to the system but close support and reorientation for the majority of staff who wanted to succeed. So the key lessons that between them the new managers learnt were:

- Staff who are managed, in whatever way, are more likely to be satisfied than those who are not.
- Staff who are focused on and taught to share the organisation's aims are likely to be more effective to those they are seeking to help.
- Change must be introduced sensitively, although sometimes the people who dislike it most are the very ones who you want to go anyway.

Sympathy is not enough – management and supervision is about encouraging staff through empathy towards clear objectives, supporting them in times of need so they can be that much more effective during the rest of their work.

addressed through the establishment of peer support groups and mentoring arrangements; whilst these do not provide managerial direction and supervision, they can offer a very effective forum for the isolated chief executive or other senior manager, and at the very least can be a sympathetic shoulder to cry on.

Different charities will place different demands on inter-staff relationships, depending on the range of activities, the speed of change, the geographical distribution of the workforce and their degree of operational autonomy. It will not always be possible to have frequent face-to-face meetings between managers and their staff, although a telephone conversation is often better than nothing (and nowadays, with advancing technology, team meetings can be conducted remotely very easily). But I would suggest that for most employees, managers should aim to have regular support meetings on a monthly or quarterly basis, however frequently they may meet on other occasions when working together. Even when they are in the same building, and in and out of each others' offices all the time, a passing chat is no substitute for a properly structured support session.

Such a session needs to aim to do several things. First, there should be an opportunity to review progress against short-term and interim targets, to discuss how obstacles can be overcome, and to agree adjustments to work programmes as appropriate. Secondly, it offers the manager a chance to pass on and add to new ideas and information coming out of the charity, and for the employee to make her contribution back to the corporate development process. (This aspect is also usually covered in the team briefing process in those charities who use that system to communicate with staff, but it does not usually allow for individual concerns to be raised in a safe and private environment.) Thirdly, there should be time for the employee to come forward with new ideas and suggestions, which can then be put into a broader corporate context as these are passed back through the charity's hierarchy. Finally, it gives the employee and her manager an opportunity to deal with employment and 'housekeeping' matters, such as pay, timesheets and holidays.

How formally this will operate will to a great extent depend on the size and nature of your charity and the personalities of the manager and the employee. It is the responsibility, ultimately, of the chief executive to ensure that all staff get the support they deserve and need, however that is achieved, and you will need to set up arrangements that reflect your organisational culture. I state, however, quite simply: if you take management seriously, then some formal system of support is essential.

There is also the need for a safety valve, for an employee to have a reference point whenever she feels the need for one, and not to have to wait until the next supervision meeting. As staff gain confidence in their own judgement and decision-making abilities, they are unlikely to use it very often, but it must always be there – so if the line manager is not available, alternative arrangements should be put in place, and the situation when any contact with the charity is possibly only for one hour a week always avoided.

You owe it to your staff to be available, to show that you care, just as they owe it to you to act responsibly and only make use of the safety valve in real emergencies. Mutual trust and mutual confidence will lead to mutually satisfactory and improving outcomes.

Formal appraisal

So far, what has been discussed has been regular management supervision, an absolutely standard prerequisite to the success of your charity. Such supervision tends to be within the context of day-to-day work and short-term targets which, for most employees for most of the time, is what is important. Everyone needs to know how they're getting on, and regular contact does that for them. But to give them a greater say in their destiny, and to give them a true sense of worth and of their overall contribution to, and potential in, the charity, you need to step back from day-to-day performance, and to conduct a broader evaluation. That is where appraisal comes in: it measures how well individuals are doing, and it sets standards that they should be achieving. Thus, by adopting a competency-based approach, not only are you evaluating progress and planning for next year, you are also measuring quality of performance against readily understood norms that relate to the specific needs of the job.

Appraisal tends to be an annual affair. In the main, this is because it's convenient that way, it can be easily diarised and it can (if you insist) be linked to pay rises, which themselves tend to be annual matters. But there is, or rather there should be, a more fundamental reason for the timing, and that is to fit in with the business planning process, since the best appraisals are those that link individual employees to the charity's corporate objectives. Most planning cycles run over twelve months, so annual appraisals make sense in that context, provided that the timing of appraisals fits in with the timing of the planning itself. Some organisations conduct appraisals throughout the year, for example on the anniversary of the employee's start date, but if your corporate objectives are developing on a planned basis, this rather misses the point, as you will want to relate the employee's activities to new objectives. Thus the more enlightened charity is likely to determine its annual objectives, and then undertake its appraisal round in a concentrated period after that.

There are many different styles of appraisal, and the introduction, development and review of them is a growing industry within the personnel profession. How systems work will depend on cultural values and management structures, but I would suggest that they all have some common elements, however these are expressed:

- Review of performance over the previous period (usually the past twelve months).
- Planning for the next period.
- Identifying resources necessary to secure success.

The most successful appraisals are those that are properly prepared for. It is good practice for both the manager and the employee to spend some time in advance considering these three aspects, so that whilst there may be differences of view as to cause, there will be common ground on the facts of the previous year; they both familiarise themselves with corporate objectives for the coming year and start to identify what these will mean locally; and they both start to identify the resources they think are necessary to get the job done. Charities often prepare an appraisal planning prompt form to help with this thinking, and encourage staff and their managers to exchange notes before the actual appraisal meeting. A possible model for you to adopt is given opposite.

In considering what has happened in the last year, no individual matters should come as a surprise to either the employee or manager if there has been a series of effective supervision sessions. But those sessions will have tended to address more immediate concerns, and the appraisal is the opportunity to take a step back and see them in the broader and longer-term context. Patterns may emerge, how realistic earlier targets were will become apparent and the reasons for success and failure can be analysed. Reasons for doing certain things, and for deciding after all not to do others, should fall into place, and the responsibility for these outcomes attributed.

Your charity may be one of an increasing number that is introducing some element of performance-related pay (PRP) for either its senior staff or more generally. Some organisations base their assessments for such rewards on this part of the (annual) appraisal; others operate a separate mechanism. If you do link PRP to appraisal, you will need to ensure that you have built up the confidence of your staff sufficiently so that they are prepared to admit to mistakes in circumstances where this could affect their remuneration – not an easy thing to do. Or you may prefer to separate a review of previous activities, which will consider all aspects of work, not just the individual's contribution but also the impact of the work environment generally, from a target-setting system that is agreed beforehand with the staff involved. PRP systems are discussed in more detail in chapter 7.

In reviewing the previous year, therefore, you will need to consider not only the employee's contribution but also what has enhanced that contribution, and what factors beyond his control have diminished it. After all, it's hardly fair to blame the

MODEL 11.2 Appraisal preparation form

The Charity
Annual performance appraisal preparation form

Please prepare your responses to the questions on this form either as the postholder or the postholder's manager, at least one week before the agreed date for your appraisal meeting, and give a copy of them to your manager/member of staff.

Post: ....

Postholder: ....

Reporting to: ....

Length of time of postholder in post:

1 Review of previous year
   Please refer to the key activities and targets agreed in last year's appraisal (attached)
   1.1 Which of these activities was fully completed, and which targets reached?
   1.2 Which were only partially completed, or not at all?
   1.3 What enabled the targets to be reached, and what prevented them?
   1.4 Which activities were reprioritised during the year, and which targets amended, and why?
   1.5 With the benefit of hindsight, which activities and targets could/should have been dealt with differently?
   1.6 How far was the identified training undertaken, and how successful was it?
   1.7 Were all identified resources secured and effectively deployed? If not, why not?
   1.8 What lessons have you learnt from last year?
   1.9 Overall, how would you rank the postholder's performance during the past year?

2 Plans for next year
   2.1 Taking into account the key themes of *The Charity's* corporate plan for next year, what are the implications for this post, both personally and for the functions/staff for which it is responsible? Please ensure that you include in this evaluation the continuation of existing activities, as well as new initiatives.
   2.2 What priorities should be given to the activities that arise from these implications?
   2.3 What other, more local, activities are you planning for next year? How do these fit in with corporate objectives, and what priority should they have?

3 Resources
   3.1 Are the current levels of staffing, finance, equipment, etc., sufficient to carry out existing responsibilities? If not, what more is needed, and why?
   3.2 What additional resources (staff, equipment, materials, money, etc.), if any, will be needed, to carry out the new activities?
   3.3 What training will the postholder need to carry out existing and new responsibilities?
   3.4 What are the key competencies needed to undertake the duties of the post successfully? What changes, if any, have there been in these since the last appraisal? How far does the postholder possess the necessary competencies and will the training proposed meet all current development needs?
   3.5 What priorities and ranking should be given to proposals for growth in resources and training activities?

individual for not meeting his targets if the charity itself has taken away the necessary resources to help him achieve them. And if that applies generally in the appraisal process, it is doubly important to avoid unfair judgements if performance is linked to pay.

Once the review of the last year has been completed and the lessons drawn from it understood, a line can be drawn under the past and you can turn to the future. It is here that the particular relevance of the charity's own programme arises. The manager and the employee will identify those parts of the corporate plan, however formally it is developed, that apply directly and individually to the employee's job, and individual targets and action plans can be agreed. These will include not only the employee's personal targets but also, in general terms, those for the staff and functions for whom he is accountable. This can then form the basis of the appraisal that will subsequently be discussed with the employee's own staff. Once all the anticipated activities and their targets have been agreed, priorities and timescales can be determined – both of which will inform the regular review of progress that will be the main plank of supervision sessions throughout the coming year.

The third element in the appraisal process is to identify the resources the employee will need to deliver effectively on all the targets agreed for the coming period. This will include training, staff, equipment, other materials and capital items and finance. Whilst, in principle, all such resources should be oriented towards the overall corporate objectives and needs, there will inevitably be some local variations and add-ons, and across the charity, these may not all be compatible with each other, nor may there necessarily be sufficient resources to meet every aspiration.

It would therefore be prudent, in dealing with this stage of the appraisal process, for the manager to make it clear that any identified resources will only be made available subject to their being approved corporately, and therefore, until this has happened, the planning process for the next year is in draft form only.

Rather, all local plans, whether arising from the appraisal round or otherwise, need to be consolidated and contradictions and bids for competing resources resolved before the process goes much further. This is particularly important when planning the charity's training programme for the next period, when the extent of collective need can be determined, and training activities laid on accordingly. It is also becoming increasingly important in areas such as information technology, where it is all too easy for a local manager to agree to the purchase of a piece of hardware or software that meets the needs of the individual, but which may not be compatible with other hardware or applications in the charity.

Only when this consolidation process has been achieved and the actual scope of possible activities determined, can the individual plans be finally agreed, and if there have had to be significant changes, the manager and the employee need to review proposed operations and priorities, to see what other ways can be identified to achieve the same or modified objectives.

Of course, if the appraisal process has been an open and positive one, there is unlikely to be any substantial difference between appraiser and appraisee. It is important that both know what the key issues are and how they are going to be addressed, and that the appraisal is not 'dumped' onto the unsuspecting employee at the last minute – that way, quite understandably, fear of appraisal lies. It may be the case that the appraisee does not always get everything she wants, but she should at least know why. If she still feels really strongly about it then, just as in a grievance process, the best appraisal arrangements allow for someone else to look at the outcome and for the possibility of adjustments. There will anyway be some such review as the collection of appraisals are put together to underpin the organisational development plan; but in really difficult cases, where there may be a genuine conflict between manager and managed, the wise organisation will provide for the manager's manager to consider the appraisal before its formal adoption. That is the time to sort out the arguments.

Some organisations are now developing appraisal of staff by people other than their managers – the current vogue phrase is 360 degree appraisal, implying that the employee is considered in the round from all perspectives. A recent survey of charity chief executives indicated that upwards of thirty per cent of them were getting some form of feedback from people other than their trustees or chair. Increasingly, people such as more junior staff, peers and external contacts are providing some form of evaluation of performance in key areas, such as: *How well do I feel managed by this person? Does she present a good image of the organisation to its public?*, and *Does the manager make a significant professional contribution to the development of good practice in the field?* Whilst the questions in the prompt form may need modification or adapting to suit the circumstances, the same principles will apply, but your charity, if it is to go down this route, does need to determine how it will handle information from different sources, how to resolve conflicting evidence and how to arrive at an overall evaluation that will be the formal appraisal. Hard enough when evaluating the performance of managers generally, but far more difficult if you are thinking of linking appraisal to reward. Would you like to have an element of your pay determined by what your staff say and think about you?

However the appraisal is finally conducted, you should finish up with a clear evaluation of what has happened, a realistic pro-

> **MODEL 11.3** An appraisal report
>
> **Name:** Phran Tick
> **Post:** Personnel Manager
> **Length of service in post:** 2.5 years
> **Appraising manager:** Attila the Hun, Corporate Services Director
> **Date of agreement of final appraisal:** 1 June
>
> 1 Review of previous year's targets and performance
>
>   1.1 *Provision of effective personnel function to The Charity*
>   Under Phran's leadership, the department has improved on most performance indicators this year. Recruitment delays have been reduced by twenty per cent, all pay changes have been implemented within agreed timescales, and all but two grievance and disciplinary hearings have been advised by personnel staff. Feedback evaluation forms from line managers have shown a three per cent increase in satisfaction overall, although there were two examples of poor advice being offered to the shops manager, which resulted in overpayments of wages.
>
>   1.2 *Introduction of new pension scheme with a target take-up of fifty per cent*
>   The details of the new scheme were successfully developed and agreed by the trustees, and widespread publicity was provided, with a series of successful staff meetings. To date, the take-up rate has been thirty-seven per cent of existing staff and sixty-nine per cent of new starters.
>
>   1.3 *Minimising role of trade union and move towards individual contracts*
>   Little progress has been made on this; the union continues to maintain a thirty per cent membership penetration and claims to represent all staff. Joint committees still take twenty per cent of the postholder's time to service, and the pay round was again determined through this process. All new starters are on individual terms and conditions, but a majority of them have joined the union.
>
>   1.4 *Comprehensive review of pay and benefits*
>   First stage of gathering and consolidating data completed, but

gramme of action for the coming year and a shopping list of resources needed to achieve that programme. An example of such an appraisal report is set out above.

Linking performance to pay and benefits

I have, I hope, guided you away from linking appraisal assessment directly to reward, on the argument that if staff are concerned about their pay levels, they are less likely to be honest and open about their successes and failures, and are likely to play safe. Indeed, there is an increasing body of evidence, particularly in

no firm proposals for progress yet developed.

2 Reasons for level of performance

Resignation of personnel officer and subsequent freezing of post to fund savings meant that the postholder spent more time on operational matters, bringing her experience at that level to bear on departmental performance. However, this also meant that she was not able to undertake a more strategic role.

A limited wage settlement meant considerable discontent amongst staff group, particularly new starters, with consequent strengthening of pro union feeling. Postholder still not personally convinced of advantages of seeking to cut union out of processes.

Occasional mistakes in advice arose from lack of training of a personnel assistant, who has now been coached to a better understanding.

3 Overall assessment

Generally a very successful year at operational level, but insufficient attention paid to strategic issues. Phran is working well at the practitioner level, demonstrating all the necessary competencies to deliver an efficient reactive personnel service, but as yet lacks the full range of skills to be able to demonstrate success at senior managerial level.

4 Key objectives for next year

Maintain quality of operational performance of Personnel Department.

Complete review of service conditions, introduce menu-based approach, secure seventy-five per cent of existing staff on to individual contracts.

Review strategy towards union, confirm charity policy, and implement.

Push pension scheme membership to seventy per cent of all staff.

5 Resources and training

Postholder to undertake 1P13 Strategic Personnel Management course on evening class basis to assist development to full personnel manager role.

Personnel officer post to be filled to release postholder to more strategic duties.

Identify and introduce recruitment management software package.

---

the voluntary sector where outputs are often difficult to relate directly to effort, but also even in the commercial world where performance is measured by bottom-line profit, that PRP, especially when badly designed and run, does not have a motivating effect. Rather, it tends to encourage conservative and safety first approaches to work, apart from those fairly rare high risk-takers, who are probably already successful. Contrary to popular belief, PRP does not seem, in the longer term, to encourage innovation.

Nevertheless, it is becoming increasingly popular in the voluntary sector, which has a habit of following what has been tried ten years before in the private sector. The fact that some private companies are now abandoning their PRP schemes seems to have passed charity trustees by, although to be fair, for every commercial organisation that gives up on it, another reviews and improves its scheme, and a third launches a new one. As any discussion about PRP must of course be linked in with consideration of salary policies generally, a more detailed discussion of the pros and cons and practicalities of operating such a scheme is given in chapter 7. For now, if you feel that PRP may a useful motivational and staff development tool for you, then the following pointers may be of assistance in determining your charity's policy.

Checklist 11.1   Performance related pay

- ☑ Which posts will the scheme apply to, and which not? If there are staff who do not have access to the chance to earn a supplement to their salary, how will you deal with any resentment that arises?

- ☑ How will you devise measures of performance that are acceptable to the staff affected? It's all very well to propose that you base the scheme only on objective statistics, but in most jobs these are only a small part of performance – quality as opposed to quantity is far more difficult to evaluate.

- ☑ How can you be sure that the end product really is the result of the efforts of the person earning the PRP bonus? For example, if the fundraising income goes up, do you give all the reward to the fundraising officer, or do other staff who have supported him, and perhaps have learnt from him how to improve their own, less direct efforts, get a bonus as well?

- ☑ What proportion of total earnings should be available for PRP? The higher the figure, the more precarious the scheme and its effect on your finances; the lower the figure, the less PRP may work as an incentive. Received wisdom seems to suggest a figure of between ten and twenty per cent, but this does vary enormously and arguments continue to rage about it.

- ☑ What safeguards can you build in against what may, reasonably or unreasonably, be perceived as managerial whim in the awarding of bonuses? Are there effective review mechanisms and appeal processes?

- ☑ How do you avoid building in a reward from one year into a base salary for the next? Many schemes make the mistake of ratcheting up overall salary levels because of good performances one year, offering what is in effect an increment for all time, even when the performance in subsequent years falls off. You should seek to keep PRP payments entirely separate from basic salary (even, I would suggest, from cost-of-living awards), or you will institutionalise them.

☑ What do you do if you find the scheme isn't providing the desired results? Unless you have a regular and rigorous review mechanism, you may find yourself paying for something you don't get.

In summary ...

- Getting staff more deeply involved in planning their work and controlling their environment is one of the best motivators to improved performance. They want to see an improved service to your charity's clients, so work with them on how their efforts can best be channelled to that end.
- Setting individual performance targets should be a process that is jointly owned by the organisation and the individual, considering each aspect of the job, and should take account of all the relevant factors. It needs to be based on current and potential ability and knowledge and how this can be enhanced.
- Targets and measures can be just as much about judgements of quality as about measurable statistics, but there has to be trust and confidence within your charity for such measures to be acceptable.
- It is always better to accentuate the positive, but charity managers should never shirk from tackling the negative aspects of performance. Unfortunately, they all too often do, but the skills of positive criticism are a major asset to any staff team.
- Supervision is about far more than correcting mistakes – it is about being constantly available to offer advice, counsel and encouragement, leading to greater self-reliance and enhancement of overall ability. Regular contact between managers and staff improves everyone's performance and commitment to the charity.
- Formal appraisal offers a framework for a more strategic review of performance, an opportunity to build on strengths, work on weaknesses and set objectives that fit in with the needs of the charity. Appraisal properly prepared for and conducted can be an extremely enriching experience.
- Relating performance to pay can be a very tricky business, and is particularly problematical in many parts of the voluntary sector. Nevertheless, there are ways of making it more likely to work, but the sensible charity will plan very carefully before introducing any radical scheme.

CHAPTER 12

Taking the tough decisions

INTRODUCTION

So far, virtually all of this book has been about working towards and achieving success in the management of your charity through the management of your staff. I have assumed that, on the whole, things have gone smoothly, that you have been able to plan where you want to be and how you will get there, and that you have processes in place that enable you to avoid being diverted from the task in hand.

But unfortunately, it's not always quite like that. Already you will have seen models of how to deal with employee misconduct or under-achievement. There's a lot more that can go wrong, and charity managers responsible for staff will from time to time have some pretty tough decisions to take – whether these are about defending an Employment Tribunal application, facing up to industrial action or making staff redundant. This chapter looks at these tough decisions and provides guidance and advice about how to approach some of the less pleasant aspects of managing staff.

We don't all see things the same way

Personnel people are often accused of being soft. Managers who are trying to achieve organisational objectives sometimes feel that the personnel department is taking the side of the staff against them. Put aside the argument that there shouldn't be sides: in virtually every organisation, including most charities, the staff will at the very least have a difference of emphasis – differing priorities – from those held by senior managers and trustees. In some cases, they will be diametrically opposed. In these circumstances, it is understandable, albeit erroneous, if a line manager becomes resentful when a personnel specialist urges caution. The point is to understand that 'the staff wouldn't accept that, why don't you do this instead' is not agreeing with the staff, it is understanding their viewpoint in an attempt to accommodate it within the charity's overall objectives. If a personnel manager counsels caution, it is because she is concerned that those objectives may not be achieved if management persists with its plans.

Personnel management is about making sure that the people in a charity and their skills are deployed in the most effective way, and the key responsibility of any manager undertaking personnel management duties is clear: to consider the balance between your charity's needs and the rights and legitimate expectations of the staff, particularly when, as in the voluntary sector, these very often include some aspect of sharing organisational goals; but then ultimately work on the premise that the charity and its needs are bigger than the staff and theirs, and put the charity first.

Reasonableness

Of course you might, even then, act completely unreasonably, with the likely result that you have generated serious difficulties for your charity and yourself. That can hardly be considered as putting the charity's needs first. That is very much a matter of judgement, and what might be reasonable in one charity could be seen as outrageous in another, and what worked last year may become unacceptable next year. Thus reasonableness has to be judged in context, and this is generally recognised in British law – there are very few hard and fast rules, let alone guidelines, as to when an action will be judged unreasonable.

Actually breaking the law, or failing to follow it, will generally be considered unreasonable. Not following the rules of natural justice, as they are applied in the employment context, may have a similar result. But, besides codes of practice, such as the ACAS one on handling employee misconduct, and some references in the legislation to actions that are automatically unfair, most of what is judged reasonable is determined by a consideration of the facts, against a few benchmarks that have been laid down by the judges in decisions setting precedent, particularly over the past twenty years or so. You should note, in passing, that whilst Employment Tribunals are supposed to consider precedent, there is sometimes no absolute obligation on them to do so; they can determine their own procedures in order to make sense of an issue before them and to enable them to draw upon the industrial lay experience of their members, but as a result, they do not set binding precedents themselves, that is left to the higher courts.

So finding yourself in an Employment Tribunal can be something of a lottery. You can significantly improve your chances of demonstrating that you have acted reasonably, both in the Tribunal and generally, if:

- You treat all staff the same, and have the statistics to prove it (if you must, you can be an absolute swine of a manager, as long as you are a swine to everyone).
- You allow staff to exhaust procedures available to them before you take action (unless to do so would make absolutely no difference to the outcome).
- You can show clearly that the action you have taken was necessary to defend the vital interests of your charity, to the point that what would normally have been reasonable no longer is – even then, you may lose, but at least the Tribunal may be understanding.

Tests of reasonableness can become quite complex, and as well as varying between situations, different Tribunals can come up with different decisions on the same set of facts. What they can't (or shouldn't) do is to substitute their decision for yours – they may not like what you have done, but provided it does not fall outside the (rather wide) band of what a reasonable employer might be expected to do, in all the circumstances, then you are probably safe. It's erroneous Tribunal decisions that err beyond these parameters and substitute their own decisions for those of employers that are probably the largest single cause of appeals against their judgments to the Employment Appeal Tribunal (EAT). But before you conclude that you don't have to worry too much because the EAT will look after you, remember that it's expensive to appeal, you can only do so on a point of law (either that the Tribunal misdirected itself or misapplied the current state of the law), and that it's better to construct an effective defence at the Tribunal in the first place, based upon expert and objective advice. And where do you get that advice? Either from specialist employment lawyers (expensive) or from those poor old maligned personnel managers.

Grasping the nettle

From the above, you might be tempted into not taking action in difficult circumstances, even though you think that an employee deserves it. Certainly, some employers, particularly in the public sector and the more 'right on' parts of the voluntary sector, have fought shy of some cases, and either failed to take any action at all, or took entirely inappropriate action, buying off or promoting crooks and underachievers. One local authority I know, sick of that approach over the years, toughened up and found itself facing countless Employment Tribunals for unfair dismissal and race discrimination claims. Because they had introduced new guidelines and procedures and publicised them widely, and because none of the staff could reasonably (there's that word again) argue that they didn't know what was expected of them, they won ninety-five per cent of the cases against them (the average is only fifty per cent). The point is that they were prepared to grasp the nettle, and for several reasons:

- If they didn't take all cases seriously, they ran the risk of being accused of taking some more seriously than others, which was but a short step to the accusation that they were informally discriminating.
- Staff who were working hard and well would become quickly demotivated if they saw others 'get away with it'.
- If they tolerated certain misconduct, they would have made it all the more difficult to address similar misconduct by others later.
- If they failed to deal with poor performance, the individuals concerned would not be aware (or would avoid the truth of being aware) that a better standard was expected, and carry on in their same old ways. This would have made it that much more difficult for their next manager to deal with them (which of us has not complained about inheriting a poor employee?).

Whilst these points relate primarily to dealing with individual cases, the same is true in collective situations. If a group of staff underperforms or misbehaves, or if they make unreasonable demands, then if management fails to respond positively, to protect the charity's overall interests, then their job the next time round will be that much harder. However tempting it may be, no manager can afford to avoid the difficult decisions, and in the end neither the charity itself, nor the other staff who are affected by the approach of a minority, will thank her for the cowardice. The decision may be, in the greater good, not to act; but if it is, it will at least have been taken in the light of all the circumstances and this rather more structured evaluation process than would otherwise have been the case.

A procedure a day keeps your troubles away?

Well, not quite. If you go too far, you'll be accused of being too bureaucratic, and probably with good reason. But when it comes to dealing with difficult situations, particularly when they relate to individual employees, there's a lot to be said for having procedures in place beforehand.

That way, a manager cannot justifiably be accused of treating one employee in a different way from another and, especially if you are using a procedure that has generally been agreed, perhaps with the employee's trade union, and then widely understood, everyone knows what is happening, the likely outcome, and how it will be determined. It's much easier to respond to 'Why are you doing this to me?' with 'It's part of the procedure, how we've agreed round here to deal with such matters, and I'll explain the steps to you' than with 'Well, I think that's how we need to handle it on this occasion'.

Of course, you will still need to apply your judgement to avoid miscarriages of (natural) justice and ensure that neither you nor the charity looks ridiculous by myopically applying something that just does not fit, but any major departures from the set procedure should be agreed in advance, be explained and be defensible. It often comes back to the test of reasonableness.

Even the law recognises the usefulness of some procedures, by making it a requirement that your disciplinary and grievance procedures should be spelt out in the employee's statement of particulars, where they exist (and drops a pretty heavy hint that they should do so). If the minimalist approach of British law insists on that, this is a strong argument in itself that a proceduralist approach is a welcome one, within a managerial framework, and I would suggest that as well as the basic set of disciplinary and grievance arrangements, your charity would also benefit from the following, most of which address questions of dealing with difficult situations of individual employees:

- Capability procedure.
- Appraisal procedure.
- Sickness management policy and process.
- Redundancy procedure.

As well as these I suggest a whole raft of procedures and work instructions designed to reflect your charity's objectives and how staff can most effectively be deployed to meet them, such as a telephone answering policy, financial regulations, security arrangements, care monitoring and so on. As all of these are more about the management of the charity through its staff rather than about staff management *per se* they are not covered further in this book, but are nevertheless vital components in the armoury of any manager with staff responsibility.

From the above list, the procedures dealing with individual employees – discipline, grievance, capability, appraisal and sickness – have already been covered in some detail elsewhere (see chapters 4 and 11). The one exception is redundancy, which is a difficult but perhaps inevitable aspect of the rapidly changing face of the voluntary sector.

Redundancy

There can be a whole range of causes for redundancy, most of which are outside the control of either a charity or its staff. You may be faced with dropping income, so can't afford to employ so many staff. Your service users' needs may change, so that what the staff have been doing is no longer required, and they may not have the skills to do something else. With the ever-increasing reliance on community care and similar contracts for charity income, voluntary sector organisations are finding more and more that their funders are seeking to dictate what services are to be provided, and how, with the inevitable impact that has on staffing matters. Or your trustees may decide that the charity should change direction, or even cease operating.

In every one of these scenarios you are likely, as a charity manager, to be faced with the problem of too many staff chasing too small a pool of funds for salaries, and/or a range of very square pegs to fit into very round holes. And the implicit presumption in law is that you will seek to avoid making redundancies, so you do need to consider carefully how you will manage your way out of this situation.

Obviously, the earlier you recognise that you have a problem, the greater are the chances of identifying an acceptable outcome. It is for this reason that the law requires any employer to give notice (to the Department for Education and Employment, and if you have one to a recognised trade union – this is likely soon to be to all staff) of impending redundancies, when these amount to significant numbers. If the number of staff likely to be affected is between twenty and ninety-nine, you need to give one month's notice; a hundred or over, three months'.

The clock starts counting backwards from when you actually intend to declare that individual employees are redundant, and from that point they are entitled to notice, the length of which is likely to depend on the length of their service, as well as any agreed redundancy payment. So, for example, if you know that a local authority grant will run out at the end of March, and that this will remove the funding for fifteen staff, some of whom have been employed for eight years, you need to give notice of impending redundancy on about 1 January at the latest, to allow one month to consult about it and, if you cannot find a solution, eight weeks' notice.

You may have heard about private sector management who close the factory on Friday and tell everyone that they're redundant from Monday. Yes, it's appalling practice, but they normally get away with it by giving staff lump sum payments in lieu of notice, added to the (usually) statutory minimum redundancy entitlement. But there is a lesson for charities here: rather than have your redundant staff leave at different times because of their differing notice entitlements, you may be able to agree with everyone a single date for closure, once you have exhausted the redundancy consultation process, at which point they all get pay in lieu plus a redundancy lump sum, all of which is usually not taxable – a small added compensation for a job loss.

But before you get there, you are expected to try to find alternatives to redundancy – unless of course, the staff involved really aren't interested. You may have frozen vacancies elsewhere in your charity, and then set up systems to measure staff's suitability to be slotted into them; you can consider appropriate and reasonable levels of training to enable them to do so; you may consider restructuring your finances and salary costs, for example, cutting back on overtime and other peripheral benefits, or even absolute salary levels, as an alternative to job losses; you may be able to identify alternative sources of funding, or find another charity willing to take on the staff and the service they provide (in which case, TUPE – see chapter 3 – will almost certainly apply). In all these endeavours, it is crucial to seek the views of the staff involved; they will have strong feelings about the situation, but they may also have very useful ideas about a way out of the problem, and often will suggest short-term sacrifices to retain longer-term jobs.

Whilst staff are under formal notice of redundancy (and, I would argue, it is appropriate as soon as any possibility of redundancy is mooted), they are entitled to reasonable time off with pay to seek alternative employment. And if you are able to offer another job within your charity or in an associated organisation, they are entitled to a reasonable trial period; if it doesn't work out, and they have to leave after all, they are still entitled to a redundancy payment. On the other hand, if an employee refuses the offer of a reasonable alternative job, he will probably lose any entitlement to redundancy pay on dismissal.

All this sounds rather reactive, which it inevitably is. Employers, even in the voluntary sector, do not as a rule take on staff in the expectation that they will be made redundant later – at some level or other, the need for redundancy comes as a shock to everyone. When that shock does arrive, it is not normally the best time to be arguing about how the details of the redundancy should be handled. Far better that you have in place a redundancy policy beforehand, so that if and when the inevitable happens, everyone knows what will happen and is aware of their entitlements, and that they have been treated no differently from other earlier groups of employees in similar circumstances. A redundancy policy is offered in model 12.1.

This model policy draws out several matters that you will need to consider or be aware of.

> **MODEL 12.1 Redundancy policy**
>
> 1. *The XYZ Charity* seeks to avoid redundancy amongst its staff, whether this be compulsory or voluntary. However, in the event of its ceasing or expecting to cease to provide services, in whole or in part, or where there is a need to reorganise staffing arrangements that cannot be fully met by redeployment and retraining, it has adopted the following redundancy procedure.
>
> 2. *The XYZ Charity* will fully consult with staff in accordance with its legal obligations, and will seek to give at least thirty calendar days' notice of any intention to declare redundancies. Any proposals for selection for redundancy will be based only on suitability or otherwise for remaining and new posts.
>
> 3. As soon as practicable after giving general notice of redundancy, *the XYZ Charity* will publish detailed proposals of changes, the timetable for implementation, the reasons for changes and the staff affected, including, as a first preference wherever possible, redeployment and retraining proposals and how staff will be selected for these. Staff, either individually or collectively, will be invited to submit alternative proposals.
>
> 4. Following this period of consultation, the director will submit final proposals to the management committee for consideration and implementation.
>
> 5. Formal notice of redundancy will then be served as appropriate. Any member of staff then facing redundancy shall be entitled to reasonable time off with pay to seek alternative employment. Any employee offered redeployment who refuses such an offer shall not be entitled to redundancy pay.
>
> 6. Staff under notice of termination of employment as a result of redundancy shall be entitled to a notice period determined by their contract. *The XYZ Charity* reserves the right to make a payment in lieu of notice.
>
> 7. In addition staff will, subject to funds being available, be entitled to the following lump sum redundancy payments. These payments will not be capped by the prevailing redundancy payment calculator statutory limit.
>
> | Length of service* | Weeks' pay |
> |---|---|
> | Up to 6 months | 0 |
> | 6 months up to 2 years | 2 |
> | 2 years up to 3 years | 4 |
> | 3 years up to 4 years | 5 |
> | 4 years up to 5 years | 6 |
> | each additional full year thereafter | 2 in addition |
>
> *As at anticipated last day of service.

Selection method

Although the model policy indicates that this will be determined separately on each occasion, you may prefer to agree one in advance. The more common are:

- *Last In, First Out* (LIFO), which minimises redundancy costs, but may lose some of your younger and more committed staff, as

well as undoing the results of any positive action programmes you may have been running.
- *First In, First Out* (FIFO), which is expensive, but in general encourages older staff to go – you can lose valuable experience this way.
- Through *volunteering* (with or without a management veto), which can be the most comfortable route for everyone, but may not enable you to end up with the actual staff team you want.
- Through *identification by management* of the least useful employees for future operation.

Consultation period

The model assumes that you will consult at least a month in advance, however many staff are involved. You don't need to do so if it is only a handful, but as a matter of good practice you may well wish to commit yourself to doing so; and if you are unfortunate enough to be facing a hundred or more job losses, you need to plan and consult much earlier.

Redundancy payment formula

There is a complicated formula to determine how much statutory redundancy pay your employees are entitled to, based on age and length of service (nobody with under two years' service has a statutory right to anything), multiplied by a limit determined by the government, which at 2001 prices relates to an annual salary not much more than £12,000. Many charities therefore ignore this and make payments related to actual salary levels rather than the capping level, which in most cases more than discharges their statutory responsibilities. The arrangements shown in the model are certainly more generous in respect of both the formula and accessibility to the scheme, even for older staff, who are entitled to one and a half statutory weeks' for each completed year of service.

If you want to know the exact statutory entitlement for each employee in every circumstance, in order to keep your payments to the legal minimum, the government publishes a useful table that sets all this out. And remember – however sympathetic you may be to staff facing the trauma of losing their jobs through no fault of their own, your first obligation – especially if you are a trustee – is towards the well-being of the charity as a whole, as the case study on pages 238–239 shows.

Outplacement and career management

Many employers are concerned that their responsibilities towards people whom they have had to make redundant should not stop the moment that the unpleasant decision has been made, or even after they have left their employ. If these people are going to be cast out through no fault of their own, then the least the employer can do is to help them find another job. Such sentiments sit well with the caring ethos of the voluntary sector, and even to some extent in the public sector, but interestingly it has been in the commercial world where, until recently, most practical steps have been taken to support employees and former employees facing the major trauma of job loss.

People no longer have jobs for life. If this was ever true, it certainly is not now, and the public and voluntary sectors are no exception: life and the world of work are changing rapidly, and the very nature of employment is undertaking a fundamental shift towards job mobility, role flexibility and multiple working – in short, people are developing portfolio careers. For them to succeed in this approach, they need job hunting and self-marketing skills more than ever before.

This is where career management comes in. Once known as outplacement counselling, reflecting the kind of assistance that employers would purchase on behalf of the staff they were 'letting go', a more pro-active and positive approach is now being developed. This recognises that individuals will need to control their own destinies, make their own luck and be prepared to move around in the course of their working lives, and that they will therefore actively manage their own careers rather than be developed and promoted within a more paternalistic framework.

With the increasing uncertainty of the workplace, staff do need something to substitute for job security. Whilst no employer can nowadays offer the kind of reassurance of twenty years ago, an indication that you do care about the futures of people who may only transitorily be your employees can go some way towards replacing it. Making career management support an additional employee benefit can seem attractive and, like sorting out redundancy arrangements, it is generally better to have a system in place before the crunch comes. You may feel, if you are a large enough organisation, that you want to provide such a service in-house and develop the specialist skills necessary. However, this often does not work very well, particularly if career counselling is offered by the personnel department – how many staff are going to feel confident in the support being given them by the very people they perceive as having told them they are not good enough to stay and have just given them the sack? An external provider of career management advice may well be a much better proposition.

There are many career counselling organisations although, since this service grew up almost exclusively in the private sector, their products tend to be heavily oriented towards supporting

CASE STUDY 12.1 Facing up to redundancy

A campaigning charity concerned with responsibility in the workplace had a precarious funding stream, largely dependent on donations from trades unions and radical employment lawyers. In order to practise what it preached, it encouraged all sixteen of its staff to join a union, and the management committee encouraged the director to negotiate generous hours and salary rates for them. The director also agreed with the union, and incorporated into individuals' employment contracts a redundancy package that far exceeded the charity's statutory obligations, comprising a commitment to no compulsory redundancy but a guarantee of redeployment, voluntary redundancy payments including three weeks' pay for every year or part year of service, not capped at the statutory limit, plus the right to pay in lieu of notice, full consultation periods based on the statutory obligations of much larger employers, and outplacement counselling worth up to £10,000 per employee.

As a result of some serious adverse publicity surrounding the mismanagement of funds by the treasurer, many key funders withdrew their support and income was severely depleted. It rapidly became clear that redundancies would be needed. The director asked for volunteers, but nobody came forward, as all the staff enjoyed their work and their conditions and did not want to carry the can for the treasurer's misdeeds. There was nowhere else for staff to be redeployed.

The charity had a small reserve that had been earmarked for parliamentary lobbying following a legacy from one of its founders. In order to meet its contractual obligations on redundancy, the charity was about to use these restricted funds when the Charity Commission got wind of it and advised strongly against it. With no other course open to her, the director declared half the staff redundant without going through the agreed three month consultation period and made statutory minimum payments to them and gave them their notice pay tax free in lieu of working their time out.

The staff took the charity to court in a blaze of publicity to enforce their employment contracts. It was ruled that the charity should make the enhanced redundancy payments and pay for the outplacement counselling, as well as give

---

commercial executives. There are few that offer support to lower-graded staff, and fewer still that understand the rather different ethos of the voluntary and public sectors. If you do decide that you want to offer your staff a benefit of this kind, you may wish to consider the following pointers:

Checklist 12.1 Using career counsellors

- ☑ What is the background of the counsellors who would be offering support to your staff? Do they understand the culture of the sector, and can they offer strategies for bridging the divide into other

them employment for the agreed three month period reserved for consultation. This amounted in all to about £150,000, far more than the charity had available, and rather than trade whilst insolvent, the management committee decided to close the organisation down. As individual trustees, they remained liable for the debts; the work of the charity was set back a generation by the image of incompetence and duplicity that emerged. To cap it all, the Inland Revenue declared that contractual payments could not be tax free, so the payments in lieu of notice were grossed up and the charity as employer faced another huge bill.

Two dissenting trustees, determined to start again, started to build up a new campaigning body and slowly took on staff; this time, they were more cautious about redundancy agreements. They had learnt some valuable lessons:

- Don't incorporate redundancy policies into employment contracts – they should be guidelines, not absolute obligations.
- Be realistic about what can be achieved, particularly over redeployment within small organisations, or a redundancy agreement will not be worth the paper it's written on.
- Don't promise what you can't deliver; lifting the cap on payment levels may well be reasonable, offering a huge multiplier may not; so be realistic about constructing your policies in light of what is reasonable for your organisation.
- Don't allow your personal beliefs to cloud your managerial judgement, and work with unions to reach a pragmatic solution rather than an unattainable ideal.
- Ensure that staff are involved in consultation from the outset, but don't allow that consultation to prevent you making managerial decisions when you have to.
- Don't offer huge sums to cover the cost of outplacement: there are far more effective and economical ways of doing it, and you can always negotiate the details with individuals as appropriate.
- Don't make payment in lieu a contractual right, or you may face extra tax demands; but do reserve the right to impose it if appropriate.

sectors, particularly the commercial world where traditionally charity workers have been viewed with suspicion?

- ☑ Can they offer programmes that are useful to more junior staff as well as to your senior executives?
- ☑ How flexible are these programmes? Are they genuinely modular, or are you in effect offered a customised off-the-shelf course? Are they prepared to offer an initial session where individual needs can be assessed and a programme constructed around them?
- ☑ Are their fees reasonable? Some private sector employers may think nothing of paying £10,000 or more for an executive programme; most eyebrows in the voluntary sector would be raised at that kind

of figure. A more reasonable figure for charities could be anywhere from £2,000 to £5,000, depending on the seniority of the staff involved, the current state of their marketability and the complexity of the agreed programme. Anything more and you will be paying for the outplacement organisation's deep-pile carpets.

Responding to complaints – Employment Tribunals and sacking fairly

However well you handle problems with staff, whether these arise from misconduct, incapability, redundancy or allegations of discrimination, their perspective on what has happened will almost invariably be different from yours. However much you try to sweeten the pill, they may well still feel aggrieved. If that feeling is strong enough, they may complain to an Employment Tribunal that their dismissal has been unfair, that they have been unfairly selected for redundancy (or that redundancy was not the real reason for the dismissal) or that they have been unfairly treated in comparison with another person of a different race or sex. They may also complain about a few other matters, mainly breaches of the Employment Rights Act or a failure to give a statement of particulars, but such complaints are rare and should not arise if you have been following good employment practices. If you get a notice that an applicant or one of your employees (or ex-employees) has made an application for a Tribunal to consider her complaint – and it will come in the shape of a Form ITI – there are three golden rules:

1 Don't panic.
2 Respond quickly.
3 Seek professional advice.

Many Tribunal applications are put in to test the waters – the employee concerned usually has nothing to lose. So if you are sure of your ground – and if you have followed the advice in this book about treating your employees fairly, you should be – then view the matter phlegmatically, and take it on board as just another rather annoying aspect of managing properly. But you do need to respond promptly. Unless you send your answer (on the Form IT3 which the Tribunal will supply) back within two weeks, you lose the chance to defend yourself if and when the case comes to trial. And because the processes have a whole load of pitfalls for the unwary, and in a book of this nature I cannot possibly include all of them, you may well feel more confident if you at least get support from a solicitor or personnel specialist in defending your case.

The first thing to satisfy yourself about is whether the applicant has the right to submit a claim. Check whether:

- She is in fact an employee or ex-employee, or is self-employed.
- The application is submitted within three months of the date of the alleged act about which the complaint has been made (usually a dismissal or an act of discrimination).
- If a complaint of unfair dismissal, that the employee has been continuously employed by you for at least two years (this time limit is currently under scrutiny).

If the application fails on one of these tests, then in most cases you should be able to get it dismissed without a full hearing, as long as you request that it be put before a Chairman of Tribunals for determination at a preliminary hearing. But you still need to put in your preliminary response within the two-week time limit, accompanied by your request for a preliminary hearing.

That response should be kept to the bare facts – you can always add information later. Give the details the form asks for (whether the person was employed by you, and if so when; whether there was a dismissal, and if so, why; what the salary and other remuneration details were) and your grounds for resisting the application (for example: 'the applicant was dismissed after only nine months with us, so does not have sufficient service to qualify her to apply to the Tribunal'; 'the applicant was summarily dismissed, following due process, having been discovered stealing from a client'; 'the applicant has been treated no differently from other staff in similar circumstances, so the question of discrimination does not arise'). Whatever you say, keep it succinct.

Sooner or later (usually later), you will learn whether the case will be taken before a preliminary hearing or will go to a full Employment Tribunal hearing. Either way, the process can be quite complex, and I would not advise any manager to expect to take the case themselves without a lot of prior training. It is at this point that you really do need external assistance, particularly if the case looks like getting at all complicated, as discrimination allegations always do, and as many cases which turn on a point of law, rather than the pure interpretation of reasonableness according to the facts, often threaten to do. You will need impartial assistance and advice during the following stages:

- Evaluating what the basis of the complaint is, and identifying what the real underlying issue may be.
- Taking witness statements and assembling proofs of evidence in preparation for examination and cross-examination before the Tribunal.
- Preparing bundles of evidence to support your case.
- Planning the presentation of that case, structuring where witnesses fit in to the presentation so that your story can be told

with clarity, both through their own oral evidence and in relation to any documentary evidence you have submitted.
- Developing an understanding of Tribunal procedure and the presentational skills for arguing your case effectively before a Tribunal, which comprises a qualified lawyer in the chair and highly experienced representatives of both employer and employee organisations, all of whom may well be sympathetic towards a poor applicant who is up against the might of a big organisation like yours.

If you do decide to do it yourself, then the very least that you should do is to learn inside out the booklet on Tribunal procedure that you should be given by the Tribunal office, and then go to watch other cases in action.

However you decide to defend your case, you will need to be aware that it can and almost certainly will be expensive. There will be a vast amount of management time taken up in preparing all the aspects of your defence; there is always a great deal of sitting around at the Tribunal waiting for your case to come on, or for your witnesses to be called (and if you don't call them they can be subpoenaed); and usually an even longer delay before you hear the result. A typical unfair dismissal case may take at least ten to twenty management days to prepare, five days in court, and up to three months for the verdict to be handed down. Discrimination cases may well take much longer. You have to ask yourself – is it worth tying up all your resources in that way, or would you do better having someone else handle the case for you? Or even, is it worth defending the case at all?

For make no mistake. In Employment Tribunals, employers never come out the winners. Even if you succeed in getting the case completely thrown out, you will still have spent enormous amounts of energy and probably advisers' fees, costs which normally are not recoverable. And if you lose, the penalties can be quite high: basic unfair dismissal awards that can be up to about £7,000 (for an older employee with long service), plus compensatory awards for loss of earnings that can be astronomical, unless they can be mitigated by the Tribunal concluding that the applicant was partly to blame for what happened. Discrimination awards, particularly on equal value claims, can often be even higher. It's no wonder that many employers decide to cut their losses and settle. However much you know that you are in the right, might it not be a better use of charitable funds for you to swallow your pride and pay the applicant a smaller amount to go away – provided that you can maintain your integrity in doing so?

A final point. Even if you do go to a Tribunal, and even if you do win, it may not stop there. Either side can appeal on a point of law to the Employment Appeal Tribunal – and some points of law can be pretty specious. That's when it starts to get really expensive.

External assistance and settling cases

On the basis that most reasonable people will wish to settle their differences in an amicable and confidential manner rather than in open court, all the rules relating to the operation of Employment Tribunals encourage the involvement of the Arbitration, Conciliation and Advisory Service (ACAS). Every time an application is submitted to the Tribunal, an ACAS officer will contact both sides and offer to broker a settlement. This can often be an attractive proposition to an employer as a way of reducing both financial cost and time and effort, but it does depend on both sides being willing to follow this route; aggrieved employees who want their day in court may be less easy to persuade, unless the ACAS officer (and they all have vast industrial and Tribunal experience) can persuade the applicant that this offers the only realistic way of getting anything.

Of the 100,000 or so cases that come before the Tribunal each year, about half are settled this way, either at the outset or nearer the trial date – some even during the Employment Tribunal hearing. Of those that do proceed to full trial, employers win something over fifty per cent, but the odds are still not so good as to provide for any complacency. Employers with good procedures and a fair approach to personnel management do rather better (it is the smaller, sweatshop types of organisation that drag the employer success statistics down); but equally, many of them, particularly in the public and voluntary sectors, seem to be more vulnerable to discrimination claims, precisely because by being good employers they have set higher standards for themselves and raised expectations of their staff, thus making themselves easier targets. What critical commentators (usually with an external political agenda) fail to mention is that such employers also have a good track record in defending such claims – partly because they get so indignant that anyone could suggest that they have discriminated. On the other hand, you may equally feel in such circumstances that you would not want even spurious allegations aired in public, and will settle quietly.

Settlements through the ACAS process – with a formal agreement signed by both parties on a COT3 form – are legally binding, and remove any further rights to submit claims to a Tribunal in respect of that complaint. They will tend to involve the payment of a sum of money (usually less than the applicant could expect to be given by a Tribunal if she won, and certainly less than it would cost you if you defended the case and lost) in return for a withdrawal of allegations and no acknowledgement of culpability on either side.

ACAS has traditionally been independent, so has been able to broker such deals. Agreements can also be reached between the parties, without the support of ACAS, provided the (ex-)employee has the advice of an independent solicitor or other professionally recognised adviser. The settlement is then in the form of a Compromise Agreement, and this route is now being quite regularly chosen for settlements of disputes between trustees and chief executives and other senior staff. This way, the embarrassment of submitting and defending an Employment Tribunal application is avoided. Trustees, if they have any sense, will come out in the open to say that the executive has to go, and the executive will save her career by agreeing, through the independent third party process, the terms of her departure, public statements about it and usually an agreed reference, all of which is binding on both parties.

ACAS is, of course, better publicly known for its role as a mediator in industrial disputes. In your charity, you will no doubt want to avoid confrontations on such a scale, but if you find yourself involved in one, then ACAS can be there to help you with that, too.

Responding to and dealing with industrial action

Industrial action in the voluntary sector may be less common that in other sectors, but it is not by any means unheard of – perhaps not so much over pay, but often about redundancies or fundamental changes in direction in organisations to which the staff taking the action have a passionate commitment. And strikes about points of principle are very often harder to resolve than those about more bread-and-butter issues.

Industrial action is not just about all-out strikes. In fact, it is very often about more subtle ways of exerting pressure, ways that minimise loss of income to the employee whilst creating maximum difficulty for the employer. Increasingly, we are witnessing carefully timed one-day strikes (where these can affect key days of the employer's business, whilst at the same time coinciding with tax pay periods so that tax rebates or reductions in tax take virtually compensate for the loss of pay when on strike); overtime bans; selective working; and refusal to carry out certain duties. In fact, in law industrial action is anything in breach of the contract of employment, so whilst an all-out strike can be obviously recognised as such a breach, if there is no contractual obligation to work overtime, the position is less clear, and whether the selection of only certain duties is in breach has to be left open to tests of reasonableness. Perhaps a rule of thumb could be: if it is intended to coerce the employer into doing something he would not otherwise want to do, it is industrial action (although that definition may not always stand up in the courts).

What is clear in the law now is that there is no immunity for trades unions (or for anyone else, for that matter) if they seek to encourage an employee to break his contract of employment, unless certain stringent conditions are met. Most unions, and non-unionised groups of employees, nowadays do seek to act responsibly before they encourage their members and fellow employees to take industrial action and abide by the various laws on such action:

- They must conduct a postal ballot of all members likely to be called upon to take industrial action, setting out clearly what action is contemplated (even if it is short of strike action) and over what period, only calling action if a majority voting approves.
- There must be a period of at least a week between the decision to take industrial action and its starting, the intention being to offer both sides a 'cooling off period' and attempt to resolve their differences. This period is currently the subject of political consideration as to whether it should be extended, and there are also proposals around to ban strikes altogether in essential public services, or to introduce either voluntary or mandatory binding arbitration. It is possible that this could apply to some key services being supplied on a contract basis by some charities.
- If requested, they must tell the employer the terms of the ballot and its result.
- If their mandate runs out, they must re-ballot before taking further action.
- If they take industrial action, they may only do so directly against the employer, and not against any of his suppliers or customers.
- Picketing at any workplace is confined to employees who normally work there, plus union officials; staff with no normal workplace may picket the head office; and the number of pickets must not be intimidatory (it is for the police to determine whether a breach of public order may occur).
- No punitive action may be taken by the union against any member who does not follow the call for industrial action.

Provided that the union (and this is taken to include all its officials, both lay and full-time) abides by these rules, their immunity against being sued remains in place, although in theory they can still fall foul of the laws of obstruction and public order.

But even if you are not faced with formal industrial action, you may well still have collective grievances to respond to and an unhappy workforce that will not be fully productive until you have sorted matters out. And do remember – if you support the idea that it is a charity's management's responsibility to manage all its assets, including its people – then it is also their responsibility to find solutions to industrial action. It is the union's responsibility to secure the best possible deal for its members, not to solve management's problems for them – although during the consultative and negotiation process they may well come up with positive ideas that will help towards this end.

Industrial unrest – a broader term that includes formal industrial action, but recognises that matters of concern can go rather wider than that – will be unique to every charity, in terms of causes, effects and solutions. There are no simple answers even to what may appear the most simple of problems, because usually unrest is symptomatic of a broader problem. It follows that there are no straightforward strategies that I can offer you as a charity manager to resolve your disputes; but I can give some pointers:

- If you are planning changes, try to be as open as possible about them. If you are secretive, it will probably leak out anyway, and may be utterly distorted by the time the staff affected hear about it. Communicate your message clearly.
- Make sure that whoever is leading the negotiations from the management side has a clear mandate on what they can discuss, what latitude they have in terms of shifting ground, and in what circumstances they should go back and to whom, to clarify a view or offer – before that view is expressed or offer made.
- Try to include those affected in as much decision-making that affects their working lives as possible. They may have ideas for ways forward that you had not thought of.
- If other parties are making what you consider to be outrageous or unacceptable demands, try to understand from their point of view why they are saying what they are.
- If you are negotiating towards a settlement, say of a dispute about pay rises or service conditions, don't put your final offer on the table until it is your final offer. The other side will not be expecting you to make such an offer up front, and if you do, they probably won't believe you – just as you won't believe they are really expecting to get that enormous pay rise. Always try to work out what their bottom line is – and keep yours close to your chest.
- Even in times of all-out industrial action, keep the lines of communication with your staff open – you need to have mechanisms such as your joint negotiating machinery to resolve the dispute and generally, the earlier it is resolved, the better it is for everyone (unless you're trying to save money by provoking a strike, that is!).

- Never denigrate the other side, however much you feel provoked. You have to live and work together afterwards. Rather, build on the positives, seek to reduce the negatives, and ensure that you get clarification about where the differences still lie.
- Throughout any dispute, maintain an effective communications system with all your staff, and beyond to your funders and service users. You should not rely on the union to get your message across – they have a different story to relay – but rather go direct to everyone with your side of the story.
- If you feel that you are getting deadlocked, consider asking for outside help. Sometimes a fresh view on a dispute can come up with surprisingly simple and novel solutions. Traditionally, ACAS has performed this role (although in the voluntary sector, some of the umbrella organisations might equally be prepared to offer you the benefit of their expertise). They can either conciliate (essentially, talking to both parties, reducing the differences and proposing compromises until they are close enough together to agree), or they can, with the agreement of both parties, arbitrate – both sides agree to let the experts go away to determine a resolution to which both sides are then committed.
- Although it is perfectly legitimate throughout a dispute for management to promote its message as vigorously as possible, conversely, once you have agreed settlement terms – and every dispute does come to an end – keep to the line, and work jointly with the union to secure support for those terms. Union negotiators will sometimes have an uphill job explaining to their members why they are recommending acceptance (especially if it's for less than they had hoped for, and sometimes even if the settlement is within the terms of their negotiating mandate), and it's against your interests to seem to be undermining them.

What is in your interests is for everyone to come out of a dispute – whether it is about an individual or the whole workforce – feeling that they have gained something, or at the very least, have minimised their losses to an acceptable level.

Going for win-win

And that, in essence, is the message of this chapter. You will inevitably be faced with many problems, many differences and difficulties, some of which may seem at the outset to be intractable. You may through economic necessity need to shed staff when the staff don't want to go; you may have to dispense with the services of long-standing employees because their skills no longer meet your requirements; you may find yourselves locked in dispute with your staff over pay rises or other issues close to their hearts.

You can take heart that, in the end, there are very few industrial problems that do not have a resolution. There may be some casualties along the way, and as a caring employer, you will seek to minimise those and their effect. And you should never be afraid of taking advice, of getting help from people who have been there before, who will help you see that light at the end of the tunnel. Believe me, it is usually a revealing and rewarding experience, and I have never known an industrial dispute yet in any charity where that light turned out to be an express train rushing towards and flattening you!

In summary ...

- Personnel management is about helping your charity to run smoothly through the best use of its human resources – which means that personnel managers deal with the exceptions to the rules just as much as with getting those rules right in the first place.
- Personnel managers are not a soft touch, nor do they take the employees' side – but they do have a critical role in counselling managers on the likely effect their actions will have on those employees.
- Actions of all managers will be judged, by both their staff and the courts, on the basis of their reasonableness in all the circumstances – and the more open the decision-making process, the easier it is to be effective under such scrutiny.
- Difficult issues should never be avoided, because of the demotivating effects of doing so have on other employees, and the greater difficulties you store up for your successor managers. Any decision to do nothing must be made consciously and as part of a broader strategic approach.
- Dealing with difficult issues through well-designed procedures can often draw the sting from what may otherwise be an unpleasant personal confrontation, and gives everyone confidence that they are being treated fairly.
- Redundancy can be a traumatic process, however it has been caused. Early consultation with everyone affected, and an agreement on how redundancy issues should be handled well in advance of its being needed, will greatly ease the pain.
- With the increasing insecurity of employment, staff will expect to move in and out of jobs far more frequently than used to be the case. They need to be equipped to do this, and outplacement and career management counselling can greatly assist.

- However hard you try, you cannot avoid being taken to an Employment Tribunal. You need to be well prepared, to see whether you can get applications knocked out before they start, and to consider securing professional support and advice.
- Many cases get settled before they are heard by the Tribunal. It may well be worth swallowing your pride and paying up now, to avoid greater expense later.
- Industrial action can take many forms, not just strikes. Although employees' room for such action is now greatly circumscribed, it is still possible, and you should ensure that everything is being run legally – but don't use the law in response unless you are sure you won't create a backlash.
- Think positively and strategically when dealing with industrial action – there will have to be a solution sometime, and you all have to live together afterwards.
- External help, such as from ACAS, can offer a fresh perspective and often solutions to apparently intractable problems.
- Always seek to find solutions to any difficult problems in which the maximum number of participants have the maximum ownership of the outcome.

CHAPTER 13

Managing volunteers

INTRODUCTION

For many small charities, the possibility of employing staff to carry out the organisation's work is a luxury that they simply cannot afford. For others, a few staff are employed to support and facilitate the main voluntary effort. Even many larger charities, employing many hundreds of staff, could not contemplate continuing the full scope of their work without the active contribution of their members, supporters and the volunteers. The National Trust, for example, depends upon its workforce of nearly 38,000 volunteers to keep its shops open, guide people around its properties and provide specialist professional advice on a whole range of events and activities, from conservation techniques to publications.

Volunteers are therefore a vital resource whatever the size of the organisation and, just like staff, they need to be managed in a way that recognises their value and ensures that they are able to play a full part in the success of the entire organisation. However, it would be a mistake simply to equate volunteers with staff and to apply, without any discrimination, the same personnel management techniques to both groups of people. The differences are sometimes subtle, but important. This chapter will point out some of the differences and similarities, and propose a framework for managing volunteers in a rewarding way for all concerned, not least the volunteers themselves.

Who are these volunteers?

Volunteers come in all shapes and sizes, all ages and both sexes. In fact, they can look remarkably like your staff. In a survey carried out across the UK in the 1990s, it was discovered that over 28 million people volunteer each year, and this figure appears to be on the increase. Overwhelmingly, the reason they gave for volunteering was devastatingly simple: somebody had asked them.

Volunteers explain why they get involved in many ways:

- They want to give something back to an organisation or community which has helped them.
- They believe in the charity's cause.
- They want to help others.

Sometimes the reasons are less altruistic:

- It's an opportunity to spend worthwhile time with the family.
- It's a way to gain work experience and new skills.
- It looks good on their CV.
- It's a way of meeting people and having fun.
- It's a stepping-stone back into work after long term absence or unemployment.
- It's a post-retirement hobby or interest.

Volunteers will decide about staying with an organisation depending on whether their needs are being met in a satisfactory way. It is because volunteers' motivations are varied and changeable that the organisation must be able to respond to them with flexibility, appreciation and in a structured way.

Table 13.1 Comparison of volunteer verses staff policies

Volunteers	Staff
Have no employment rights but may have access to courts through human rights or discrimination laws	Have full statutory and contractual rights under employment law
Motivations for working are diverse	Motivations for working are more predictable in terms of career development and reward
Their work must be made interesting and challenging if they are to be recruited and retained	Boring, repetitive tasks can be tolerated if other conditions are satisfactory
Formalities and documentation should be minimised	Policies, contracts and procedures need to be consistently applied
Screening of volunteers is essential	Screening of staff is just as important
Allocation of work is very flexible and often discontinuous, with allowances made for individual capabilities and special needs	Staff allocation of work is more predictable and continuous
De-selection of volunteers should take place quickly before problems become deep-seated	Dismissal of staff should be regarded as a last resort after all the disciplinary procedures have been exhausted
Volunteers can receive expenses and benefits in kind but must not be paid remuneration in any form	Payment of wages is an essential feature of the employment contract
Volunteering should be enjoyable at all times	!!!!!!!

Let's get organised

In the beginning, there should be a plan. While it is perfectly possible to organise volunteer activity on little more than enthusiasm and inspiration on the day, this is not a satisfactory basis for a long-term effective volunteer programme. This plan should reflect the agreed policy of the organisation towards volunteer involvement. But it is unrealistic to proceed very far without the clear understanding and commitment of the trustee board and senior management to volunteers.

The plan should start with a clear explanation as to why the organisation wants to involve volunteers at all. A tough question to answer is this: *if the charity had all the money it needed to employ staff to do its work, would it still want to use volunteers?* Hopefully, the answer is yes. But it is worth taking the time to debate within the organisation just why volunteers are needed:

- They can supplement staff work.
- They can add value by bringing in new skills and experience.
- They can reduce the cost of providing existing services.
- They can make possible the provision of new services not otherwise affordable.
- They can provide a reminder of the original ethos or founding spirit of the organisation.
- They can assist in building contacts and partnerships within a local community or across to other organisations.
- They can work with clients/users on a more personal basis.

The reasons that emerge will shape the plan and determine, to a large extent, the attitude of the organisation to volunteer activity.

The plan should provide a clear organisational framework located and integrated within the management structure. This is an important point. Unless a senior member of management is clearly identified as having responsibility for the management of volunteer activity, staff and volunteers will not take the matter seriously. The involvement of senior volunteers (and the specific tasking of a trustee) in the volunteer management process is good practice, but it is not a substitute for direct managerial accountability.

Depending upon the number and location of the active volunteers, a system for volunteer co-ordinators (or supervisors), organised on a geographical or functional basis, should be established and allowed to grow organically. Volunteer co-ordinators, often volunteers themselves, need to be in regular touch with the volunteers allocated to them, particularly within the first few months. They can also be the source of information on volunteer preferences, selection for assignments, volunteer training, evaluation of work and feedback on achievements and successes.

As part of the policy building process, it is vital to remember to consult with staff on the use of volunteers, particularly if there are recognised representative bodies. Staff can easily regard volunteers as a threat to their own job security, and can quickly scupper even the best-laid plans. Staff support and acceptance of a volunteer programme is essential and is usually readily given. But concerns should be given a full airing and genuine problems must be seen to be addressed.

The plan should contain some basic principles, for example:

- That there are no barriers or constraints on the work that volunteers can do (if there are any 'no-go' areas, set them out clearly and explain why).
- Volunteers will not be used to substitute for paid staff (this may not be an issue for smaller charities).
- Volunteers will work to the same standards as would be expected of staff (it is important to establish and maintain the respect of staff towards volunteer performance).
- There is a mutual obligation between the organisation and each volunteer to carry out the work entered into (the equivalent of the employment contract).
- The act of volunteering is not sufficient in itself – volunteers must be selected, trained and evaluated for the work they carry out, and de-selected if they are found to be unsuitable.
- The organisation will commit itself to ensuring that it will apply best management practice to the volunteer programme in terms of:
    - open and honest communication
    - health and safety measures
    - suitability of the work
    - resources available (including a specific budget allocation)
    - appropriate supervision
    - resolution of grievances
    - recognition of achievements.

A sample volunteer policy statement is outlined in model 13.1 (overleaf).

I will now look at some of these points in more detail.

Designing the jobs

Can you imagine opening up the appointment page of a newspaper or magazine to discover an advertisement with the stark message:

STAFF WANTED
Please apply to the Personnel Department

Not much chance of many people replying to that! And yet for some strange reason it seems quite acceptable for organisations to expect people to respond to a similar call:

> **VOLUNTEERS NEEDED**
> Please apply for work

MODEL 13.1 Sample volunteer policy statement

XYZ Charity

Volunteers are an integral part of *XYZ Charity*. The organisation is fully committed to their involvement in all aspects our work in ensuring that our services meet the needs of our users.

As a volunteer you will offer your time freely and without any formal obligation. However, there will be an expectation on both your part and on that of *XYZ Charity* that mutual support and commitment will exist. By recognising these reciprocal responsibilities we will jointly ensure that *XYZ Charity* continues to provide a high standard of service and facilities to all its users.

XYZ Charity's responsibilities

To carry out your work effectively *XYZ Charity* will provide:

- A volunteer co-ordinator or member of staff to whom you are responsible and with whom you will have regular contact.
- Consultation, supervision and support to enable you to carry out your tasks.
- Safe working conditions.
- Training and induction relevant to your work.
- Information about the work of *XYZ Charity* and how you fit in.
- Regular information to keep you up to date.
- A variety of activities that will appeal to your talents and skills.
- Publicity of a volunteer's contributions to acknowledge and appreciate your achievements.
- Confidentiality of volunteer records.

Your responsibilities

In return, we ask that you recognise certain responsibilities to *XYZ Charity*:

- Maintain a high standard of efficiency and quality in all aspects of your work.
- Give a reliable commitment of time when the task demands regular attendance.
- Work within *XYZ's* policies and procedures to carry out agreed tasks.
- Be aware that the ultimate authority for the management of your task will rest with an *XYZ Charity* member of staff (or trustee).
- Provide references when requested.
- Attend training sessions when possible to fulfil the needs of a task.
- Maintain the confidentiality of information when advised.

General procedures

All volunteers will complete an *XYZ Charity* registration form. This will include a declaration that there are no criminal records, whether spent or unspent, which will have a detrimental effect on the work of *XYZ Charity*.

It's as though volunteers, unlike staff, are a homogenous group of individuals sufficiently malleable to be bent into whatever shape is needed. The implication, of course, is that the volunteer contribution is limited to those areas of work that require no previous experience, no skills and no knowledge.

A more positive approach is to decide, after consulting with staff, what specific jobs or projects are available for volunteers. A

All volunteers will supply at least two references, including one from a current or previous employer.

All volunteers will have their travel and other out of pocket expenses reimbursed.

All volunteers will receive an induction into *XYZ Charity* and their own area of work.

To help you perform certain activities to the standard required by *XYZ Charity*, you might receive specialist training either 'on the job' or on *XYZ's* training courses. The training courses will be informal, providing an enjoyable opportunity for you to meet other volunteers and staff and share experiences and best practice.

To ensure that both you and *XYZ Charity* are happy with your appointment to a particular activity, periodic reviews may be held between yourself and the volunteer co-ordinator. These reviews will enable both parties to discuss the current work, or activity areas you may wish to become involved in, and any training or development needs you may have.

The majority of staff and volunteers working for *XYZ Charity* find their work enjoyable and fulfilling. Any difficulties that occur are normally resolved informally and quickly between colleagues. Very occasionally there can be problems that require more formal discussions. A volunteer grievance procedure has been introduced to deal with any such eventualities and guarantees the fair and equitable treatment of volunteers across *XYZ Charity*.

You can volunteer for as little or as much time as you like but it is important to agree your commitment with your volunteer co-ordinator when you first start. You may have a few hours a week to offer on a long-term basis or wish to work an odd number of weekends or evenings during the course of the year. Whichever you choose, please remember that reliability is important.

All volunteers are covered by *XYZ's* insurance policy whilst they are on the premises or engaged in work on *XYZ's* behalf.

Volunteers are covered by *XYZ's* health and safety policy.

XYZ Charity operates an equal opportunities policy in respect of both staff and volunteers.

Volunteers may have to use their own vehicles when travelling to and from certain activities.

If you would like to have a greater say in the policies of *XYZ Charity* or help to monitor the service to our users, you are welcome to participate in the organisation's governance procedures. Opportunities to ask questions, express opinions or stand for election to the trustee board happen every year. If you are interested in attending an AGM please contact *XYZ* Head Office.

Welcome to volunteering in *XYZ Charity*

good way of doing this is to conduct a brainstorming session to ask the question 'what needs to be done around here?'.

Having compiled a list of tasks, it is then possible to select which would constitute rewarding and worthwhile volunteer jobs. This sort of exercise can help to free up attitudes about what jobs volunteers can be 'trusted' with. It should lead to the realisation that many jobs are left undone because of lack of time, that some jobs are avoided because no one likes doing them, and that some jobs are not tackled because no one has the necessary skills.

The next step is to compile a list of tasks or projects that could be integrated into the general work programme. Volunteers will look for jobs that are interesting and challenging, and which provide an end result. Boring, meaningless, repetitive tasks, the leftovers after staff have cherry-picked the best, are likely to lead to disenchantment. To attract and retain good volunteers, they must be provided with jobs they want to do.

We have already looked at job descriptions and person specifications as they apply to staff (see chapter 8). The same principles apply for volunteers, although I would recommend that you use term 'role description' instead. This helps to underline a legal difference between volunteers and staff. The format can be simplified, as it does not have to comply with employment legislation. However, it should contain the following elements:

Checklist 13.1 Volunteer role description

- [x] Brief description of activity, including standards of work expected and the required end result.
- [x] Qualifications or skills required.
- [x] Likely timescale.
- [x] Location of work.
- [x] Number of hours of work involved.
- [x] Resources provided (equipment, expenses, transport, etc.).
- [x] Whether other volunteers/staff will be involved.
- [x] Reporting arrangements – for supervision and evaluation.

Recruitment and selection of volunteers

There is one crucial difference between recruiting volunteers and recruiting staff. Whereas potential employees need to have the benefits of working for your organisation 'sold' to them, volunteers are being asked to do something that they (potentially) already want to do. The first aim of the recruitment process is therefore to find ways to reach out to those people who are likely to be motivated by what the organisation can offer in the way of interesting activities. The second aim is to achieve a balance between the number of volunteers attracted and the number of jobs or opportunities available. The third aim is to find ways to separate out those volunteers who are not suitable from those who are. We will look at these three elements in turn.

Finding volunteers

There are many ways to ask people to come forward and give their time freely to the organisation.

By word of mouth

Existing volunteers and staff who enjoy what they do can tell their family and friends. This is undoubtedly a very effective method, and is in itself a positive demonstration that the organisation values and respects its volunteers. Any charity that is unable to recruit volunteers in this way has a serious credibility problem and should look very closely at its volunteering policies or, even more fundamentally, at the mission of the charity itself. The ability of a charity to enlist the support and involvement of new volunteers is a valuable 'reality check' on the health of the organisation.

Using a database of members or supporters

Many charities are membership organisations, whose members perhaps pay a subscription or fee. These are people who are already committed in some way to the aims of the organisation or who at least use its services. A database of this kind is a valuable source of new recruits and the cost of contacting them may be minimal. If necessary, it may be possible to 'piggyback' on a mailing (e.g. subscription renewal) that is being sent out anyway.

Talks and presentations

This can be an effective recruitment method, whether in small or large groups. It can perhaps form part of a more general public relations campaign. Why not conclude a talk by describing the work that volunteers can do? It is an alternative way of asking people to contribute rather than simply asking for a donation.

A good presentation must be informative, realistic and, above all, inspirational. The old, no doubt mythical, story goes that the volunteer working in the visitor centre at NASA in Florida, selling postcards to the tourists, was quite clear that her reason for volunteering was to help America to put a man on the moon. It's a reminder to keep the 'big picture' firmly in the forefront of the prospective volunteer's mind.

Advertising

Local press and radio are useful means of getting a message across to a large audience. It is of course very untargeted and the response rate will be correspondingly low. Charities can often gain preferential rates for advertising through determined negotiation. Even better is to wrap up the recruitment campaign as a newsworthy event. All editors are keen to fill up the space in their columns of print or their radio airtime and are always on the lookout for good wholesome stories. And the best part is that this sort of media exposure is free!

Local ads in shop windows, libraries, health centres, village halls, etc. can also be a very effective means of raising awareness and bringing in enquiries.

Promotional material

It is extremely helpful to have some leaflets and posters available as handouts for volunteer recruiters or to send to enquirers who want a little more information (and need a little more persuasion). Colour and a lively text with photographs of active volunteers are essential ingredients. For targeted recruitment, the information needs to be specific to the job in question.

Whatever method of recruitment is used, the message to the prospective volunteer must be clearly defined and articulated. It must also be encouraging and flexible for those who are not sure about whether they can make the commitment involved. They have to be able to see themselves as being a part of a solution to the organisation's problem or need. The message must also be realistic. It serves no one's interest if an unpleasant, difficult or physically demanding job is portrayed in terms that glamorise or give a false impression. In any case, this sort of job will have its own distinctive appeal to those volunteers who relish a highly challenging task.

Keeping a balance

Every organisation has a different profile for volunteers. Some need many helpful hands for a specific day or week in the year. Other charities might need volunteers for long-term specialised or sensitive roles that require an investment in time and money in training. Most organisations probably come somewhere in the middle of that spectrum, hoping to recruit throughout the year and to convince first time volunteers into staying and doing a more skilled job in the future. Whatever the requirement, the approach to recruitment must be adjusted to suit. If five volunteers are needed, and fifty show an interest, then some rethinking is needed just as much as if it were the other way around.

Effective recruitment is when the demand for volunteers of a particular kind is roughly equal to the supply of worthwhile jobs to be done. An imbalance can be frustrating for the volunteer, who will quickly become disillusioned if his 'offer' is not taken up. It will also be expensive and time-consuming to process a large number of enquiries and interview and screen the applicants, just in order to select a few suitable volunteers. Of course, it would be an even bigger mistake to take on volunteers when there isn't enough work to go round, just in order to keep them happy. They won't stay happy for long, and their impression of the competence of your organisation will suffer as a result. In addition, they will tell their friends.

So the key is to know how to turn the recruitment tap on and off as and when volunteers are needed, and preferably to have more than one type of recruitment method available.

Interviewing volunteers

No doubt there are examples of volunteering jobs where all that is needed is a willing pair of hands. However, it is more likely that volunteers will be asked to do jobs that require knowledge, competence and general life skills. There has to be a method of determining whether the volunteer who has been recruited matches the job that needs to be done. For many organisations, an informal interview is the best way, because it serves a number of purposes:

- It is an introduction to the organisation, its values and style of operation.
- It offers a chance to assess the suitability of the volunteer in terms of their interest in a job and whether they have the necessary skills, etc.
- It provides an opportunity to discover whether the volunteer has other interests and skills that might be of even greater value to the organisation.

Some type of application or registration form should be completed by each volunteer, which can serve as a basis for the interview, as well as acting as an input document to a simple database, preferably computerised (see model 13.2, overleaf).

It should go without saying that the interviewer, whether a member of staff or volunteer, should be fully trained in interviewing skills and techniques. In this respect, particular flexibility is required on the part of the interviewer in terms of agreeing the time of day for the interview, the location and the interview schedule if more than one person is being interviewed. The interviewer should also have a rounded knowledge of the organisation so as to be able to identify alternative opportunities if unexpected information is revealed in the discussion. The interview plan itself should be similar to that of an employment interview in structure, content and style. Building rapport is especially important.

A fuller discussion of interviews and other selection techniques is given in chapter 9, and many of these principles apply to

---

MODEL 13.2 Sample volunteer registration form

Private and confidential

XYZ Charity
Volunteer registration form

Thank you for your interest in becoming an *XYZ* volunteer.

We would be grateful if you could answer a few questions about yourself, so that we can find out about the types of work/activities you would like to do, and in order to place you on our volunteer register database.

Please complete this form in block capitals

Full name ....

Address ....

....

.... Postcode ....

Date of birth ....

Daytime telephone number .... evening telephone number ....

Fax number .... E mail address ....

When is a good time to ring? ....

Occupation or qualifications (current or pre-retirement)

....

....

....

Are you in full time employment/ part-time employment/ retired/ student/ other?

Do you possess a current driving licence? .... yes/no

Had you had any endorsements in the last three years? .... yes/no

(if yes, please give details) ....

....

....

If you have access to a car would you be willing to use it when volunteering for *XYZ*? yes/no

....

Have you any disabilities or ailments we need to consider?

....

....

selecting volunteers as well as staff. The main difference between interviewing a potential volunteer and a potential employee is the need to focus more on the question of their motivation. It is less a matter of whether the individual can do the job and more

References

XYZ Charity has an obligation to ensure that appropriate references are obtained for all volunteers. In addition, XYZ requires from all volunteers a declaration that they have no criminal record, whether spent or unspent, which would prejudice their work for XYZ.

I declare that I have no criminal record which would prejudice my work for the *XYZ Charity*

I consent to checks being made with the police to determine if there is any record of convictions or cautions against me.

Work activities

Please indicate the type of work in which you are interested
(tick as many boxes as you like)

Fundraising	☐	Environmental practices	☐
Social inclusion programme	☐	Computing	☐
Publicity and promotions	☐	Book-keeping/ accounts	☐
Education/ training	☐	Administration	☐
Community activities	☐	Committee work	☐
Professional services	☐	No preference	☐

A few words about yourself

please mention any relevant skills, interests or areas of expertise

....

....

....

....

Have you volunteered for *XYZ* before? .... yes/no

Availability

At what times are you interested in volunteering for *XYZ*?

Weekdays?	☐	Evenings?	☐	Other?	☐
Weekends?	☐	Flexible?	☐		

Are there times when you cannot do volunteer work?

Is it worth contacting you if an activity is organised at short notice?

Signed .... Date ....

Please send this form to: National Volunteer Co-ordinator, *XYZ Charity*, ...

about 'why do they want to do it?'. An experienced interviewer is always on the lookout for any hidden agendas.

If it is impossible to arrange a face-to-face interview, a telephone interview is the next best alternative. In such cases, a note should be made to arrange for someone to meet the volunteer as soon as possible afterwards, and preferably before they start work.

The interview should finish, like all good interviews, with a summary of what has been decided and what remains to be done before the volunteer starts work. In particular, reference checks will need to be completed, and possibly some further discussions may need to take place with staff or other volunteers. Whatever the procedure, the volunteer needs be clear about what is going to happen next and when he will hear from you.

Screening volunteers

Reference checks are essential. There is no short cut to this requirement. At least two references should be obtained before the volunteer starts work (having received the express permission of the volunteer), from an authoritative source who is not family or a personal friend. References can be taken from a current or previous employer, family doctor, teacher or other professional person, or from a government or other official agency. If evidence is required for a driving licence, nationality status, age or qualifi-

---

CASE STUDY 13.1 Talking to volunteers

The interviewer – perhaps you could tell me what sort of volunteer work you're interested in doing?

The volunteer – I have a clean driving licence and I enjoy driving. It seemed to me that I might be able to help *XYZ* in taking some of their clients who have mobility problems and have no transport of their own. I am free every Tuesday and some weekends.

The interviewer – I am sorry, I should have picked that up from your registration form. Unfortunately all our forms have become a little disorganised, and our database has just fallen over, again.

The volunteer – what's the problem with the database?

The interviewer – Oh it seems to be a recurring problem. We need a more secure and robust software package than the one that we have.

The volunteer – perhaps I can help. I work for a software house as a computer programmer. I didn't mention this on my registration form because I didn't really want a continuation of my usual work. I wanted a change. However if you have a problem I am sure I could select some appropriate software and get you going again.

It's only by talking to your volunteers that you begin to realise the full range of their talents.

cations, then appropriate documentation should be requested and provided.

Many charities are involved in providing services to children, older people or to people who are vulnerable through some form of incapacity. If this is the case, then the charity has a duty to ensure that appropriate steps are taken to safeguard the health and security of their users. This will include seeking access to criminal records as part of the screening procedure. It is sensible to include as part of the application or registration form a declaration for the volunteer to sign regarding their compliance with the requirements of the Children Act and which, at the same time, gives permission for criminal record checks to be taken. A declaration of this kind can act as a useful deterrent in cases where volunteers would be working with children.

The Criminal Records Bureau (CRB) will be in operation by summer 2001. The CRB will be able to provide a Disclosure service to registered organisations having a need for such information due to the nature of their work. There will be three levels of Disclosure – Standard, Enhanced and Basic.

The screening of volunteers is a sensitive issue, but the risks of inaction will usually far outweigh the potential problems. For example, an organisation will appear to have been less than professionally competent if a rogue volunteer commits some dreadful act on a child and it transpires that no check was made or no references were taken out. Moreover, insurance companies might be unwilling to accept liability for the consequential costs of litigation if the charity had the means to carry out a screening process but had chosen not to. In the worst-case scenario the work of a charity could be terminally damaged.

Induction and training

New volunteers, no matter how familiar they may be with the organisation, will need some help in learning how things are done and how to fit in alongside staff and other volunteers. An induction programme should be designed along similar principles as for staff. It should include the following:

Checklist 13.2   Volunteer induction programme

- ☑ Background on the charity, its purpose, organisation and development.
- ☑ Information on the products or services provided.
- ☑ Future plans.

- ☑ How the volunteer can help.
- ☑ What volunteers have done within the organisation over the years.
- ☑ Details of administration requirements, forms to be completed, procedures to be observed, etc.
- ☑ Information on volunteer benefits (if any!).
- ☑ An opportunity to ask questions on matters that concern the volunteer.

It is ideal if induction sessions can be arranged to include groups of new volunteers. It makes it more of an occasion and it can be steered into being a pleasant social event, with perhaps a senior volunteer or member of staff presiding over the welcome, introductions, etc. It all adds to team spirit and is an early opportunity to make all volunteers feel welcome and valued.

In many charities, volunteers will also need to be enrolled into a training event of some kind, to learn the specific job for which they have been recruited. The length and formality of the training will of course vary from job to job, and be different for each organisation. Some voluntary organisations require training of perhaps half a day per week for over a year before the volunteer is allowed anywhere near a client group. Other volunteer jobs require a qualification before starting work. In this respect it should be noted that volunteers who offer professional services as their contribution should check whether they need to obtain special professional indemnity cover from their Institute or Chartered Association.

It is good practice if new volunteers who are to work by themselves can be given a trial period, or a supervised 'test-drive' before they are left to do the job. A shadowing scheme, where volunteers double-up with an experienced volunteer or member of staff, is also a good arrangement.

However short or long the training process is for volunteers, someone in the organisation should be allocated to each individual as a mentor, to advise, encourage and check progress. The training period is another important opportunity to screen volunteers and decide whether they are suitable for the job.

It must be mentioned that training can sometimes be regarded as a benefit-in-kind, i.e. equivalent to remuneration. We then enter a potential legal minefield, since a volunteer who receives remuneration may suddenly be transformed into an employee, with all the rights and benefits of employment legislation (see chapter 3). This is not usually what is intended. One answer is to ensure that the training is no more (and no less) than what is absolutely necessary in order for the voluntary job to be done properly. Once the training goes beyond this, perhaps to provide support towards gaining an ancillary skill or a qualification, then the risk is run. Another possibility is to include volunteers on training that is being provided for staff in any event, and this has the added value of mixing staff and volunteers together.

Supervision and evaluation

No matter how confident you might be about the suitability of the selected volunteers, and irrespective of how small the job or responsibility might be, some form of supervisory control is essential. Whether or not you formalise it into a management structure, every volunteer must be accountable to someone within the organisation for their work and their mistakes.

The equivalent of a line manager role can be taken by a more senior volunteer or by a member of staff. The status of the line manager is of less significance than the role that person takes in respect of:

- Allocating suitable volunteers to do jobs that become available.
- Ensuring that the details of the job, the resources required, etc. have been organised.
- Ensuring that other people in the organisation who need to know about the job are fully briefed.
- Making sure that the standards required for the job are clearly communicated to the volunteer, and that targets are agreed.
- Checking that the work has been done and obtaining feedback from the volunteer and from anyone else who may have been involved, e.g. site manager or client leader.
- Recording the hours contributed by the volunteer – an invaluable benchmark and publicity tool.

From the volunteer perspective, the importance of a supervisor or co-ordinator is considerable. It demonstrates that the organisation values his contribution and cares about whether he does his job well or badly. It also provides the volunteer with someone who will listen to grievances or problems encountered with the work, with staff, or with other volunteers. The supervisor will also be the person who will conduct regular appraisals, preferably on similar lines and for similar reasons as for staff (see chapter 11). Volunteers may not always recognise their own strengths and weaknesses and may not realise when it is appropriate for them to move on to another type of job.

Like any employee, volunteers need a support structure to prevent them from becoming isolated or from engaging in work that has become irrelevant or unnecessary. Supervision and evaluation are even more important when other staff or volunteers rarely see the volunteer. This may be because their work is being done off-site or at some remote or distant place. Communication systems providing regular contact become even more important, if only to prevent a possible feeling of exclusion from the organisation from developing into a problem.

Retaining volunteers

All volunteers should be welcomed into the organisation no matter how large or small their contribution. However, good volunteers should be encouraged to stay in order to give their time and skill over a long period. The reasons why a volunteer will stay for the longer term will no doubt change over the years, but the reasons for returning to the organisation in the short term will depend on the extent to which the initial motivations for volunteering have been satisfied.

Volunteers will stay with an organisation if:

- They can make a difference to the work of the organisation.
- Their work is recognised and appreciated.
- Their work is interesting, challenging and enjoyable.
- Their supervisor, and the voluntary management system, allows them to get on with the job.

Volunteers will leave, even if the above features are present, if:

- Too much is expected of them in terms of workload.
- Too much time is required for travel.
- Genuine expenses are either not payable or not provided at an adequate level.
- Working conditions are unpleasant or unreasonably difficult.

The key to retention is to keep up regular communication with volunteers at a personal level. A telephone call after the first training session, or a chat about the first assignment, can make all the difference as to how the volunteer feels about his contribution and whether he wishes to repeat the experience. If there are failures in the management system, they can usually be put right provided questions are regularly asked of the volunteers and their answers listened to.

Longer-term volunteers can be made to feel part of the organisation by being consulted about possible new developments or projects, whether or not they are directly volunteer-related. Volunteers have a different perspective from staff from which to view the activities of an organisation, and can sometimes voice a more independent opinion about proposed new changes.

Volunteering should also be celebrated within the organisation at every opportunity. This can, and should, take as many forms as possible, e.g.:

- Special volunteer badges.
- Formal and informal parties, at relevant anniversaries or at the completion of a project.
- Presentation ceremonies, e.g. long-service, or volunteer of the month awards.
- Publicity in the annual report, and other organisational literature.
- Thank-you letters at appropriate occasions from a senior member of the organisation (see model 13.3).

Be sure that you include everyone in invitations to events and are seen to recognise everyone's contributions: favoured treatment breeds resentment.

De-selecting volunteers

Despite every best effort, some volunteers will prove unsuitable for the task to which they have been assigned. It may be a simple

---

MODEL 13.3 Sample thank-you letter

Dear Jackie

I just had to write to you on my return from the weekend fundraising event at New Haven to say how much I enjoyed meeting so many new friends and supporters of *XYZ Charity*.

I'm sure that the organisation of this event only went so smoothly because of the work that you and your team of volunteers put into all aspects of the planning and publicity. It was a great achievement, and in the process we have not only made a real impact on the local community, but also raised over £1,000 for further development work. The photographs of the kids' corner will make good material for our next newsletter. I really hope that you take time out for a good break – you deserve it!

I will be in touch again in a couple of weeks' time, and perhaps we could talk about some of your other ideas.

Many thanks again

With all good wishes

Volunteer Co-ordinator

Note:

Thank-you letters should be:
- *Personal*
- *Prompt*
- *Proportional to the achievement*

lack of competence or knowledge, or it may be a more profound problem of personality or inappropriate behaviour. Whatever the reason, the organisation must be clear about how to manage the process of de-selection. Whilst in most cases problems can be resolved informally and quickly, or performance monitored to encourage improvement, there are instances where the individual concerned may not be prepared to accept the management view and a more serious grievance develops.

A decision to de-select a volunteer that has been 'badly handled' can be just as damaging to morale as a bad decision. So, de-selection should not be seen as a last resort when all other options have failed. It is usually much better to take action early rather than to wait until other volunteers and staff have become thoroughly disaffected.

However, volunteers have rights even though they may not have an employment contract. Charities would do well to remember this. Even a basic system for de-selecting volunteers should include the following features:

- Some reliable evidence of unsatisfactory performance or inappropriate behaviour.
- A mechanism for the volunteer to be informed of the problem.
- An opportunity for the volunteer to give an explanation.
- A consideration of possible alternatives, e.g. reassignment to another supervisor, another task or another location.

Sometimes volunteers need to be persuaded to retire or to take a break, particularly if they appear to be becoming overly possessive about their role or status.

Consideration should also be given as to who should carry out the de-selection. It should be someone sufficiently senior and some distance removed from the operational details. It does not matter too much whether the decision to de-select is made by a member of staff or a volunteer, although the former is probably preferable in most situations. Charities, especially those who are also membership organisations, should also ensure that there is an appeal system in place, and that this does not in any way conflict with any provisions within their own constitution or articles of association.

There is an increasing tendency for volunteers to apply for redress for grievances to Employment Tribunals when they believe their rights have been infringed. Usually they are unable to proceed very far because they first have to demonstrate that they are eligible for a hearing, i.e. that they are employees and not volunteers. This barrier may become less important as the impact of human rights legislation becomes embedded into our legal system over the next few years.

CASE STUDY 13.2 De-selecting volunteers

A volunteer complained to the head office of a charity that he had not been selected for a particular work programme in which a team of people were going to spend a weekend repairing the fabric of a building owned by the charity. He had volunteered for this sort of work before and had thoroughly enjoyed it.

The charity had received complaints from the volunteer co-ordinator who had supervised the work project on which this volunteer had previously been involved. It seemed that he had spent most of the time talking to other people rather than doing the work. Furthermore, the team had had to redo the work that this volunteer had eventually undertaken. Apparently his behaviour in relation to the rest of the team had been considered inappropriate and unhelpful. The volunteer co-ordinator had decided not to contact again him for a while, perhaps in the hope that he would lose interest.

The charity advised the individual volunteer that they were unable to use him for this sort of work in future but were prepared to consider him for some other kind of volunteering for which he might be more suitable. The letter did not state the reasons why this approach was being taken in order not to hurt his feelings.

The volunteer responded by applying to an Employment Tribunal to complain of unfair dismissal and unlawful discrimination on the grounds of his disability.

After a preliminary enquiry, the Tribunal ruled that the volunteer's case was not eligible for a full hearing, primarily on the grounds that he could not show a mutuality of obligation with the charity such as would be evidenced by a contract of employment.

Charities may find that their treatment of volunteers will come under a similar degree of legal scrutiny as people become more aware of their right to challenge organisations.

The legal position of volunteers

It is an extraordinary fact that the legal definition of a volunteer simply does not exist. For the most part, such legalities are not of any great consequence to voluntary organisations. The question only arises when there is a problem, but then it can be too late to make changes.

The main difficulty is where volunteers have a grievance, and decide to apply to an Employment Tribunal for unfair dismissal or unlawful discrimination. The Tribunal then has to decide whether the volunteer has eligibility for a hearing, and this will in turn rest upon all the circumstances of the case. The Tribunal will examine the nature of the employment, the extent to which there is a mutuality of obligation on both parties and whether payment or some other compensation has been made to the volunteer. Benefits enjoyed by the volunteer, such as training, expenses or accommodation can point to an employment contract. The greater the formality of documentation surrounding the appointment of the volunteer, the greater will be the weight of the argument suggesting that an employment contract is in existence. This means that voluntary organisations should go to great lengths not to invest a volunteer with the usual formal and legal trappings of employees. For example, they should avoid references to job descriptions, application forms, grievance procedures, payments (perhaps in the innocent form of honoraria), etc. Once a contract of employment is found to exist, then the volunteer suddenly becomes entitled to all the other employment rights, such as paid holidays, sickness benefits, contractual notice, working hours, minimum pay and the like.

Oddly enough, it has been the introduction of the National Minimum Wage Act 1998 that has helped to clarify matters substantially. The authors of this Act did not intend to require organisations to pay minimum rates to volunteers. Accordingly, Section 44 of the Act specifically excludes voluntary workers, and in the process it defines a volunteer as '*a worker employed by a charity, a voluntary organisation, an associated fundraising body or a statutory body*' who receives:

- No monetary payments (other than expenses actually incurred).
- No benefits-in-kind (other than subsistence or accommodation as is reasonable in the circumstances).
- No training (other than as necessarily acquired in the course of their work).

Some other issues

Insurance

Volunteers can have – and can cause – accidents. While organisations are normally reminded by their insurers to include liability insurance for staff, the inclusion of volunteers in the schedule of insurances is easily overlooked. The insurance cover should also include loss or damage to equipment, especially vehicles, which may be provided for use by volunteers.

Expenses

The simple truth is that if your charity does not have a system for paying out-of-pocket expenses to volunteers, then some will decide not to work for you because they cannot afford the cost of travel and reasonable subsistence. This bears down hardest on the least well-off, and often socially excluded, sectors of society. It is also potentially discriminatory, as well as a potential PR risk.

There are other risks if you pay more in expenses than has actually been incurred, since this could be regarded as a form of remuneration under a contract of employment. The following are examples of legitimate expenses:

- Travel to and from the place of volunteering.
- Meals and accommodation taken while volunteering.
- Postage, fax, and telephone costs (if working from home).
- Protective clothing or other essential equipment.

Volunteers who genuinely do not wish to claim expenses for themselves can always repay the equivalent sum as a donation.

Welfare benefits

It is a sad fact that many volunteers have run into difficulties because they may have infringed some of the rules and regulations of the Benefits Agency or other statutory body. The most common problem is for unemployed volunteers who, by volunteering their work to a charity, can possibly put their jobseekers' allowance at risk. They have to be able to prove that they are actively seeking paid work each week and be able to start a job within a week. This can preclude them from certain volunteering projects, especially if they are located some distance from their home. A sympathetic ear is needed in government to remove this unnecessary barrier to volunteering.

Health and safety

Volunteers tend by their very nature to be enthusiastic about the work they do. However, they may be at greater risk to accidents and injuries than employees simply as a result of lack of experience, training or familiarity with equipment. This is where volunteer co-ordinators should play their part by getting to know what jobs can be safely offered to volunteers, and by relating jobs to personal circumstances, e.g. volunteer A has a bad back, volunteer B is colour-blind.

Equal opportunities

Using volunteers is a great way to increase the degree of diversity within your organisation. It may be a way of better reflecting the composition of the local community or the major users of the charity. Seen in this way, volunteers can help an organisation with the development of positive policies to promote equal opportunities within the workforce, whether in terms of gender balance, racial mix or the deployment of disabled people. Volunteers can also help to change attitudes among employees about the value of older people and young people, both of whom can make important contributions to the work of the charity.

Some final remarks

Volunteering is great fun. Managing volunteers can be enjoyable too, but it should be seen in its proper perspective, i.e. it is a special form of people management, with its own distinctive blend of persuasion, problem solving and added value. All voluntary organisations are facing competitive pressures, not least of which is the demand for increasingly scarce and expensive employees. It may well be the case that the most successful charities in the start to this new millennium will be those who can best attract, retain and utilise the skills and experience of their volunteers.

In summary …

Volunteers can be a vital source of added value, but only if:

- The charity has a clear strategic commitment to a volunteer programme.
- The senior member of the management team (or trustee board) is given responsibility for implementing and championing the volunteer programme.
- An organisational structure, with volunteer co-ordinators as required, is put in place.
- The operating principles and standards of the volunteer programme are established and communicated.
- Consistent policies are adopted in relation to recruitment, selection, screening, training and evaluation of volunteer work.
- Staff are consulted about the roles and responsibilities of volunteers, especially when there are changes.
- The formalities of volunteer management are kept to a minimum, and kept distinctive from those of employed staff.
- The volunteer contribution is regularly recognised and celebrated as a valued part of the life of the charity.

No matter how much volunteers want to help, they will not continue to offer their services if they feel their chosen charity is not treating them with respect and professionalism.

Developing a personnel strategy

CHAPTER 14

INTRODUCTION

From the outset I have sought to make this book one which offers practical advice and support to managers who are not personnel specialists in dealing with what can be the most challenging but rewarding part of their role: that of getting the best out of their staff. It has not been a book about management theory, neither has it sought to do much more than equip those managers with a range of tools that will ensure that all charity assets are managed in the most efficient and effective way, towards the universally supported objective of maximising quality products to the service users for whom the charity exists.

A valid criticism of this approach is that it is reactive, that personnel as a discipline is no more than a set of skills and procedures. For some smaller organisations with limited resources, it could be argued that this approach might be appropriate. However, this more mechanistic approach to people management seems less satisfactory in the light of the rapidly changing nature of employment and the ever more complex challenges facing staff and the managers who support them.

Many organisations in every sector are coming to realise that unless they adopt a strategic approach to personnel issues, they will rapidly fall behind the game. So personnel is beginning to come back into its own, both informing and being informed by the corporate strategic planning process. This chapter looks at how your organisation can develop a personnel strategy which is in line with your organisational objectives and which takes into account the changing nature of work today.

Matching a personnel strategy to your organisational needs

I have stressed throughout this book that all personnel policies, procedures and approaches need to be culturally sensitive to your individual charity. I very much hope by now that you will have taken this to heart and, rather than simply lifting the models I have offered and adopting them as your own, you will ensure that they feel right for your organisation. That may well mean considerable modification – of course within the limits permissible by law – and determined by what you interpret as good practice.

If yours is a small organisation with few personnel needs, this may well be sufficient. If you are unlikely to need more than a couple of procedures, you should be able to introduce them effectively after referring to the appropriate chapter, and they are unlikely to be at all contradictory. But if it is your intention to develop, either at once or over time, a whole raft of procedures and individual personnel policies, the sensible place to start is not with those policies and procedures themselves, but with a strategic overview that sets key objectives and common standards.

Since this is not a book about strategic planning, it would not be appropriate to develop this theme much further here. The principles and practice of strategic planning are set out well in the literature, and apply equally to personnel as to any other discipline. They need to be applied to the key themes of this book: deploying staff resources effectively and building on their enthusiasm through the fair and equitable application of legal, moral and practical constraints, with a package of rewards that properly combines a reflection of the worth of staff's contribution with the values of the voluntary sector. If that approach is adopted, personnel can and will make a major contribution towards helping your charity to maintain a clear sense of vision and a plan for working towards it and, insofar as it is possible with the rich variety of human experience and belief that abounds everywhere (but much more so in the voluntary sector), keeping everyone involved on the same track and in the same direction.

However, although I do not intend to offer advice on strategic planning, for the sake of completeness I offer on pages 276–278 a model personnel strategy, which should at least enable you to start thinking along these lines if you consider it appropriate to do so, inserting your own organisation's priorities and emphasis. The model starts with an overall strategic policy statement and then, having established a set of operating principles, identifies where and how these should be applied, and offers the basis for further development of detailed policies later. It is of course critical that any such personnel strategy should be entirely complementary to your charity's overall development plan.

The changing nature of work

Most of the issues discussed in this book are likely to be relevant, irrespective of the nature of your charity or how you go about managing it. You will always need to recruit, train and retain staff, you will need to motivate and control them, you will need to know your rights and obligations as an employer seeking to adopt best practice approaches. But it would be remiss of me to ignore major developments in the way that work is organised, as these will in themselves pose major challenges to personnel management in the future, and not just in the voluntary sector.

Flexible contracts

Increasingly, charity staff are being employed on fixed or short-term contracts, either because some employers think that this is a more efficient (and perhaps cheaper) way of controlling their workforce or, perhaps more legitimately, because the changing nature of charities' services and how they are funded means that organisations have to defend themselves against financial insecurity. Many a charity has run into difficulties when it has taken staff on with permanent contracts when the funding has been tapered; at the very least, they are likely to face redundancy costs, and often will have problems of discontent and underperformance as funding comes to an end. It can therefore make sense to engage staff either to perform a particular task, or on a fixed-term basis that reflects the anticipated income flow. But beware: because of abuses by some rogue employers (not, I am pleased to say, very often found in the charity world), the law has been changed to prevent employers getting out of their legal obligations on employment protection by issuing fixed-term contracts and then re-engaging the same staff on further contracts year after year. If, however, you can be satisfied that there is a genuine need for a contract for a defined period, and you are open about this, then there is every reason why you should follow this trend in employment patterns by adopting such contracts in specific circumstances where they help you to meet your charitable objectives.

Agency and interim staff

Another developing trend is the use of agency or interim staff, the latter particularly for covering managerial vacancies. If you

MODEL 14.1 A personnel strategy

The XYZ Charity's personnel strategy

Personnel policy objective

The XYZ Charity, as a responsible employer, recognises that its greatest asset in maximising the effective delivery of quality services to its clients is its staff, both paid and volunteer.

The key objective towards which all its personnel policies are aimed is, therefore, to ensure that they comprehensively reflect best practice and the interests of both clients and employees.

To this end, it will regularly review personnel policies, practices and procedures, to ensure that they continue to remain relevant to the twin objectives of quality service and good employment practice.

Statement of operating principles

The XYZ Charity bases its personnel practices on the following principles:

- Equality of opportunity in all aspects of employment.
- Maximum clarity and openness.
- Full consultation with staff over all matters that affect them.
- The highest standards of professional conduct, in both the management of its staff and in its expectations of their work.
- Extensive investment in staff training and development.
- Fair and effective service and salary conditions.

Scope of policy application

The XYZ Charity will ensure that it has in place up-to-date policies and procedures that cover all key areas of its employment responsibilities, particularly for:

- Recruitment, retention, salaries and benefits.
- Performance appraisal, personal development and staff training.
- Health, welfare and safety.
- Staff conduct in disciplinary, grievance and capability matters.
- Employee and organisational communications and access to information.
- Union recognition, employee representation and consultation processes.
- Staff and organisational responses to client needs and concerns.
- Responsibilities of the management committee, the director and all staff in financial and managerial matters.
- Clarity of roles and flexibility of operation to meet the needs of *The XYZ Charity* and its clients.

All these policy areas will be informed and underpinned by *The XYZ Charity's* equal opportunities in employment policy, and are set out in more detail below.

Equal opportunities in employment

The XYZ Charity recognises that the nature of society results in disadvantage, both at work and beyond, being experienced by certain groups. It will seek to ensure that all its employment practices treat potential, current and past employees with dignity and only on merit, and will avoid any discrimination, positive or negative, direct or indirect, on grounds of race, gender, religion, sexuality, disability, marital status or age.

Recruitment, retention, salaries and benefits

The XYZ Charity will adopt policies that ensure that all staff are recruited in accordance with best practice principles, and that selection methods ensure candidates are appointed who fully meet the needs of the organisation. *The XYZ Charity's* system of salary determination and non-salary benefits will be designed to ensure that capable staff are encouraged to maximise their contribution towards its objectives for its clients by remaining with the organisation. This will be achieved by reflecting best and most appropriate practice, drawing upon the experience of appropriate comparators in the voluntary sector and elsewhere.

Performance appraisal, personal development and staff training

The XYZ Charity recognises that its staff need support and guidance for them to be most effective in their jobs. It will provide a non-judgemental performance appraisal system, which will offer annual reviews and regular support meetings to all staff, from both a professional and managerial perspective. The appraisal process will be the basis for determining both organisational training needs identification and personal development programmes.

Health, welfare and safety

The XYZ Charity will ensure that it provides a safe and secure working environment for its staff, which they will be encouraged to determine and maintain. *The XYZ Charity* will also ensure that both it and its staff will at all times work within the requirements of the Health & Safety at Work Act and associated legislation, and requirements under various EU Directives. It will ensure that full risk assessments are regularly conducted and complied with.

Staff conduct in disciplinary, grievance and capability matters

The XYZ Charity will introduce procedures for dealing with matters of indiscipline, grievance and incapability related to individual employees. It will ensure that these are in an accessible form designed to support the avoidance of disputes and the resolution of differences in preference to the punishment of offence.

Employee and organisational communications and access to information

The XYZ Charity will ensure that systems are introduced that provide for the maximum effective exchange of information between itself and staff; and which encourage staff participation and contribution in policy development and organisational management. It has a general policy of maximum openness of information, subject only to the constraints of client confidentiality, managerial responsibility and the provisions of the Data Protection Act.

Union recognition, employee representation and consultation processes

The XYZ Charity believes that for many matters, collective discussion through trade union representation is the most effective way of developing the organisation. It will therefore enter into union recognition agreements and establish procedural arrangements for consultation and negotiation, which will include the right to representation for individual employees.

Staff and organisational responses to client needs and concerns

The XYZ Charity will establish a framework of guidance for all staff, which will set out standards for relationships with clients and other members of the public, recognising their special needs and how to respond to them, including an effective and fair complaints procedure. These principles will also apply to relationships between colleagues.

> **MODEL 14.1** A personnel strategy [continued]
>
> **Managerial responsibilities**
>
> *The XYZ Charity* will set out the level and nature of responsibility for management and financial matters devolved to the director and to individual postholders, and the role and responsibilities of the management committee.
>
> **Clarity of roles and flexibility of operation**
>
> *The XYZ Charity* will establish revision mechanisms for its bank of job descriptions and person specifications, with the objective of providing maximum job satisfaction through flexibility of role and a broad range of activities for each employee, commensurate with their status within the organisation. This flexibility will be to ensure that the needs of *The XYZ Charity* and its clients will always be met.

have a fluctuating demand for your services, then it may make more sense for someone else to carry the burden of additional and otherwise surplus staffing costs, leaving you to find funding for your core and regular activities. This can be particularly attractive when the additional skills that you need are fairly universal, such as clerical support at the time of a large mail out, extra social workers following a drive to raise awareness about your charity's specialist client group or more play workers for summer play schemes. Some types of employee are more available from agencies than are others, and you may on occasion need to resort to recruiting temporary staff yourself; but the use of agency staff is at least worth considering in many instances. You will pay a premium on top of the normal wage rates, but you will not bear other overheads (although you must be clear with the agency whether they are continuing as the employer or whether they are placing staff on your payroll). You should also not necessarily expect these staff to fit in immediately – if you are not careful there can be resentment amongst your permanent staff about different wage rates and other conditions; and they may not always be culturally sensitive to your needs. Hence it is a good idea to establish a firm relationship with a reputable placing agency that understands what your charity is about, and helps its placed staff to acclimatise themselves.

Interim management is another growing trend. Whether it is because you are between managers, or one is away for an extended period (perhaps on maternity leave), you still need the job to be done. You can consider recruiting a temporary replacement, if you are ready to go through the whole process only for a limited period and can devote resources to training the newcomer (always provided you don't have someone inside the organisation who could cover the vacancy and gain senior work experience that way). Alternatively, there is nowadays a breed of manager, often people who have retired early, who can bring a wealth of experience to a role on an interim basis. Generally self-employed, they will cost more on a day rate basis that direct employment, but they will have little if anything to learn, and all good interim managers make a point of being very flexible and being able to fit in with your particular needs, so there will be no training costs.

Work experience

Then there is the move towards widening out work experience. There are still the 'traditional' government sponsored methods, whether under the New Deal or whatever the next initiative may be called, which aim to link otherwise unemployed people with job vacancies. Since these programmes now place heavy emphasis on skills training there is every chance, if carefully planned, that you could grow a new employee to meet your needs, someone who will come equipped with many of the basic skills and who will be keen to get involved. However, what you should not consider is using such trainee employees just to cover the menial jobs or as a temporary measure. Don't simply be tempted by the grants that often come with such placements, but rather recognise that for them to work, you should be offering genuine and permanent (insofar as anything is permanent in the world of work nowadays) employment to someone who will be glad of the chance and is in nearly every case likely to turn out to be one of your most valuable employees.

Some people are now prepared to organise their own work experience, not through sponsorship and its associated rewards, but by working as a volunteer in what might otherwise be a paid position. Of course, the voluntary sector is well used to having paid and volunteer staff working side by side, and this 'intern' process, as it is known from its origins in the United States, can be beneficial to all concerned – cheap labour for the charity, good experience for the worker. Do beware the pitfalls, however – interns may not always be reliable, at least until they have developed a degree of commitment (at which point they may start to seek paid employment with you or elsewhere in the sector), there may be resentment from paid staff that they are being denied further work opportunities, and there can be horrific implications around the minimum wage, particularly if the interns are being paid their expenses.

Career flexibility

Increasingly, all employees' expectations of their relationship with their employer are changing towards far greater flexibility.

Whereas thirty years ago, perhaps even less, a young person starting out on their career would expect to be doing the same kind of thing for the rest of their working life, perhaps with the same employer, nowadays that has virtually vanished. People expect a flexibility that will enable them to do new things in new ways, that will give them a wider range of opportunities to follow, not just sequentially but all at once. Rather than one contract with one employer, some people are now building significant 'portfolio careers' on several part-time jobs with different organisations, doing other things as well, and perhaps with a mix of being an employee and self-employment. Traditionalists frown at this, because they are worried about lack of commitment and about one part of the working life being played off against the other. However, there is increasing evidence that people who work in this way are more contented, probably because they have a greater degree of control over their lives, are therefore more productive, and can offer a cross-fertilisation of ideas and experience that might be lacking if they just stayed full time with one employer. It is already widespread in the commercial sector and is starting to appear in the voluntary sector. Provided issues around confidentiality and conflict of interest can be resolved, it is likely to continue to grow here.

Homeworking and remote management

I have left the most significant development in patterns of working to last. The information technology revolution is fundamentally changing the nature of the world of work, and the voluntary sector has not gone untouched. Increasingly, computers, modems and mobile phones mean that for many staff, going to the office is no longer a regular feature, indeed, in the commercial and telecommunications sectors, the virtual office has already nearly become a reality. However, it is interesting to note that, whilst the technology exists for people to work remotely on even the most complex of services, call centres still occupy large buildings with large numbers of staff working from banks of desks in them. Someone has recognised that human contact that goes beyond a disembodied voice remains crucial if employees are to remain 'on message'. Not many charities have got this far, and indeed, there is likely always to be the need for a substantial degree of human contact, because of the very nature of the kinds of product that the sector offers. You can't, after all, offer personal social services on the end of a computer link.

But what you can do is to make it easier for field staff to do their jobs, by providing them with better communications and support systems so they can get information about clients and reduce the time they have to spend on travel and administration.

Why, for example, should home care workers have to come to an office every morning when a list of clients to be visited can be e-mailed to their homes? And if plans change, what could be simpler than calling them on their mobile phones to enable them to reschedule? Applied sensibly in such ways, the availability of cheap and efficient information technology will not only improve efficiency, it will also greatly empower staff to organise their own working lives, thereby increasing job satisfaction.

It's not just staff visiting clients who don't need to go in to the office every day. Finance staff can just as easily check accounts through a landline from their own homes as from a desk in head office. IT specialists (unless they are dealing with hardware) can resolve all users' concerns over the phone. Fundraising calls can be just as effective from home as from an office desk – and can be done at more flexible hours when targets are more likely to be at home. The list goes on; probably the only person who needs regularly to be at the centre is the poor old personnel manager, if you have one, and even she is often just as able to advise on some issues over the phone as face to face.

This does not mean to say that you can do away with the office altogether, and certainly not with some get-togethers. There is likely to remain a need for a physical centre, particularly if you are dealing with shifting a lot of written information, for some time to come, and staff need to feel part of the organisation, not just by having the label but by meeting with colleagues. Remote management, with all its attractions, also has its limitations, and face-to-face contact will continue to pay dividends in terms of motivation and performance. The point is not to throw away all the aspects of the old workplace, where everyone came together to work and then went away again; rather, it is to ensure that this coming together can be at its most productive. Used sensitively this way, the new technology can be a really significant enhancement in how you deploy your staff towards the objectives of your charity.

Beware, however, that some aspects of new ways of working can damage relationships. In particular e-mail, whilst a great boon in sharing necessary data and getting general messages across through bulletin boards and the like, can lead to overload of irrelevant information and the ensuing stress of having to cope. It can also act as a substitute for simple human intercourse: many an office relationship has been soured by the thoughtless wording of an e-mail to the person sitting at the next desk, when a quick word, with its associated body language and other aspects of non-verbal communication, would never have caused a problem. You may already be aware of these problems – if you are not, you soon will be, and I would suggest that they can largely be overcome, and indeed the whole question of the management of information technology can be addressed, through the development of effective protocols that are well communicated, heavily trained on and effectively policed.

Delivering a personnel service

This book has, in general, been written on the assumption that you are a manager who doesn't have access to a personnel department. Since the vast majority of charities who employ staff have fewer than ten employees, this is a valid assumption. Most personnel work has to be done by the director or, at best, another senior employee with a portfolio of other responsibilities as well. I hope that this book will help such managers.

However, there are a few charities with sufficient staff numbers to justify a personnel specialist being employed in her own right. Although such an appointment will of course add to central overhead costs, it will mean that much of the work that was being covered by senior managers will be devolved, allowing them to get on with their main task. It is of course critical that, in passing on the personnel management role, those managers do not abdicate their leadership responsibilities – they need to remain sensitive to staff expectations and keep a hold on the strategic development of their charity through the management of its staff. But much of the routine work can be lifted from them and their own support staff, and the strategic development can, within the cultural context of the charity and subject to overall approval by its most senior management, be worked up by the specialists in it.

Recent survey evidence indicates that, excluding administrative support staff, larger organisations in the public and voluntary sectors employ one personnel specialist for about every seventy-five to one hundred and fifty staff; the larger charities, with their greater complexity, more in-house provision and a (perhaps inevitable) tendency towards bureaucratisation, will have proportionately larger personnel departments. But organisations of that size are utterly untypical of the sector as a whole, where fifty staff is considered large. In such charities, it is becoming more and more common for a part-time personnel officer to be employed.

A typical example of a charity I know well is set out below. This organisation has grown rapidly as a result of effective campaigning to increase awareness of its services, expanding its membership base five-fold, and has secured a wide range of contracts through community care legislation. It has thus significantly diversified its operations, and the pattern of how it provides central services such as personnel reflects this pattern quite clearly (it also applies to its growth in other key functions such as finance, public relations and information technology).

Table 14.1 Personnel management in the XYZ Charity

Year	Staff numbers	Management of the personnel function
1988	15	By director, with administrative support from her PA
1992	40	By director's PA, now part-qualified CIPD, supported by director
1995	70	By personnel officer, formerly director's PA and now fully qualified
2000	100	By personnel manager, with part-time personnel assistant

Personnel consultants

Providing an in-house service is not the only option, even for those charities big enough to consider doing so. In fact, even in the largest organisations, in every sector very few personnel departments are either able or appropriate to provide every aspect of personnel work. Specialist training, payroll bureau and remuneration determination work is often bought in to complement the work of the core personnel team. And the smaller the charity, and hence the smaller its personnel team, the less likely it will be that that team has all the necessary expertise and experience to tackle all the issues. The model is very typical – with the best will in the world, a part-qualified and inexperienced personnel officer will not always be equipped to confront the major issues.

That is where personnel consultants come into their own. Whether it is to provide a one-off service on a particular project, to offer general locum support or to be available on a standby or peripatetic basis, it can be more effective to use their specialist skills as and when you need to rather than bear all the costs of keeping an in-house resource yourself. As a charity manager, you will be very aware of the skills and techniques needed for the effective management of consultants, and I do not need to go much further into that here. My only word of advice is that you select them carefully. Whilst there are many freelance personnel specialists and trainers around, regrettably there are very few with much experience of the voluntary sector, and I have seen far too many examples of insensitive approaches to the culture of charities by so-called experts (not to mention their insensitivity to pricing for their services – the voluntary sector cannot afford the private sector rates many of them still think they should charge!).

You may find it helpful to be reminded of the guidelines offered by the Institute of Management Consultancy; what they call their Golden Rules. These are:

1. Clearly define the objectives you hope to achieve.
2. Consult with others in your organisation to agree those objectives.
3. Shortlist no more than three consultants, and ask them to provide written proposals.
4. Brief the consultants properly.
5. See the individual consultant who will do the job and make sure the chemistry is right.
6. Ask for references from the chosen consultant(s) and follow them up.
7. Review and agree a written contract before the assignment starts.
8. Be involved and in touch during the assignment.
9. Ensure that the consultant does not save surprises for the final report.
10. Implement the recommendations and involve your management as well as the consultant.

Whilst this guidance was prepared primarily with organisational development consultancy in mind, it is of just as much use where you are bringing someone in to tackle a particular problem or issue, and even serves well if you are thinking about employing an interim manager. If you are not comfortable with a consultant, don't use them – if you are, then you are likely to get a great deal out of the relationship, even if you don't implement every recommendation, and working closely with them should ensure that there aren't any nasty surprises at the end of the process.

In summary ...

- Planning ahead on personnel strategy will, just as with any other area of management, pay enormous dividends. You, your staff and your organisation will all know where you are going, and if things do go wrong, you'll have a framework in which to put them right.
- Decide carefully how (not whether) you will secure appropriate levels of personnel expertise, and bear in mind that the overheads of an in-house resource are likely to be too high for all but the biggest charities.

Directory

Further reading

The Chartered Institute of Personnel and Development (CIPD) has a vast library covering every aspect of personnel management, but charges a very high fee for non-members, should you need to consult a specialist reference. There are also many general personnel textbooks which outline the basic principles, but do not look specifically at the charity sector.

Good general overviews of charity management include:

- Handy, C. *Understanding Voluntary Organisations* (Penguin Books, 2000)
- *Voluntary Matters: management and good practice in the voluntary sector* (Directory of Social Change, 1997)
- *The Charities Manual* (ICSA Publishing – loose leaf information service with regular updates)

Journals

- *Briefing Plus*, Industrial Society
- *Employment Gazette*, published monthly by the Department for Education and Employment
- *Industrial Relations Law Report*, the specialist and definitive publication on legal developments, published by Industrial Relations Services
- *Industrial Relations Services*, a range of specialist and more general publications appearing twice monthly: 18-20 Highbury Place, London N5 1QP, 020 7354 5858
- *Management Today,* Institute of Management (see 'Institutes', below)
- *People Management*, CIPD (see 'Institutes', below)

- *Personnel Today*, published twice monthly as an independent magazine, available from Quadrant House, The Quadrant, Sutton, Surrey SM2 5AS, 020 8652 3946
- *Voluntary Sector,* NCVO (see 'Voluntary sector umbrella bodies', below)

Employment law reference manuals

There are several very detailed employment law reference manuals (but their application is usually best left to the employment law or personnel specialist), including:

- *Employment Law Service*, CIPD (see 'Institutes', below)
- *Croner Publications*, Croner House, London Road, Kingston upon Thames, Surrey KT2 6SR, 020 8547 3333. Croner Publications publishes several volumes on employment law, health and safety, and general personnel issues.

Useful addresses

Institutes

It may be useful either to join, or qualify for membership of, one of the following, or at least to seek to recruit trustees or members of staff who are members:

- *Chartered Institute of Personnel and Development* (CIPD), CIPD House, 35 Camp Road, London SW19 4UW, 020 8971900, www.ipd.co.uk
- *Institute of Chartered Secretaries and Administrators* (ICSA), 16 Park Crescent, London W1N 4AH, 020 7580 4741, www.icsa.org.uk
- *Institute of Management*, Management House, Cottingharn Road, Corby NN17 1TT, 01536 204222, www.inst-mgt.org.uk

Voluntary sector umbrella bodies

If you work in a charity that has some interests and activities in common with others, or if you want a general view on the kinds of issues you face from a voluntary sector perspective, the following may be of assistance:

- *Association of Charitable Foundations* (ACF), 2 Plough Yard, Shoreditch High Street, London EC2A 3LP, 020 7422 8600, www.acf.org.uk
- *Association of Chief Executives of Voluntary Organisations* (ACEVO), 130 College Road, Harrow, Middlesex HA1 1BQ, 020 8424 2334, www.acevo.org.uk
- *Association of Medical Research Charities*, 61 Gray's Inn Road, London WC1X 8TL, 020 7242 2472, www.amrc.org.uk
- *Charities Aid Foundation* (CAF), Kings Hill, West Malling, Kent ME19 4TA, 01732 520000. www.caf.org.uk

- *Federation of Independent Advice Centres* (FIAC), 4 Deans Court, St Paul's Churchyard, London EC4V 4AA, 020 7489 1800, www.fiac.org.uk
- *Genetic Interest Group*, 4d Leroy House, 436 Essex Road, London N1 3QP, 020 7704 3141, www.gig.org.uk
- *Museums Association*, 42 Clerkenwell Close, London EC1R 0PA, 020 7608 2933, www.museumsassociation.org
- *National Council for Voluntary Organisations* (NCVO), Regent's Wharf, 8 All Saints Street, London N1 9RL, 020 7713 6161, www.ncvo-vol.org.uk
- *National Council of Voluntary Child Care Organisations* (NCVCCO), Unit 4, Pride Court, 80-82 White Lion Street, London N1 9PF, 020 7833 3319, www.ncvcco.org
- *National Housing Federation*, 175 Gray's Inn Road, London WC1X 8UP, 020 7278 6571, www.housing.org.uk

The above is just a small selection of the many umbrella organisations that offer mutual support amongst charities with similar interests. For a more comprehensive list, consult the *Voluntary Agencies Directory*, published annually by NCVO.

Voluntary sector personnel consultants

There are many consultants working within the voluntary sector, but relatively few with any specialist knowledge. These include the following:

- *Industrial Society*, Robert Hyde House, 48 Bryanston Square, London W1H 7LN, 020 7262 2401, www.indsoc.co.uk
- *Judith Lovelace Associates*, 30 Strawberry Hill Close, Twickenham, Middlesex TW1 4PX, 020 8892 3671
- *Management Development Network*, 39 Gabriel House, 10 Odessa Street, London SE16 7HQ, 020 7232 0726, www.mdn.org.uk
- *National Council for Voluntary Organisations* (NCVO), Regent's Wharf, 8 All Saints Street, London N1 9RL, 020 7713 6161, www.ncvo-vol.org.uk
- *Personnel Solutions*, 21 Harmer Green Lane, Digswell, Herts AL6 0AS, 01438 840848
- *Specialist Information Training Resource Agency* (SITRA), Bramah House, 2nd Floor, 65-71 Bermondsey Street, London SE1 3XF, 020 7357 8922, www.sitra.org.uk

Other consultants are listed in the *Trainers and Consultants Directory* published by the National Association of Councils for Voluntary Service and the Charities Information Bureau, available from NACVS, Third Floor, Arundel Court, 177 Arundel Street, Sheffield S1 2NU, 0114 278 6636, nacvs@nacvs.org.uk

Voluntary sector recruitment specialists

There are literally hundreds of private recruitment organisations offering a wide range of executive selection services, but very few with a detailed knowledge and understanding of charities. Amongst those with such sector relevant experience are:

- *Charity and Fundraising Appointments*, Longcroft House, Victoria Avenue, Bishopsgate, London EC2M 4NS, 020 7623 9292, www.charity-executives.co.uk. Also offers a trustee recruitment service.
- *Charity People*, 38 Bedford Place, London WC1B 5JH, 020 7636 3900, www.charitypeople.com
- *Charity Recruitment*, 40 Rosebery Avenue, London EC1R 4RX, 020 7833 0770, www.charityrecruitment.com

Trades unions

The three unions with by far the largest membership in the sector are:

- *ACTS*, 128 Theobald's Road, London WC1X 8TN, 020 7611 2500, www.tgwu.org.uk (part of the Transport & General Workers Union)
- *Manufacturing, Science and Finance Union* (MSF), 33-37 Morland Street, London EC1V 8BB, 020 7505 3030, www.msf.org.uk
- *Unison*, 1 Mabledon Place, London WC1H 9AJ, 020 7388 2366, www.unison.org.uk

Training organisations specialising in working with charities

Most of the specialist charity consultants will offer support and courses, and give advice on training needs analysis and selection of training provider. Dedicated training organisations particularly working with the sector include:

- *Centre for Strategy & Communication*, Unit 301, 16 Baldwin's Gardens, London EC1N 7RJ, 020 7242 7733, www.cscpebble.com
- *Charity Consultants*, Little Holme, Station Road, Shiplake, Henley-on-Thames, Oxon RG9 3JS, 0118 9401016, www.charity-consultants.co.uk
- *Directory of Social Change*, 24 Stephenson Way, London NW1 2DP, 020 7209 4949, www.dsc.org.uk
- *Happy Computers*, Cityside House, 40 Adler Street, London E1 1EE, 020 7375 7300, www.happy.co.uk
- *National Council for Voluntary Organisations* (NCVO), Regent's Wharf, 8 All Saints Street, London N1 9RL, 020 7713 6161, www.ncvo-vol.org.uk

- *National Housing Federation,* 175 Gray's Inn Road, London WC1X 8UP, 020 7278 6571, www.housing.org.uk
- *Specialist Information Training Resource Agency* (SITRA), Bramah House, 2nd Floor, 65-71 Bermondsey Street, London SE1 3XF, 020 7357 8922, www.sitra.org.uk

Higher education voluntary sector management courses

If you are considering more in depth and longer term training for key staff, a postgraduate programme may be appropriate. Universities change their courses every year; at the time of writing the following institutions were known to offer postgraduate accreditation, although it is worth checking elsewhere as well.

- *Centre for Charity and Trust Research,* South Bank University, 103 Borough Road, London SE1 0AA, 020 7928 8989, www.sbu.ac.uk
- *Centre for Civil Society,* London School of Economics, Houghton Street, London WC2A 2AE, 020 7955 7575, www.lse.ac.uk/depts/css
- *Centre for Voluntary Sector and Not-for-Profit Management* (VOLPROF), City University Business School, Frobisher Crescent, Barbican Centre, London EC2Y 8HB, 020 7477 8667, www.business.city.ac.uk

Pension organisations

Most charities are too small to set up a company pension scheme, but may consider paying into employees' private pensions. The choice of pensions broker and provider needs careful consideration; you may obtain some guidance from the industry regulatory body: *Personal Investment Authority* (PIA), 25 The North Colonnade, Canary Wharf, London E14 5HS, 020 7676 1000, www.fsa.gov.uk

If you are considering setting up a final salary or group scheme, the organisation with most experience of running pensions on behalf of a large number of charity clients is: *The Pensions Trust,* Verity House, 6 Canal Wharf, Leeds LS11 5BQ, 0113 234 5500, www.thepensionstrust.org.uk

For those concerned about advice on public accountability, fund performance and ethical investment, help is available from:

- *Ethical Investment Research Service* (EIRIS), 80-84 Bondway, London SW8 1SF, 020 7840 5700, www.eiris.org
- *Pensions Investment Research Consultants,* 4th Floor, Cityside, 40 Adler Street, London E1 1EE, 020 7247 2323, www.pirc.co.uk

Career management advisers

There are many career management (or outplacement) organisations around, most of them operating with blue chip companies, with a few now entering the public sector market. However, very few have as yet much experience of offering advice to voluntary sector and potential voluntary sector staff. Exceptions are:

- *Charity and Fundraising Appointments*, Longcroft House, Victoria Avenue, Bishopsgate, London EC2M 4NS, 020 7623 9292, www.charity-executives.co.uk
- *Judith Lovelace Associates*, 30 Strawberry Hill Close, Twickenham, Middlesex TW1 4PX, 020 8892 3671

Statutory bodies

- *Advisory, Conciliation and Arbitration Service* (ACAS): several regional offices; head office: 180 Borough High Street, London SE1 1LW, 020 7210 3000, 020 7396 5100 (public enquiry point), www.acas.org.uk
- *Commission for Racial Equality*, Elliot House, 10–12 Allington Street, London SW1E 5EH, 020 7828 7022, www.cre.gov.uk
- *Department for Education and Employment*, Head Office, Sanctuary Buildings, Great Smith Street, London SW1P 3BT, 020 7925 5000, www.dfee.gov.uk
- *Department of Trade and Industry*, 1 Victoria Street, London SW1H OET, 020 7215 5000, www.dti.gov.uk
- *Disability Rights Commission*, 222 Gray's Inn Road, London WC1X 8HL, 08457 622 633, www.drc-gb.org
- *Employers' Forum on Disability*, Nutmeg House, 60 Gainsford Street, London SE1 2NY, 020 7403 3020, www.employers-forum.co.uk
- *Employment Tribunals*, (many regional offices), Central Office, 100 Southgate Street, Bury St Edmunds, Suffolk, 1P33 2AQ, 01284 762300
- *Equal Opportunities Commission*, Overseas House, Quay Street, Manchester M3 3HN, 0161 833 9244, www.eoc.org.uk
- *Health and Safety Executive* (many regional offices); to obtain local details call: 0541 545500, www.hse.gov.uk

Psychometric test publishers

There are some very reputable test publishers and, regrettably, some that produce instruments that are poorly designed and validated. If in doubt, contact: *British Psychological Society* (BPS), St Andrews House, 48 Princess Road, East Leicester LE1 7DR, 0116 254 9568, www.bps.org.uk

The best test publishers are those who will not release material to you without a licence from the BPS, but they will give you guidance on what you might use and who can help you to use it. These include:

- *Oxford Psychologists Press*, Elsfield Hall, 15–17 Elsfield Way, Oxford OX2 8EP, 01865 404500
- *Saville & Holdsworth Ltd* (SHL), The Pavilion, 1 Atwell Place, Thames Ditton, Surrey KT7 0NE, 020 8398 4170, www.shlgroup.com
- *Test Agency Ltd*, Cray House, Woodlands Road, Harpsden Woods, Henley-on-Thames, Oxon RG9 4AE, 01491 413413, www.testagency.com

These agencies both publish their own tests (such as SHL's Occupational Personality Questionnaire) and market other well-established instruments such as Myers-Briggs Personality Type Indicator and Catell's 16PF.

Networks and trustees

Voluntary sector managers are probably the best in the world at sharing ideas and information and offering mutual support. Do not be afraid to ask – everyone feels vulnerable, ignorant and isolated at times, and your colleagues will be only too willing to help. Your trustees will also often be an invaluable source of information and technical expertise.

Epilogue

And that is just about it. If you've read this book from start to finish, you've reached the last lap, and you probably deserve a medal. I hope that it has offered you both stimulating ideas for managing staff and some of the techniques to achieve success. You may just have dipped into different sections as you needed to (which is how I anticipated the book would be used, and indeed was how it was written). Whatever your approach, I hope that you have found what you have been looking for.

But however you've got here, I would stress once again:

- *Never be afraid to ask* – managing people is a complicated business.
- *Don't panic* – there's always a solution to be found.
- *Think positive* – your staff are your charity's greatest asset: they want you to succeed, and it is your job to help them do just that.

Good luck!

And finally ...

If you liked the author's style and approach (or even if you didn't) and want to comment direct – or if you would like him to offer you direct support in tackling your personnel management issues, he can be contacted through his own consultancy:

Personnel Solutions
21 Harmer Green Lane
Digswell
Herts AL6 0AS
01438 840848

Index

ACAS *see* Arbitration, Conciliation and Advisory Service (ACAS)
accountability, chain of command 4
advertising
　recruitment 134–40
　for volunteers 258
altruism 4, 251
anti-discrimination legislation 31
appraisal of staff
　formal 219–24
　model form 221
　model report 224–5
　performance-related pay 220
Arbitration, Conciliation and Advisory Service (ACAS) 25, 290
　codes of practice 28, 32, 54, 94, 229
　conciliation role 49, 243–4, 247
　Discipline at Work handbook 28
assessment centres *see* recruitment
Association of Chief Executives of Voluntary Organisations 135

Belbin, Meredith 202
benefits to employees
　choice for staff 122–5
　tax position 122
　transport 119–21
bicycle loans 119–21

capability procedures 54–7, 59
car loans 119–21
career management

advisers 290
counselling (in case of redundancy) 236–40
development within organisation 6, 208
flexibility 279–80
charitable objectives 67, 178, 183
Charities Act (1992), trustees' obligations 11–12, 14
Charities Aid Foundation 2
Charity Commissioners
　charitable objectives 67, 178, 183
　estimates of charity revenues 2
　scrutiny of charities 11
charity sector *see* voluntary sector
Chartered Institute of Personnel and Development 135
chief executive
　Association of Chief Executives of Voluntary Organisations 135
　directly responsible to trustees 79
　employment conditions 22–4
　pay 5
　recruitment 6
　staff appraisal 223
　support systems 215–19
childcare 122
Children Act, compliance with 263
Commission for Racial Equality 169, 290
commitment 5–6, 8
Confederation of British Industry (CBI), training target proposal 184–5

confidentiality
    personal employee details 69
    references 158-61
conflicts of interest 12-14
contracts of employment 12, 26-8, 81-97, 117, 124-5, 275
criminal convictions/allegations
    checks for (relevant to work) 46, 263
    unconnected with work 45
Criminal Records Bureau 263

Data Protection Act 158
decision-making 228-49, 268-9
delegation 14-24, 28, 79
dependants' leave 92
development strategy
    Belbin team type model 201-2
    corporate plan extract 190
    departmental model plans 191-2
    model policy 188-9
    staff appraisal 219-27
    SWOT analysis 186-7
    target-setting and performance evaluation 210-12
    team development 200-2
    see also training
directory of further reading and useful organisations 285-91
disability rights 31, 66, 290
disciplinary procedures 28, 43-63, 94, 230-1

e-mail, overload risk 281
employees see staff
employer
    disciplinary procedures 28, 43-63
    duty of care 27-8
    liability 28
    trade union recognition question 71-4
employment rights 33-5, 38, 81-97
Employment Relations Act (1999) 35
Employment Rights Act (1996) 27, 31-2, 34-5, 81, 96, 240
Employment Tribunals 35-6, 240-4
    aggrieved staff 65
    appeals 35-6, 230
    contract of employment 26, 84
    directory 290
    disciplinary process 48-9, 231

reasonableness test 45, 229-31
sickness 55, 117
unfair dismissals 32-3, 77, 240-4
volunteers 268-9
equal opportunities 66-70, 170-72
    anti-discrimination legislation 31
    best practice 39-40
    case study 141
    decision-making 167
    motivation and development 180-2
    recruitment 138, 168-72, 208
    training 173, 206
    voluntary sector compared with private sector 5
    volunteers 271-2
    what it means 66-70, 80
Equal Opportunities Commission 169, 290
Equal Pay Act (1970) 29
equal treatment, pensions 92-3, 119
ethical management 37, 61, 67
European Union (EU)
    law 28-9, 35-6, 69, 73
    Social Chapter 69
evaluation and appraisal
    chief executive 23-4
    employees 219-27

financial/budget implications
    expenditure authorisation procedures 24
    redundancy payments 236
    salary policy 99-104
    training and development 182-6, 207-8, 222
    transport policy (mileage etc) 119-21
    volunteers 264-5, 269-71
fixed-term contracts 26, 32, 95, 275
founder member syndrome 16-17

grievance procedures 57, 61, 62-3, 232
gross misconduct 32, 45, 46, 50, 51, 62

health and safety
    electrical appliances 30
    hazardous substances 30

Health and Safety at Work Act (1974) 29-30
Health and Safety Executive 290
manual handling operations 30
VDUs 30
volunteers 271
holidays 88, 95, 114-15
homeworking and remote management 280-2
hours of work *see* working hours
housing associations, legal restraints and obligations 12, 183
Housing Corporation 12, 183
human rights 35, 268
Human Rights Act (1998) 35

incapability 54
industrial action 244-7
industrial relations 44-5, 64-5, 75-7, 80
Industrial Society 175
information technology 281, 282
Institute of Management Consultancy 283-4
insurance
  criminal checks 263
  volunteers 270
interviews *see* recruitment
Investors in People (IiP) 182

job analysis 127-8, 211-212, 213
job description 85, 128-30
job evaluation 107-11, 112-13
job satisfaction 5, 8, 214-15

law and legal obligations
  anti-discrimination legislation 31
  employment law 25-36, 38
  European legislation 28-9
  liability 28
  reasonableness 229-30
  reference manuals 286
  statutory sick pay 116-17
  trustees 11-12
  volunteers 269-70
  see also health and safety
liability, employment law 28
loans, transport 119-21
Local Government and Housing Act (1989) 14

management
  best practice (rules and procedures of staff management) 37-63
  communication and employee relations 64-80, 246-7
  decision-making 228-49
  delegation 14-24
  motivational 176-82, 206, 208-10
  reasonableness 229-30
  reference policy 158-61
  support role 213-19
maternity rights 34, 88-91, 92-3, 115
medical reports 157
member organisations, particular difficulties of 15
minimum wage 35
motivation 174-82, 206, 208-10, 227, 231, 266-7
MSF (Manufacturing, Science and Finance) Union 3

National Council of Voluntary Organisations 2, 135, 139
national insurance
  maternity pay and allowance 89-90
  pensions contributions 91-2

openness and sharing of information 68-70, 80

pay *see* salaries
pensions and retirement 91-4, 118-19, 289-90
personality profiling 164-5
personnel consultants 283-4, 287, 292
personnel managers
  advice 228-9
  role 248-9, 282-3
personnel strategy 273-84
police checks 157
see also criminal convictions
politics, and charitable work 7, 9
professionalism 5-7, 8-9, 65
psychometrics as selection tool 161-6, 173
  aptitude/ability tests 162-3, 169
  checklist of suitable tests 165-6
  personality profiling 164-5
  test publishers 291

public relations 68, 138–40, 258–9, 282

race relations 31, 67
recruitment 126–73
   advertising and finding candidates 134–40
   application forms or CVs? 144–5
   consultants 134–7, 153
   decision-making 166–8
   equal opportunities
     case study 141
     debate 66–8, 170–72
     decision-making 167
   evaluation 147, 155, 159
   external or internal 6
   faulty process 55
   feedback on candidates by current staff 156–7
   information for candidates 143–6, 150
   interviewing 149–52, 153, 169, 172, 259–62
   job analysis 127–8, 162
   job description 128–30
   person specification 131–4, 162–3, 172
   planning 140–3, 147, 152, 155, 172
   promotion or? 145–6
   references 157–61
   selection process 152–66
     aptitude/ability tests 162–3, 169
     assessment centre 152, 166, 169, 172–3
     astrology 157
     case study 170–1
     graphology 157
     group exercises 156
     in-tray exercises 154–5
     medical reports 157
     personality profiling 164–5
     presentations by candidates 153–4
     psychometrics as selection tool 161–6
     report preparation test 154
     selection panel 142–3
     simulation exercises 155–6
     spy observations 156
   staff feedback 156–7
   see also interviewing; references *above*
   tests, reports and exercises by candidates 154–7, 162–3, 171
   voluntary sector recruitment specialists 288
   volunteers 256–63
redundancy 34–5, 115, 233–40
references 157–61
   providing 160–1
   requesting and obtaining 158–60
   volunteers 261, 262–3
remuneration *see* salaries

safety *see* health and safety
salaries
   compared with commercial sector 5, 8, 39
   confidentiality/openness question 69
   job evaluation 107–11, 112–13
   maternity pay 89–90
   methods of payment 96
   minimum wage 35
   negotiations over 75
   performance assessment/reward 103–7, 224–7
   policy 99–104
   reviews 111–14
   scale of remuneration 87–8, 111–14
   temporary staff 278
Saville & Holdsworth Ltd Occupational Personality Questionnaire 166, 168–9
selection *see* recruitment
sickness and incapacity 32, 55–8, 91, 116–18
staff
   agency/interim 275, 278–9
   appraisal 219–27
   benefits 114–25
   career development 208
   career management 236–40
   choice and benefits 122–4
   commitment 178
   conditions 98–125
   confidentiality 69
   contracts of employment 33–4, 77, 82–3, 124–5, 275

discipline and rules 28, 43–63, 94, 230–1
employee involvement/consultation 38–9, 44, 64–80
employee rights 3, 33–5, 38, 81–97
employment law 25–36
flexibility 279–80
grievance procedures 57, 61, 62–3, 232, 240–4
handbooks 40–1, 125
homeworking and remote management 280–2
incapability 49, 54–7, 59–60
industrial action 76–7
minimum wage 35
motivation 208–10, 231
notice 91
performance assessment 103–7
probation 94
redundancy 34–5, 115, 233–40
role and place within organisation 175–6
skills information 193–8
statement of particulars 84–96, 124, 232
supervision case study 216–17
target-setting and performance evaluation 210–12
temporary 90, 95, 275, 278–9
transfers (TUPE regulations) 33–4, 82–3, 95–6, 234
unfair dismissal 31–2
see also equal opportunities; recruitment; salaries; training
statement of particulars
changing conditions case study 124–5
collective agreements 95
disciplinary procedures 94, 232
employment dates 85
holidays 88, 95
job title 85
maternity rights 88–91, 92–3
model 86–7
notice 91
pensions and retirement 91–4
place of work 85–7
probation 94
remuneration 87–8
sickness and injury 91
signatures 95
working hours 88
Statutory Maternity Pay see maternity rights
Statutory Sick Pay see sickness and incapacity
strikes see industrial action

taxation, on benefits (e.g. childcare) 122
trades unions
changes to employment conditions 124–5
collective agreements 95
directory 288
industrial action 244–6
law and legislation 34
recognition by employer question 71–4
redundancy 233
right to employer information 68–9
salary/wage negotiations 100
transfers of staff (TUPE regulations) 33–4, 82–3, 95–6
see also industrial relations
training 174–227
assessment 204–6
coaching 203
costs/value 182–6, 207–8, 222
courses 199–200, 289
directory of organisations 288–9
equal opportunities 173
identification of training needs 193–8
investment in 182–3
mentoring 203–4
model departmental plan 192
on-the-job skills training 202–3
performance evaluation 210–12
policy 187–92
professional qualifications 198–9
SWOT analysis 186–7
team development 200–2
techniques 198–204
volunteers 263–6
why train? 183–6

Transfer of Undertakings
    (Protection of Employment)
    Regulations (TUPE) 33–4,
    82–3, 95, 234
transport policy 119–21
trustees
    conflicts of interest 12–14
    legal constraints and obligations
        11–12
    liability 28
    as managers 18–19
    networking 291
    personal liability 12
    recruitment panel 143
    relations with senior managers
        14–24
    rights 178–9
    role and responsibilities 4, 11–24,
        78–9, 142–3
    see also management

unfair dismissal 31–2, 94, 240–4

voluntary sector
    size of sector 2–3, 8
    uniqueness of 1–9
    users' views 178–9
volunteers
    conflicts with paid staff 15
    de-selecting 267–9
    equal opportunities 271–2
    expenses 270–1
    financial implications 264–5,
        269–71
    health and safety 271
    induction and training 263–5
    insurance 270
    interviewing 259–62
    legal position 269–70
    management of 250–72
    motivation 179–80, 266–7
    policy 252–6, 272
    recruitment and selection
        256–63
    registration form (sample) 260–1
    retaining 266–7
    role description 256
    role in charities 3, 5–6, 250–1
    screening 262–3
    supervision and evaluation
        265–6
    welfare benefits 271
VDUs – see health and safety

women
    carers 66
    see also equal opportunities
work experience 279
working hours 30, 88, 115–16
Working Time Regulations 88, 116